Cognition, Value, and Price

Cognition, Value, and Price
A General Theory of Value

Henry K. H. Woo

Ann Arbor

THE UNIVERSITY OF MICHIGAN PRESS

Published in the United States of America by
The University of Michigan Press
Manufactured in the United States of America

1995 1994 1993 1992 4 3 2 1

Library of Congress Cataloging-in-Publication Data
Woo, Henry K. H., 1946–
Cognition, value, and price : a general theory of value / Henry K. H. Woo.
p. cm.
Includes bibliographical references and index.
ISBN 0-472-10331-8 (alk. paper)
1. Value. I. Title.
HB201.W69 1992
338.5'21—dc20 92-4047
CIP

Contents

Introduction

Probably no economist would disagree that price theory constitutes the cornerstone of economics, but not all economists, notably those in the mainstream, agree that we need to take a theory of value seriously, if, by a theory of value, we mean something more than a theory of price determination. More specifically, a neoclassical economist would consider it irrelevant for economics to concern itself with the study of how patterns of value are formed in the human mind or to consider how our cognitive architecture governs our perception and judgement of prices. Surely, there was a problem of value in the way the classical economists formulated it, but perhaps, as John Stuart Mill declared more than a century ago, "there is nothing in the laws of value which remains for the present or any future writer to clear up" (Mill [1848] 1967, 3:456). Thus, neoclassicists might consider the problem of value largely a pseudoproblem that has been dissolved. It has been dissolved because value is rightly a subjective concept, and the classical search for an absolute standard is nothing but a futile enterprise. Even if the problem were a genuine one, it has been ingeniously solved by the neoclassical approach to the determination of market prices, which takes into account both demand-side and supply-side considerations. Within the neoclassical framework, value is found to be identical to price in the state of market equilibrium and is measured by it.

No doubt the neoclassical framework rests upon the unreal assumption of taking the consumer's preferences to be given. But the unreality of the assumption seems to be a price worth paying if one considers that economics could hardly have progressed with an imprecise concept of value. Equally objectionable, a commonsense concept of value involving dimensions that relate to our beliefs, wants, and ideologies would subject economics to the vicissitudes of discoveries of new psychological and sociological facts and variables and would thereby discredit the status of economics as an autonomous discipline. From the methodological point of view, the neoclassical framework is a simple but formidable framework. Together with the simple rule that choices are automatically deducible upon applying given preferences to well-defined opportunity sets, the neoclassical theory, equipped with the optimization technique, is able not only to derive the important law of demand, but also to provide unified solutions to the questions of production and distribution. By extension, it allows one to build sophisticated general equilibrium theories with far-reaching theoretical consequences without recourse to studying the properties of the mind or how ideas of utility spring in the mind of the consumer. Such, indeed, is the hallmark of the core of theoretical economics since the so called marginal revolution in the 1870s.

The validity of these unreal assumptions and the attendant reductionist methodology is, however, increasingly being called into question. Even if it were a sound theory on its own terms, it seems that neoclassical theory will still have a dear price to pay. If we take it that prices are formed during exchange and that exchange takes place when differences exist in valuation among the transactors in question, such differences in valuation must be attributable, at least in part, to the fact that different economic actors possess different valuational frameworks. To understand the price phenomena, it is natural that we take into account the properties of these valuational frameworks and, by extension, material, psychological, sociological, and ethical factors that may have a bearing on these frameworks. Without doubt, there is a need in many cases to confine the study of the price phenomenon to strictly economic variables in order to avoid the question of value formation in the human mind, but a wholesale abandonment of the discourse of value formation in price determination stands in conflict with our commonsense concept. Clearly, these two approaches are complementary to each other and, in the least, something needs to be done to define the relationship between them. Work of this nature is yet to be done.

With hindsight, one might say that the development of economics from the stage of positing subjective theories of value as an alternative to the classical, cost-of-production theories to the stage of developing a full-fledged general equilibrium theory with virtually no subjective components had been heavily influenced by the positivist, behaviorist trends in philosophy, the dominant intellectual theme of the time. Since the marginal revolution in the 1870s, there have been economists who made serious attempts to study the valuational frameworks of economic actors in order to put the understanding of the subjective roots of prices on more solid ground, but this direction of research was eventually replaced by the subsequent positivist, reductionist quest to purge the psychological and less-than-fully verifiable foundations of choice. The result was a metamorphosis of the neoclassical research program, which eventually led to abandoning the discourse of value in mainstream economics (except in the narrow sense of price determination).

The approach of positing minimal, if not blatantly wrong, assumptions about man's valuational and decision-making apparatus has far-reaching ramifications for subsequent developments in economics. Restricting the understanding of the price phenomenon to the perspective of a strict logic of choice means that neoclassical economics is deprived of fruitful interfaces with other important sources of knowledge and, as a consequence, of the causal power necessary to explain the multifarious aspects of price formation in real life. (Hence, we have such strange situations as Frank Hahn making the statement that general equilibrium theory is not making causal claims.) Following this approach also means that value and prices are tacitly assumed to operate in a single direction, namely, prices are the result of the economic actors' valuations and decisions pertaining to exchange situations. It discourages inquiry from the opposite direction, namely, how an existing pattern of prices will affect the formation of value on the part of economic actors. Ignoring the multicausality of price and value means that one tends to oversimplify the complexities involved in how a system of prices at a particular time affects the formation of prices in subsequent periods. It is, therefore, not surprising that general equilibrium theory, which rules out by definition such sequential relations, is unable to make causal claims about the real world.

Not all economists bypass the problem of value in the broader sense. Unfortunately, an unbridgeable gap divides the minority of contemporary economists who hold that the problem of value is a genuine one and deserves greater attention. One camp wants to revive the classical tradition by upholding the objective theory of value, and they believe that, in spite of surface changes across different markets and economies, the human condition is such that certain deep and invariable patterns of factors must objectively exist. With ingenuity, we could probably unearth such factors and patterns and use them to analyze long-term price movements (e.g., Pasinetti). Opposed to this camp are the subjectivists, notably the Austrians and neo-Austrians, who believe that value springs from the mind and that choices are necessarily mediated through value patterns in the mind. For any particular set of prices, exchange would not be possible without prior differences in the perception of utilities of the economic actors concerned. Hence, equations of exchange as descriptions of equilibrium are deceptive. In spite of such insights, the Austrians, generally entertaining a relativist notion of subjectivity, have not advanced far in their search for the subjective roots of prices. In particular, they have not been able to formulate a theory of value formation, and are generally unwary of the effects of long-term changes in the socioeconomic environment on the "inner subjective orders" of humanity and thereby the effects on price determination. Such a challenge, however, is beginning to be taken up, albeit in a rather piecemeal manner, by a new group of subjectivists who are intent on reviving the relationship between economics and sociological and psychological variables (e.g., Earl).

The fact that such conceptual camps exist at all suggests that there must have been, all along, some simplistic understanding of the subjective and the objective and their complex relations. One fruitful route of research that may resolve such a controversy might be to articulate the meaning of the subjective and the objective and to explore their deeper relations, to the extent that any extreme position would eventually look absurd. Another fruitful route might be to spell out the methodological canons by which a tenable theory of value is to be appraised. Such routes are explored in chapter 3. An important methodological proposal I make is the canon that any tenable theory of value must command both sufficient causal depth and breadth. It is seen that the classical theories of value (cost-of-production theories), while commanding causal breadth, lack causal depth. On the other hand, the subjective theories of value, while possessing more causal depth, lack causal breadth, especially insofar as they ignore the impacts brought about by long-term changes in socioeconomic institutions, a considerable part of which is necessarily of a conventional or man-made nature. All existing theories of value are invariably found to underemphasize or fail to capture the importance of our valuational apparatus.

If given preferences and prewired choice behaviors as postulated by the neoclassical theory are not helpful assumptions to our deeper understanding of the price phenomenon, what assumptions should be put in their stead? The second part of the book attempts to provide an alternative framework. Instead of assuming given preferences and prewired choice behaviors, the new framework sets out to study the relevance of true-to-life cognitive architecture and processes to choice behaviors in consumption, to analyze cognitive factors involved in the formation of preferences, and to examine how cognitive principles explain rationality and irrationality in consumer behavior. These approaches constitute an altogether new "cognition paradigm" for value theory and price determination and provide a new perspective for understanding the question of consumer rationality. With these formulations, we could claim a theory of value that goes beyond the narrow sense of price determination. Alternatively put, by postulating a more realistic and less restrictive theory of the mind, new possibilities are opened up for explaining more interestingly and convincingly the peculiarities of the modern consumption economy, including among others, pricing strategies of suppliers, extensive marketing and advertising activities, less-than-fully rational consumer behavior, and so forth–phenomena that baffled neoclassical theory and that compelled it to resort invariably to ad hoc hypotheses in order to save its core theoretical assumptions.

The starting point of the new cognition paradigm and the neoclassical paradigm differ little; both of them assume the mind to be an optimizing apparatus. The latter takes the optimizing mind to be one-dimensional, namely, to operate in a static, situation-bound setting with given preferences. In contrast, my paradigm posits a multidimensional mind. Architecturally, the mind is posited to be so constituted that it strives to allocate its energy expenditure optimally between its conscious and unconscious strata. Operationally, it can be seen to strive toward maximal welfare by allocating resources in a more or less optimal manner among different sets of parameters, value compartments, and time frames that it possesses or perceives. These facets of optimization manifest themselves in different cognitive strategies that we consciously or unconsciously adopt in different choice situations, strategies that are blatantly ignored in the neoclassical framework. Such an overarching optimizing strategy of the mind, upon which the phenomenon of human rationality seems so strongly rooted, is further shown to be the result of human evolution and our adaptation to survival pressures.

Whereas human rationality and, by extension, consumer rationality is firmly rooted in the optimizing mind operating in situations of given or fixed parameters, the man-made environment that humanity has developed gives rise to a proliferation of values and a multiplicity of time frames within which such values materialize and poses challenges to the bedrock of consumer rationality. This issue is taken up in detail in chapter 4. I show that, short of involving our cognitive characteristics and their evolution, any discussion of the question of consumer rationality and the challenges that the modern economy pose to it can hardly claim to be comprehensive. Such, indeed, constitutes one of the major shortcomings of the neoclassical approach.

The prevalence of less-than-fully rational consumer behavior, phenomena that are ruled out by definition under the neoclassical framework, can be accounted for by a fundamental feature of the mind, namely, it is characteristically fragmentary. This very feature of the mind is seen as built upon and evolving from the basic optimizing principle. Specifically and importantly, the mind is seen to balance its energy allocation between the need to operate efficiently and the need to openly adapt itself to the environment by way of conceptualizing and anticipating problems. It is a fine design that accounts for man's success in the process of evolution. But the same design also has unintended consequences for human development in the social setting we create. In particular, it permits the infiltration of alien values into the unguarded, unconscious stratum of the mind and, thereby, allows the subversion of existing patterns of values. On the one hand, this design facilitates the process of socialization, leading to the creation of a heterogeneous set of cultural conventions and civilizations in the human species. But on the other hand, the same architecture permits both the existence of a compartmentalized value system and the easy domination of certain types of conventions in behavior. Such features, to no small extent, account for the mode of value formation in the consumer under the bombardment of modern marketing and advertising, as well as for the way he or she comes up with compartmentalized value maps embodying "convention-laden scarcities." These explanations are developed in chapter 5.

Fragmentation is not the only property that makes the mind of the consumer susceptible to socialization and supplier manipulation. The "imagistic" mode of mental organization, meaning that what we store in our value maps are largely concrete experiences or images, also explains why advertisers employ vivid pictures in putting their messages across. Also important is the fact that the effectiveness of repetitive advertisements can be accounted for by the peculiar structure of human memory, which, at the retrieving point, is linearly organized instead of distributively organized, permitting only a small amount of data to be retrieved in a sequential manner at any time. In short, the rationality and irrationality of our choice behaviors can be said to rest importantly on the subtleties of our cognitive design—the fragmentary nature of our value maps, the asymmetry between our conscious and unconscious operations, the overarching optimizing principle that incessantly guides us in making compromises between the conflicting concerns for efficiency and quality of judgement, and so on.

That consumer rationality is susceptible to being weakened by the socialization process has profound consequences on the evolution of the modern consumer society. The present theory, without resorting to ad hoc hypotheses, explains the proliferation of marketing and advertising in modern business, the subversion of the sovereignty of the consumer, the creation of "apparent" values, the emphasis on nonprice competition, the rise of the "manipulative firm," the domination of the production function by the distribution function, and the power of the distributor-producer in the present-day consumption economy. Together, these facts speak for an evolutionary and long-term approach to the study of value formation in the economy. This approach also enables us to capture the dynamic and subtle relations between price and cost and renders absurd the simplistic frameworks held by both the conventional objective (cost-of-production) and subjective theories of value. Predictably, too, these phenomena and their emergence lie outside the explanatory power of neoclassical economics; such impotence is traceable to the fact that it bears cognitive assumptions that are not descriptive of our mental properties and operations.

Another central aspect of human cognition is learning and anticipation. In embodying these dimensions, my new theory posits that consumers, in their acts of consumption, will build up expertise and skills that amount to certain forms of capital. On the one hand, such "consumer capital" tends to sustain and refine certain patterns of preferences on the part of the consumer. On the other hand, the awareness of the existence and development of such capital in consumers induces forward-looking suppliers to orient their production and innovation in anticipation of changes in the stock of such capital. It encourages them to refine their products and services and to inculcate more sophisticated tastes among their target consumers. Some kind of coevolution thus takes place between the expectations of the customers and the suppliers, fostering more intense competition and more rapid technological changes. Such dynamic relations can also be shown to favor the trend toward nonprice competition and to favor improvements in quality rather than in cost reduction as a preferable business strategy in modern consumption society. Chapter 6 is devoted to the analysis of these different aspects of consumer capital and supplier strategies.

The cognitive assumptions embodied by my new paradigm are compatible with or derivable from the knowledge of present-day cognitive science and evolutionary epistemology. Most of them are squarely opposed to the assumptions tacitly embodied by neoclassical economic theory, in particular a given pattern of preferences and a strictly computational theory of choice and consumer rationality. Some economists may worry that accepting my new assumptions imply that we would again subject economics to the validity of propositions and theories in other disciplines. On the same basis, it may also be contended that my proposed theory shares the same objectionable features of positivism. These objections, however, can be taken care of if we consider the set of cognitive assumptions constituting my new paradigm to be of a metaphysical order (considering the level of abstraction) and as constituting a coherent part of a broad metaphysical system pertaining to human cognition. The justifications for metaphysics in the inquiries of man, though falling outside the scope of my discussion, are briefly covered in chapter 3.

With the support of my new paradigm, chapter 7 formulates a new framework for analyzing the question of price determination. The problem of price determination is now seen as the study of the conditions under which a sufficiently large number of consumers accept offers made by suppliers to warrant the latter enough revenue to sustain their business, and the study of how the suppliers, taking into account the conditions of price acceptance on the part of the consumers, set their prices in the belief that these prices will come to be accepted by their target consumers. Central to the analysis of price acceptance is the notion of price sensitivity, which defines the relative importance of the price factor to other, nonprice factors that are relevant to the consumer's decisions. Price sensitivity also elucidates the extent to which price changes alter consumers' perception of the relative importance of nonprice factors. Important conditions that affect price sensitivity are discussed, including budgetary constraint, price stability, consumer capital formation, competition, and manipulation. Cost sensitivity on the part of the supplier, a counterpart to the notion of price sensitivity, is also discussed. With these theoretical tools, a manipulation theory of price determination, emphasizing the conventionality and arbitrariness of prices and the mechanisms responsible for such arbitrariness, is finally advanced to explain the price phenomenon in the realm of consumption in the modern economy.

A few disclaimers and qualifications, however, need to be made here. Although my proposed theory is claimed to be a general one, it is general only in relation to neoclassical theory or to any theory of value within the sphere of economics. The idea of value explored in the book is restricted to the notion of utility and, therefore, subscribes essentially to utilitarian doctrine. As such, I have not considered those aspects of value that are related to, say, what is morally preferable (such as the notion of rights) or to what is ultimately preferable (such as the interests of humans as a species), although these considerations will inescapably have impacts on the notion of value as utility perceived by the individual. Nor has the idea of value formation related to say, changes in technology, been fully discussed in this book. All these issues, worthwhile as they are, do not fall within the scope of this book. In light of their importance, I recommend that they be further and separately researched.

I am chiefly concerned with the theory of value formation. As such, I put relatively less emphasis on the relationships between value formation and price determination. Although chapter 7 does attempt to present a crude, first framework, it is clear that a lot of work remains to be done. Given the vast scope of the topic, the study of price determination has to be left to an independent study, but for fruitfulness, subsequent studies are well advised to take into account the importance of value formation as I discuss it or to take findings of a similar kind as points of departure.

In the course of writing and revising this book, I received comments, suggestions, and materials from many people. I would like to thank all of them: Gary Becker, Alain Bienayme, Kenneth Boulding, A. W. Coats, David Colander, Peter Earl, Amitai Etzioni, William Frazer, K. K. Fung, Daniel Fusfeld, Nicholas Georgescu-Roegen, Henri Guitton, Norton Jacobi, Charles Kindleberger, Jürgen Kuczynski, Jan Larosse, S. C. Littlechild, Thomas Mayer, Eugene Meehan, Laurence S. Moss, Luigi Pasinetti, Prasanta K. Pattanaik, Mark Perlman, William Peterson, Anghel N. Rugina, Amartya Sen, H. Van Der Wee, Sidney Weintraub, and Peter Wiles. I would also like to thank my associates at the Hong Kong Institute of Economic Science for their help and encouragement in this project, in particular Alan Wong, P. C. Lund, Carson Chan, Rex Li, Po-Keung Ip, Adolf Tsang, Man-Hung Sze, Wan-Chaw Shea, Louis Lau, and John Ma for their invaluable comments. In addition, I would like to thank Colin Day, director of the University of Michigan Press and his team of editors and readers whose advice and patience have contributed greatly to the present shape and organization of the book. Last but not least, I must express my deep gratitude to Linda Lee, my former secretary, for typing numerous manuscripts and revisions and to Mazy Lee for taking care of the final phase of the work.

Part 1
A Critique of Existing Theories of Value

CHAPTER 1

In Search of an Invariable Measure? The Objective Theories of Value

Two conceptual polarities have dominated the debate in value theory in the history of economic thought. At one pole are what are commonly known as objective theories of value. These theories formulate their problem as the determination of the relative value of commodities in terms of some invariable, supply-side factors that do not change over time. They are opposed to subjective theories of value that stress the importance of demand-side factors in the determination of relative prices. Classical economics usually espouses some different versions of the objective theories of value, whereas neoclassical economics was rooted in a subjective theory of value. Among economists, the consensus is that the objective theories of value, regardless of version, were largely abortive attempts to address the question of value in general and the question of price determination in particular. In contrast, the neoclassical, subjective theory of value is believed to have solved, once and for all, the so-called problem of value. As of today, the word *value* is seldom used in formal literature except in treatises on the history of economic thought. It must be surprising to the noneconomist, therefore, that the word *value* in economics is used almost synonymously with the word *price*, and, to the economist, a theory of value is, strictly speaking, a theory of price determination or value in exchange.

However, it would be a gross generalization to infer from this polarized characterization and the lack of interest among economists today that the classical economists or their predecessors were simplistic in their treatment of the issue of value or that the problem they formulated was a mere pseudoproblem. Adam Smith himself was surely fully aware of the multiplicity of issues involved in formulating a theory of value. He certainly was aware of the distinction between "value in use" and "value in exchange" and their paradoxical relation. The question that he asked with regard to the exchangeable value of commodities clearly shows the depth of his understanding of the problems involved, regardless of the final position that he settled upon.

> First, what is the real measure of this exchangeable value; or, wherein consists the real price of all commodities. Secondly, what are the differ-

> ent parts of which this real price is composed, or made up. And, lastly, what are the different circumstances which sometimes raise some or all of these different parts of price above, and sometimes sink them below, their natural or ordinary rate; or, what are the causes which sometimes hinder the market price, that is, the actual price of commodities from coinciding exactly with what may be called their natural price. (Smith [1776] 1976, 1:30)

Twenty-five years before Adam Smith published his *Wealth of Nations,* Ferdinando Galiani displayed sophisticated insights in his analysis of the basic ingredients related to the question of value. Although his value theory was never developed into a full-fledged price theory, he hinted at a number of principles that, in a fully developed form, are part of the modern subjective theory of value as it emerged in the 1870s. Of particular importance is the fact that he recognized the powerful effect of social forces and stressed the role of fashion as a determinant of people's desires and, thus, of value. Similarly, he was aware of the significance of what Veblen was to call "invidious comparisons" and what is now known as the demonstration effect (Spiegel 1983). In praise of his insights, Pasinetti wrote,

> one can discern in his [i.e., Ferdinando Galiani] writings the concept of utility, the concept of decreasing marginal utilities, and the relativity of all these concepts; one can also see the concept of cost of production, and more particularly, the principle of labour cost, which is defined as nothing less than the only one that gives value to things. One can . . . see in all this the interplay of demand and supply, the concept of elasticity of demand with respect to both prices and income, and in fact also a clear enunciation of the hierarchy among goods. (1986, 413–14)

Nor was it the case that David Ricardo, a major classical economist after Smith, thought of value as solely governed by the cost of production without reference to demand, as Jevons would have us believe. In some interpretations, the economics of Ricardo, as well as that of Mill, are seen to comprise (in its essentials) an exchange system consistent with the marginalist view. Hollander, for example, contends that the cost-price analysis done by Ricardo is preeminently an analysis of the allocation of scarce resources, proceeding in terms of general equilibrium, with allowance for final demand and the interdependence of factor and commodity markets (Hollander 1987). Even if one does not agree with such a strong interpretation, one might agree in a much milder way with, say, Sowell that Ricardo did seriously consider the relevance of demand to price determination. In Sowell's interpretation, Ricardian economics regarded supply and demand as a causally neutral mechanism through which other variables determine value. Supply and demand independently determine value only where the other determinants (such as cost of production or utility) were rendered ineffective by noncompetitive market structures or fixed supply (Sowell 1974).

If classical economists were not entirely unaware of the importance of demand-side considerations in the determination of value, the intriguing question becomes what made them each arrive at or insist on, in a seemingly uncompromising way, an objective theory of value? What, for instance, were the considerations that led them toward a production-oriented, cost-of-production or even labor theory of value? In addition, did the major classical economists all share the same considerations? Before answering this set of questions, let us first look at the respective theories held by Smith, Ricardo, and Marx. Before I begin, I must point out that my goal is to examine the problem situations of these economists and to place their value theories in the context of their overall frameworks. Hence, the discussion will focus on the outline rather than the details of their value theories.

Smith's Theory of Value

Adam Smith's position has been very controversial. Although in his earlier works he had held scarcity to be the source of value, he was explicit in favor of holding value as labor content that is required in the production of a commodity in his later works.

> Labour, . . . is the real measure of the exchangeable value of all commodities. The real price of everything, what everything costs to the man who wants to acquire it is the toil and trouble of acquiring it. What everything is really worth to the man who has acquired it, and who wants to dispose of it or exchange it for something else, is the toil and trouble which it can save to himself, and which it can impose upon other people. (Smith [1776] 1976, 1:32)

In another passage, he also mentioned that

> if among a nation of hunters, for example, it usually costs twice the labour to kill a beaver which it does to kill a deer, one beaver should naturally exchange for or be worth two deer. It is natural that what is usually the produce of two days or two hours labour, should be worth double of what is usually the produce of one day's or one hour's labour. (49)

The latter context in which this strict proportionality was assumed is, however, implied to be "that early and rude state of society which precedes both the accumulation of stock and the appropriation of land" (51). From these passages, it is quite clear that labor as a measure of value was meant by Smith to be a mere hypothetical approximation approaching strict proportionality only in special or extreme cases.

By corollary, if the value or real price of a commodity is determined by its relative labor content, the "labor commanded" by a commodity should provide a convenient yardstick by which one can tell the purchasing power of the commodities possessed by a person. This point is well illustrated in the following.

> Every man is rich or poor according to the degree in which he can afford to enjoy the necessaries, conveniences, and amusements of human life. But after the division of labour has once thoroughly taken place, it is but a very small part of these with which a man's own labour can supply him. The far greater part of them he must derive from the labour of other people, and he must be rich or poor according to the quantity of that labour which he can command, or which he can afford to purchase. The value of any commodity, therefore, to the person who possesses it, and who means not to use or consume it himself, but to exchange it for other commodities, is equal to the quantity of labour which it enables him to purchase or command. (32)

Clearly, Smith's intent was to develop a standard measure or index of the purchasing power of individuals for an economy that has reached a certain level of sophistication in its division of labor. This standard is useful because it helps to provide intertemporal comparisons of welfare. Labor provides the best yardstick because it is the basic, though not the exclusive, factor of production.

> Labour alone, therefore, never varying in its own value, is alone the ultimate and real standard by which the value of all commodities can at all times and places be estimated and compared. It is their real price; money is their nominal price only. (37)

What made Smith think that labor does not vary in its value? In part, one might attribute this belief to his implicitly postulating a state of standard technology and, thereby, a constant cost function in his analysis. Growth, in Smith's view, was brought about jointly by the process of division and specialization of labor as well as by the expansion of the market. Under such assumptions, higher productivity is engendered by either the upgrading or by different arrangements of existing labor. Although the same commodity could be produced with less labor, the basic idea that the value of a commodity is determined by its labor embodiment remains unchanged, as long as labor remains the essential contributing factor to production.

From this, one might hastily conclude that Smith ignored other factors of production. This, however, is not the case. Smith was clearly aware of the distinction between value or real price and exchangeable value or market price. He was well aware of the fact that, at any particular moment, market price is affected by factors of production other than labor that are subject to contingencies in a growing and more complex economy. Smith, in fact, analyzed exchangeable value in three cost components (i.e., wages, profits, and rents).

> As the price or exchangeable value of every particular commodity, taken separately, resolves itself into some one or other, or all of these three parts; so that of all the commodities which compose complexly, must resolve itself into the same three parts, and be parcelled out among different inhabitants of the country, either as the wages of their labour, the profits or their stock, or the rent of their land. . . . Wages, profit, and rent, are the three original sources of all revenue as well as of all exchangeable value. All other revenue is ultimately derived from one or other of these. (54)

At this point, one might wonder how Smith could reconcile his apparently inconsistent positions. On one hand, he attributed to labor the measure of value and the ultimate source of the real price. On the other hand, he clearly recognized that wages are not the only cost component in production. Moreover, to have merely posited labor as a measure of value, or to have analyzed different cost components that enter exchangeable value or market price, does not warrant one to say that Smith possessed a theory of value.[1] To qualify as a theory of value, Smith had to be able to say in what way each of the cost components determines, jointly or separately, exchangeable value. Taking into account that Smith had not gone that far, could one still say that Smith possessed a theory of value?

In a sense, the answer is a qualified yes. Smith's theory of value is hinged upon his general theory of a harmonious and self-regulating economic order and is subordinate to it. To Smith, short-term fluctuations in exchangeable values or market prices are subject to the contingent movements of factor costs. Hence, these exchangeable values or market prices that fluctuate accordingly cannot be the real prices. To him, value or natural price is

> the central price, to which the price of all commodities are continually gravitating. Different accidents may sometimes keep them suspended a

1. It could, of course, be described as a simple cost or production theory. Or, as Sraffa put it, as an "Adding-up Theory" (Dobb 1973, 46). It is, however, debatable if the mere juxtaposition of different cost components should be conferred the status of a theory.

> good deal above it, and sometimes force them down even somewhat below it. But whatever may be the obstacles which hinder them from settling in this centre of repose and continuance, they are constantly tending towards it. (60)

But in the long run, these contingent factors are likely to be averaged out. Given that labor is implicitly the dominant and constant factor, fluctuations in market prices naturally will have to oscillate around the constant factor of labor content that can be taken to reflect the real prices. In other words, out of myriad possible market prices, there exists one set of natural prices that is in line with the labor factor to which market prices will converge, as the economy regulates itself toward the most harmonious order. In this interpretation, the set of natural prices reflecting some constant labor factor represents the logical outcome of the self-regulating economic order. Deviations from the natural prices, on the other hand, could be viewed as temporary states of disequilibrium that prompt movements of factor prices and direct the system toward some kind of equilibrium. Value, in this view, can be interpreted in present-day terminology to be prices in a long-run, stable equilibrium, the point at which resources in an economy, in particular labor, are supposed to settle at a state of efficient utilization.

Ricardo's Search for an Invariable Measure of Value

Like Smith, Ricardo subscribed to a cost-of-production theory of value. To him, utility is the necessary but not sufficient condition for exchangeable value.

> Utility . . . is not the measure of exchangeable value, although it is absolutely essential to it. . . . Possessing utility, commodities derive their exchangeable value from two sources: from their scarcity, and from the quantity of labour required to obtain them. (Ricardo 1951, 1:11–12)

Scarcity, however, only applies to certain unique products, such as works of art or particular kinds of wine, whose supply is highly restricted. Otherwise, the source of value embodied in a commodity is invariably derived from human labor and the amount of value embodied varies directly with the amount of labor required to produce it. Ricardo demonstrated through a process of reduction that each cost component that enters into exchangeable value could be expressed in terms of labor cost alone. First of all, he eliminated rent as a bona fide cost of production. He then proceeded to reduce one component of capital, namely circulating capital, to labor cost, the former being the amount of corn or the wage fund required to sustain the current labor force. However, he had difficulty in reducing fixed capital to labor. According to him,

> this difference in the degree of durability of fixed capital, and this variety in the proportions in which the two sorts of capital (fixed and circulating) may be combined, introduce another cause, besides the greater or less quantity of labour necessary to produce commodities, for the variations in their relative values—this cause is the rise or fall in the value of labour. (1:30)

While Ricardo accepted that differences in the durability of fixed capital and differences in the fixed capital-to-labor ratio do affect exchangeable value, these differences represent, in his opinion, but a small fraction of, say, 6 to 7 percent of the overall cost that accounts for exchangeable value. As an expedient, or the rule of thumb, one could perhaps say that the labor content is all that one need to take into account.

But if what Ricardo was after was merely some rule-of-thumb standard, then one would have difficulty understanding his continuing obsession in searching for an invariable measure of value, nothwithstanding his recognition that there could be no perfect empirical embodiment of the concept of an invariable measure of value. One could not understand, for instance, why he attached such importance to this particular pursuit, to the extent that he believed his entire theory would stand or fall with its validity (i.e., his theory of value; see Ricardo 1951, 7:250–51). Nor could one easily understand the kind of obstinacy he displayed in pursuing this subject. In his last letter to James Mill, he said,

> I have been thinking a good deal on this subject lately but without much improvement—I see the same difficulties as before and am more confirmed than ever that strictly speaking there is not in nature any correct measure of value nor can any ingenuity suggest one, for what constitutes a correct measure for some things is a reason why it cannot be a correct one for others. (9:387)

The plausible reason for Ricardo's persistent effort to deal with something that one might dismiss as an expedient is that his theory of value, notwithstanding its instrumental character, is critical to the success or failure of his ultimate project, namely his theory of distribution. In the original preface to the *Principles of Political Economy and Taxation* (1817), he stated that the principal problem in political economy is to determine the laws that regulate the distribution of the produce of the earth among landowners, capitalists, and laborers. Ricardo was concerned with distribution for two prime reasons. On one hand, he was pessimistic about the prospects of an industrial economy. In his view, the long-term state of the economy is one with limited growth potential, if not a stationary one. The stagnating mechanism that brings about such a state was conceived to be the law of diminishing returns, which characterizes agricultural production and which dominated much of classical economic thought. With dim prospects of growth, the problem of the division of the national product between antagonistic social classes, for example landowners and capitalists, naturally assumes importance, for how the distribution is made becomes the sole remaining determinant of living standards.

In spite of his pessimism about the long-term prospects of the industrial economy, Ricardo was still very much concerned about the extent to which growth was possible and about the effects on income distribution brought about by the process of economic growth. As a result, he was concerned about building a theory of profit and explaining the rate of profit in the national product. Being aware of the important role played by the accumulation of capital in the new economic situation brought about by the industrial revolution and of the role of profit in the process of capital accumulation, he naturally considered that an increase or decrease in the rate of profit has important repercussions for the development of the economy. To explain or to predict the rate of profit, he considered it necessary to develop a measure of value that would be independent of changes in the division of the social product so that he could use it in a theory of distribution.

He went about this first by developing the corn "rate of profit" in his *Essay on Profits* (1815). Using the Malthusian theory of rent and population, he demonstrated the inverse relation between the share of rents and the rate of profit by using a simple corn example. He then generalized the determination of profit to a more complex economy. He showed that, given a particular level of output and a given state of technology, the rate of profit varies inversely with the share of wages in the net product. His labor theory of value is fundamental in this demonstration because it provides him a common denominator by which the different heterogeneous aggregates that enter the profit-rate determination could all be expressed in homogeneous labor magnitudes. Alternatively put, the assumption of a common, constant denominator is crucial to the validity of Ricardo's theory of profit, which, in turn, is crucial to his theory of growth and distribution. Seen in this way, Ricardo's untiring search for an invariable measure of value can be readily understood. However, if this interpretation were correct, Ricardo's theory of value would take on an indisputably instrumental character. One might, then, wonder whether or not Ricardo's theory could be qualified, after all, as a bona fide theory of value. As O'Brien puts it, "Ricardo is often credited with having advanced a labour theory of value, although this is not, as we shall see, a strictly accurate description of what he produced" (1975, 84).

A Grand Rationalizing Instrument: Marx's Labor Theory of Value

Marx followed Ricardo in adopting a labor theory of value and made some corrections to his formulation. To Marx, the concept of labor should be analyzed at a more abstract level. In a commodity-producing society, it is labor in general rather than concrete, specific labor that should be perceived to produce value. Besides, labor that produces value should be social rather than private and necessary rather than wasted. By social labor, Marx means only labor that is devoted to the production of commodities that are actually exchanged. By necessary labor, Marx means that the mere expenditure of labor time does not add to the value of commodities unless that labor time is necessary for the production of the commodity under a given state of technology.

On the surface, Marx advanced his labor theory of value in order to account for the exchange values that commodities possess in commodity-producing societies. In a nutshell, he asserted that the value possessed by a commodity is the amount of exchange value it has. In a metaphorical sense, it is a kind of "social substance" that resides in the commodities. He further asserted that the amount of value that a commodity possesses at any time is determined by the amount of socially necessary labor that is required at that time to produce a sample of that commodity, socially necessary labor to be defined as the number of man-hours of averagely skilled and intense labor needed to produce a sample of that commodity using the standard tools and technology of the time. Marx further asserted that, in its normal state, the exchange of commodities is the exchange of commodities of equal value.

Marx's labor theory of value was generally criticized as resting on too many oversimplifying assumptions. One familiar criticism is that he assumed that the average skilled labor in a capitalist economy is unskilled labor. Another criticism is that Marx assumed that more complex labor is nothing more than the summation of simple labor. As Elster aptly puts it,

> notice, . . . the extreme simplifications in this story. Raw materials are assumed to be available freely and costlessly. Production is assumed to take place without the use of produced means of production. The two kinds of works are assumed to be equally irksome or unpleasant. Acquired skills are ignored, as are inborn talents. When we introduce the complications that the story assumed away, the labour theory of value becomes difficult to defend, or even to state coherently. (1986, 64).

Moreover, the arguments implied in the theory, namely, that the only property that is common to all of the different quantities of commodities that are capable of being exchanged for one another is the property of being producible by means of labor and that different commodities that are exchanged for one another embody the same amount of value, are remarkably weak and simplistic assertions. It simply is not justifiable to assume that all commodities that are capable of being exchanged possess some common property in equal magnitude in order for them to have the same exchange value.

Notwithstanding its basic weakness, the theory was meant to be the fundamental pillar of Marxist economics. It is the very basis upon which Marx's theory of surplus value rests. Without the idea that, in the aggregate, commodities exchanged at their values could be solely accounted for by labor, Marx could not have explained the origin of surplus value. Without the latter, he could hardly have advanced the thesis that the capitalist system of production, although appearing on the surface to establish an equality between all individuals as property owners, rests "in reality" on the private appropriation of the social surplus produced by a particular class. It would then be meaningless for him to make the distinction between labor power (the commodity that is available to capitalists on the market) and labor (the actual expenditure of human effort in production that adds value to commodities) or to contend that surplus value is possible within the capitalist system in the exploitation of workers through the institution of wage labor. With the existence of surplus value (derived solely from labor) "proven," he was able to further argue that, by virtue of its very organization, the capitalist system has a tendency to increase the rate of surplus value, resulting in either a shortening of the labor time necessary to produce a given set of use values or substituting entirely new products for existing ones. From this fundamental fact starts the dynamic and suicidal process of capitalist development, as the accumulation of the surplus brings into focus the inherently conflicting relationships between the capitalists and the laborers, and among the capitalist themselves.

Considered in this manner, the pivotal but instrumental role of Marx's labor theory of value is transparent. Supported by this conceptual instrument, Marx was able to demonstrate the exploitive character of capitalist society as well as the inexorable fall of capitalism as a socioeconomic institution. One might, of course, say that Marx derived his conclusions about capitalism from the very premises he made. But given the remarkable weakness of the conceptual foundation of the labor theory of value, one has reason to suspect that what Marx actually did was to work backward from his conclusion to the premise. That this is so is not surprising. Contrary to his preaching that appearances are deceptive, Marx, himself, was, without much exaggeration, obsessed by a superficial and apparently pathological image that the capitalism of his day presented him. Out of his particular experiences and perhaps also out of his strong sense of humanity, he thoroughly rejected the kind of capitalism he personally encountered and, by extension, capitalism in general. Much of his theoretical work, tacitly guided by his pathological image of capitalism, could be suspected to work backward from his foregone decision to demonstrate the inescapability of its downfall. The labor theory of value, the very foundational conceptual tool by which he works out the conflicting relations between capital and labor leading to the ultimate, inevitable demise of capitalism, is the product of his foregone conclusion rather than a theory that is meant to have independent explanatory power of its own.[2]

Is There a Unified Theme in the Classical Theories of Value?

From the preceding discussion, it should be clear that, as far as the purposes and problem situations of these thinkers are concerned, one could discern little similarity among the respective theories they posited. In Smith's framework, the value theory seems to be the by-product of his conception of growth as well as his conception of the self-regulating economic order. In Ricardo's framework, value is the accounting instrument employed to derive a theory of profit and, by extension, a general theory of distribution of social product, the latter being importantly governed by Ricardo's larger concern about the possibilities of growth of an industrial economy. To Marx, the significance of the labor theory of value lies in providing the theoretical tool for demonstrating the fundamental defect of the capitalist system, which, through a series of self-propelling steps, leads to the demise of itself.

Each of these thinkers, living in the budding stage of capitalism, was only able to have a dim grasp of its possible shape. Notwithstanding their natural limitations, they were compelled by the very logic of their studies to make speculative conjectures about the overall shape and the future of the new industrial system that was dawning at their time. Each believed he had grasped the fundamental property of this new system and held the key to its future path. These "ontological" conjectures, needless to say, affected, to no small extent, the formulation of their problems and the choice of their theoretical tools. Their value theories are, in a sense, either the by-products of these metaphysical images or the theoretical tools that they use to justify their large metaphysical pictures. As such, they play only a subordinate role in the overall "parent" frameworks. In spite of their alleged claim to the status of theory, they are actually either the logical consequence (as in the case of Smith) or the instrument (as in the cases of Ricardo or Marx) employed to justify or to rationalize a set of preconceived metaphysical and ontological suppositions. As subordinate theory, they stand or fall by the broad metaphysical presuppositions that constitute the ultimate pillars of the parent framework.

It can, of course, be argued that from the stance of theory justification,

2. From the stance of theory justification, the validity of the theory itself does not depend on, and is therefore not affected by, such relations.

the validity of each of these theories should be considered or appraised in its own right, independent of its parent framework. But ironically, once we adopt such a perspective, each of these theories immediately loses much of its power or appeal. Smith's theory is turned, almost instantaneously, into a nonfalsifiable theory whose truth is to be dependent on ex-post facts, while the falsity of the Marxist postulate taken independently is transparent. And once removed from its original context, Ricardo's search for an accounting essence turns out to be a naive and futile enterprise, as Ricardo himself admitted in the last years of his hopeless search. In other words, none of these value theories, considered as independent theories, possesses interesting explanatory value or sound predictive power or even a falsifiable status. Their appeal is derived as part of a total package of the respective economics upon which they depend but to which they lend powerful rationalization. Joan Robinson's remark on this subject is most insightful.

> Prices are the most obvious surface phenomena in economic life. Every school of economic theory was obliged to give some account of the determination of prices, but each school was concerned with wider questions; a theory of value was merely incidental to a general view of how the economic system operates. (1978, 182)[3]

If each of these theories are so different in their respective problem situations, was it a mistake to lump them together, as we sometimes did, into a "classical" theory of value? Are we still justified in subsuming them under one common framework, beyond the superficial reason that they are all cost-of-production, objective theories of value? And, more important, can any objective theory of value hold in principle, even if none of those held by the classical scholars could stand?

Notwithstanding the dependent status of the classical value theories, there is one overwhelming reason why we could still meaningfully lump all of them into one single category. I have said that all these classical economists, in spite of their very different grasps of the essence of the capitalist economy, shared the common mission of projecting the future shape of the new system. As such, they characteristically took a long view of economic variables and problems. Long-term development being their prime concern, it is only natural that they were more interested in the questions of how productive possibilities could be enhanced, what limits there were to these possibilities, and how they could be overcome. Hence, their focus was more on identifying factors that remain unchanged over time. Market prices that fluctuate under the forces of supply and demand were considered secondary phenomena and,

3. I owe this citation to Alan Wong.

therefore, less interesting issues because they were contingent upon particular circumstances or short-term factors. More concerned about the broad shape of the future, the classical scholars were understandably interested in factors that enable them to bridge the present and the future. Subjective utilities, and indeed all demand-side factors, varying from moment to moment, are too whimsical to provide either an invariable measure of value or intertemporal comparisons of welfare. Only an understanding of supply-side factors could help throw light on the trends and patterns of long-term development. Seen in this way, their search for a deeper understanding of the operating laws of the economy or for some common denominators that facilitate intertemporal comparisons of value is by no means an unsound strategy.

Are Objective Theories of Value Tenable?

The pursuit of the classical economists interpreted in this generalized sense sounds plausible. But the plausibility of the aim of an inquiry does not mean that there will necessarily be tenable solutions. While it clearly makes sense to posit or search for long-range patterns that govern value or price formation in an economy, it does not make sense to infer from this premise that only supply-side factors matter or to leap into the monistic thesis that only one type of supply-side factor, labor, matters to the exclusion of other factors. One fundamental defect of the kind of cost-of-production theory of value held by the classical economists is that if the source of value is said to reside exclusively in one factor of production, then that theory would have difficulty explaining why and how that factor could stay unchanged in the flux of the industrial economy whose operation rests clearly on the dynamic interaction between different factors of production. Moreover, since the deliberate exclusion, or abstraction, of certain factors in the construction of these theories is not the outcome of a careful weighing of different candidates, but is merely contingent upon the heuristics of the parent metaphysical frameworks, these monistic classical theories cannot be said to spring from impartial considerations of the different first principles that might be involved in a theory of value. It is not the case that their authors, having carefully considered various alternatives, came to accept a particular factor as overridingly crucial and hence dwarfing the importance of other factors.

Another intrinsic difficulty of any cost-of-production theory of value is this: if a theory of value posits that the source of value is said to be derived from a package of cost factors, the determination of which is nonspecific, that theory will immediately lose its rigor and appeal. To avoid this difficulty, one might propose, after Pasinetti, that prices are some kind of indices showing the relative "tangible" efforts (i.e., labor) that society is obliged to put into producing different goods. However, at such a level of abstraction, the theory no longer has much content and is at the risk of being taken as a tautology. On the other hand, if one wants to say more by insisting on a monistic position such as that held by the classical economists, what one ends up having will be an interesting but false thesis. This, perhaps, is the inherent paradox facing theorists who posit a cost-of-production theory of value.

Recent major efforts to revive the cost-of-production theories of value were made by Sraffa and Pasinetti, among others. It is often alleged that, with Sraffa (1960), interest in Ricardo's theory is rekindled. Sraffa employed a system with a static structure of production that is capable of self-reproduction and generates a surplus that can be used for capacity expansion or consumption. He took as given a pattern of output, technological conditions, and the rate of profit. On the assumption that competition will equalize profit rates in all sectors, prices in this system were shown to be determined entirely by technological considerations and the given profit rate without reference to demand-side factors. From this system and by constructing the idea of a "standard commodity," he also attempted to examine Ricardo's "absolute value," and to show that this idea is possible under certain analytical interpretations of the system. In effect, Sraffa's "natural" prices can be shown to be equal to the average costs of production.

Pasinetti (1986) placed high hopes on the possibility of developing a general theory of value to be based on supply-side factors alone, in particular labor.[4] According to him, prices emerge out of the necessity of an extensive division of labor. As such, they are indices of costs.

> Prices, that is the rates of exchange among commodities, arise from the fact that each individual specializes in producing only one (or even a fraction of one) consumption good, but at the same time needs all consumption goods, which must therefore be obtained through exchange. Production and exchange are inherently linked by labour specialization. In this context, prices express the "toil and trouble" of production. Hence the physical quantity of labour emerges as the clearest objective standard with which to compare all goods and services. (1986, 423)

He was confident that, by applying his method of generalizing a pure labor theory of value (1981), it is possible to develop a labor theory of the rate of profit, a labor theory of the rate of interest, and, ultimately upon these foundations, a complete generalization of the labor theory of value and, by extension, to reach the extreme of completely covering all economic phenomena.

---

4. Pasinetti believes it is legitimate to assume that a technologically advanced society has the characteristic of using only labor, and, therefore, there is no need to refer such a model to a primitive society, as Adam Smith did.

Interesting as these attempts are, they must be considered misplaced efforts from the perspective I have just developed. Taken in isolation, Ricardo's idea of, and his search for, the absolute value is meaningless. As a result, any subsequent reinterpretation of the idea would only yield tautologies such as those given by Sraffa, sophisticated and technically interesting as they might be. Expectedly, these tautologies cannot alter the basic flaws in the fundamental concepts. The same can be said of Pasinetti's theories.

But cost-of-production theories of value need not be equated with objective theories of value. The synonymous use of the two phrases has been rather unfortunate; it unwittingly reinforces the view that cost-of-production theories are all there is to objective theories of value. From the preceding discussion, it is, of course, naive to say that there can be purely objective theories without regard to subjective considerations. On the other hand, there is no a priori reason why we cannot study the objective patterns of human preferences at the social level and their changes over time, in spite of the fact that many human preferences are either very much subjective phenomena or are products of human conventions governed by contingent circumstances. One goal of this book is to inquire into the possibility of objectively studying such patterns.

CHAPTER 2

The Neoclassical Solution to the Problem of Value and Its Metamorphosis

The Neoclassical Solution

From the discussion in chapter 1, one might say that classical economists as a whole, taking a long-view perspective of the economy, were prone to ignore day-to-day changes in the economy and were, thereby, prone to dismiss fluctuations of market prices. To them, supply and demand can hardly constitute an adequate framework for the understanding of the long-term movement of prices. This position might be further defended on the ground that classical economists implicitly take demand and demand-side factors to be of a rather whimsical character and free of lawful regularities. To go beyond the whims of demand and to make meaningful intertemporal comparisons of value or welfare, one must locate some intrinsic, invariable substance that exists in lawful regularities in different types of commodities across different economic systems.

Convincing as this rationale for ignoring fluctuations of market prices might at first seem, a serious thinker would have difficulty in accepting, without question, why there has to be an absence of order or regularities in the subjective and demand-side factors and why one could not offer an alternative account that takes the role of subjective factors seriously in the understanding of price determination. Even in the heyday of classical economics, such a position did not go unchallenged. Samuel Bailey, convinced that value is a relative concept, held that it is contradictory to speak of an invariable standard of value amid universal fluctuation (1825). Before Mill's dogmatic claim "there is nothing in the law of value which remains for the present or any future writer to clean up" ([1848] 1967, 456), Nassau Senior had already brought the notion of utility back to the theory of value ([1836] 1938). An intellectual revolution was soon in the making. Gossen elaborated his new laws of value based on the principle of diminishing utility (1854). Shortly afterward, Jevons began to embark on his famous attack on Ricardian orthodoxy. A marginal revolution was said to take place with a subjective theory of value completely replacing the cost-of-production theories espoused by classical economists.

Not all economic historians are convinced that the way the subjective theory of value and its subsequent neoclassical framework emerged reached revolutionary magnitude. This dissent could be defended on the ground that ideas have subtle, lineal relations, and it has seldom been the case that an important idea in history was born entirely anew. However, from the stance of intellectual impact, the revolutionary character of the neoclassical framework can hardly be denied. Within the realm of value theory, the rise of the neoclassical theory means not merely the end of the cost-of-production theories, but the entire question of value was rendered a pseudoquestion to be legitimately bypassed. It was no coincidence that, with the ascendancy of the neoclassical theory, the idea of value in the sense of "intrinsic worth" or "real worth," as understood by other branches of social science or philosophy, was no longer considered relevant to economic discourse.[1] As I have mentioned, the word *value* is seldom used in the formal literature except as equivalent to the word *price*. It might seem, therefore, unbelievable to the noneconomist, but Gerald Debreu's seminal work entitled *The Theory of Value* (1959) does not give an explanation of what value is.[2] Nor is one able to find a definition of value in John Hicks's famous *Value and Capital* (1939).

The neoclassical reformulation of the problem of value consisted in several steps. First, value was considered to be essentially a relative concept, expressing a relation between an object and a subject (e.g., Jevons [1871] 1970). With this change, the idea of intrinsic worth became something of a misplaced emphasis. The thrust of the inquiry then moved from value to exchange and from "natural" price to "market" price. The second step was to

1. Sociologists, psychologists, anthropologists, philosophers, and laymen all operate with a commonsense version of the word *value* that is far from the economist's meaning. The former talk about value in the broad sense of real worth, which clearly goes beyond the idea of price or price formation. Roger Sperry, for example, talks about value in relation to our beliefs, wants, needs, and ideology. He sees values inherent in the pattern of the mind being key determinants in all human decisions and actions (Sperry 1983). And when philosophers and social scientists inquire about questions of value, they would concentrate upon such questions as how do we obtain a sense of value; under what conditions do we attach value to certain objects or situations; how are different values ordered in our mind; how is value intersubjectively, socially, or culturally transmitted; how does one set of values come to dominate a society or economy, and how is it replaced over time by a new set; how does a set of values rigidify into norms that guide our behavior, action, or choice; and by what criteria do we appraise values.

2. Except for the strictly formalist definition of the value of an action: "The value of an action a relative to price system p is

$$\sum_{h=1}^{l} ph^{a}h,$$

i.e., the inner product $p \cdot a$" (Debreu 1959, 33, 35, 100).

take value to be measurable in terms of utility and, in particular, marginal utility. This was achieved by assuming that "just as the Theory of Statics is made to rest upon the equality of indefinitely small amounts of energy" (Jevons [1871] 1970, vii), utility could be subdivided in the same manner. Having broken up utility into divisible units, it was further posited that utility at the margin decreases with increased consumption of a given commodity for a consumer. The third step, one of synthesis, was taken by Marshall and Walras. With Marshall, the problem was to show the interdependence of supply and demand and to show how market prices are determined by an interaction between cost and utility. In Marshall's account, the equilibrium price is determined in a competitive market at the point of intersection of the supply and demand curves (Marshall 1923). In a different direction, Walras attempted to define a general equilibrium system for the economy by way of using simultaneous algebraic equations (see Walras 1874). In either case, value was found to be identical to the price determined under the equilibrium condition and measured by it.

In a slightly different formulation, one can say that the seminal idea of neoclassical value theory consists in the maximization of utility and in the law of diminishing marginal utility. Its key analytical tool is marginal analysis. Subject to a budget constraint, utility is said to be maximized by the consumer for a particular basket of commodities to be consumed at the point of equilibrium, for example, where the ratio of marginal utilities is equated to the ratio of prices. In this account, prices are indices of relative scarcity with respect to consumer preferences, while changes in relative prices can be said to be caused by consumer substitution. The same mode of analysis can be extended to production, positing profit-maximizing behavior on the part of the firm. From the vantage of the firm, profit is maximized when the value of the marginal physical productivity of each factor input is equated to its price. Expansion of output in a particular sector is caused by increases in the relative prices for that sector's output. Prices are determined in the market, where consumers and entrepreneurs meet and exchange commodities. Assuming perfect competition to prevail, partial equilibrium is obtained for a particular market when its aggregate demand equals its aggregate supply, and general equilibrium is reached when aggregate demand is equated to aggregate supply simultaneously in all markets. Equilibrium prices are then the sets of prices determined in such states.

The superiority of the neoclassical value theory over the classical value theory is beyond dispute. In one sense, it is now possible to say that the classical problem is largely a pseudoproblem. It is a pseudoproblem because, value being a relative concept, the search for an absolute standard inevitably turns out to be a futile enterprise. Thus, the problem was *dissolved*. In another sense, one could also say that neoclassical theory *solved* the problem of value through a synthesis of both supply-side and demand-side considerations. In the neoclassical framework, the determination of market prices simultaneously takes into account utility on the part of the consumer and cost on the part of the supplier; the equilibrium that thus ensues represents an optimal solution to these dual aspects. In a further sense, it is also possible to say that neoclassical theory, rooted in the bedrock of individual experience,[3] is more solidly grounded than the classical counterpart. Value as a subjective quality is clearly more defensible than value as a metaphysical substance or constant in the context of an evolving human society subject to continual changes in individual tastes on the one hand and technological know-how on the other. Moreover, the law of diminishing marginal utility upon which neoclassical value theory rests is more easily demonstrated and tested than any law positing an invariable measure or standard. It can be shown to rest on a biological fact that can hardly be disputed.

Of remarkable importance is the fact that the neoclassical solution of the value problem is based on an analytical technique that turns out to have far-reaching ramifications and applications. Marginal analysis turns out to be a special case in the broader technique of optimization, which provides the necessary technique, definition, and theoretical foundation for building a sophisticated economics. The equimarginal principle in neoclassical value theory, being an optimizing principle, not only provides a regulative guide by which one allocates resources or makes choices in specific situations, but it also provides the important theoretical idea of seeing cost as foregone opportunity. With the concept of cost elevated to this plane of understanding, it is possible to reformulate the nature of economic problems, in particular the nature of economic efficiency and the nature of economic rationality. A kind of Pandora's box in the positive sense is thus opened, with immense explanatory power to be tapped and vast technical potential to be unfolded. Seen from this broad perspective, neoclassical value theory was the first crucial step in the chain of reformulations and discoveries that led to the extensive buildup of the neoclassical edifice that we now have. Starting from the analysis of consumer behavior, the idea of balance at the margin and the optimization principle embodied therein was soon extended to the question of exchange and then to questions of production and distribution, eventually yielding a unified analytical framework for major realms of economic discourse. This unity brings an extra bonus. The neoclassical framework is not only formidable in solving and dissolving the question of value and its ability to encompass major realms of economic discourse, but it satisfies major, extraempirical as

3. This assumption is never considered problematic by neoclassical theory. This is a strange position, because it is clear that experiences must be interpreted. If experiences have to be interpreted, their interpretations may be fallible. But neoclassical theory never questions such fallibility and its ramifications.

well as methodological criteria that we usually employ in evaluating the epistemic status of theories, namely, simplicity, symmetry, aesthetic elegance, amenability to formal analysis, minimal assumptions, and so forth.

The unified application of the marginal technique of analysis yields a further insight into the fundamental character of an economy. That is, the economic system could be seen as one where everything depends on everything else and where each part is interconnected to other parts. The determination of rent, wages, and profit was no longer seen as a series of separate problems, sharply distinguished from each other and each with a separate law confined to itself. This insight was not easily attained, and it took some time before the formal equivalence between utility maximization and profit maximization was recognized and before Marshallian partial equilibrium was finally integrated with Walrasian general equilibrium. However, what subsequently unfolded could somehow be anticipated, given the way the marginalists first formulated their problem of value and solved it.

The Metamorphosis of the Neoclassical Position

Given the superiority of the neoclassical insight over the classical one and given the remarkable explanatory power of its theoretical framework, one would hardly expect that the neoclassical paradigm would, at this time, come under sustained challenges from different quarters and with increasing intensity. I will bypass discussion of these various challenges and will confine my inquiry to the logic of the development of neoclassical value theory. I contend that much of the undermining of the original neoclassical insight in value theory in the course of its subsequent development as the neoclassical paradigm is the result of a wrong choice of research direction that was unwittingly inspired by the dominant intellectual theme of the time.

Once the potential of neoclassical value theory is recognized, several routes of research are open to practitioners. One route would be to further refine the subjective foundation of the value theory by way of, say, extracting or positing further aspects of the human mind that reflect upon and respond to price data or changes in price data. In this regard, the proper research direction would be to discover new subjective variables and patterns and to analyze how these variables and patterns interact with objective changes in economic reality. In this direction, the original neoclassical theory would have to refine its initial concept of utility and to make provision for modifying, from time to time, its assertions of subjective states in light of new findings in psychology or neurophysiology. If such a research direction had been pursued, the gradual uncovering of the complexity of the subjective aspect of internalizing price information and its subsequent effect on the valuational apparatus of the consumer would have shown that the first equation of ratios of marginal utility to price ratios was nothing more than a rule-of-thumb approximation and should not have been looked upon as a sound scientific fact upon which further logical deductions could be unquestioningly based. This route of inquiry, however, was not pursued.

Instead of that approach, two other routes were separately pursued by neoclassical theorists. The first simply took it for granted that the subjective theory of value in a form that enables us to derive the law of demand or to establish the existence of a consumer's equilibrium is the last word on the subject. There is no further need to explore whether or not there are deeper relationships between price and utility. One might say that such an approach was first adopted by Walras, who actually abandoned the search for the origin of value in favor of a purely formal but completely general theory of functional interdependence. The original problem of analyzing the origin of price from its subjective value roots was, to all intents and purposes, abandoned in this approach.

The other approach accepted the need to develop the subjective foundation of neoclassical value theory in order for subsequent analysis of objective measures, such as prices and quantities bought and sold, could stand on firm theoretical grounds. Unfortunately, the philosophy that inspired development was logical positivism, the dominant intellectual idea of the 1950s and 1960s. There are two major tenets in logical positivism that have a bearing on the development of neoclassical economics. First, propositions incapable of verification by sensory experience were considered to be metaphysical and meaningless. In light of this doctrine, assertions of utility or states of satisfaction must be considered as bordering on the metaphysical and, as such, should be minimized, if not altogether avoided. Interpersonal comparisons of utility, for example, were judged to be essentially "normative" or "ethical" statements that fell outside the purview of economics as a science. Second, meaningful knowledge consists, in part, in logical statements that can be derived from elementary statements directly based on sensory experience. From these two tenets, the logical positivist's approach to meaningful knowledge is to elaborate a system of logical statements upon certain incorrigible and elementary facts of experience. It is in this spirit and by this approach that neoclassical value theory developed, and the search for tenable, subjective roots of prices was transformed into the logic of choice.

The transformation took several steps. The first crucial step was taken when the cardinal concept of utility was replaced by the concept of ordinal utility. In this regard, Pareto's work was instrumental (1906). Holding a methodological position in favor of an absolutely formal and positive theory and of purging economics of all ethical elements, Pareto demonstrated that a purely ordinal conception of utility suffices for the formulation of a theory of choice. Alternately put, a scale of preferences can be deduced for each individual without the assumption of determinate utility functions. Adopting the concept of indifference curves first used by Edgeworth (1881), Pareto showed that in the case of two goods, an individual's system of preferences with respect to these two goods can be represented by an indifference map that will show different levels of satisfaction, from which it is possible to write a number of differential equations that will represent an equilibrium system in terms of indifference rather than utility functions. With the advent of the ordinal approach, attempts to arrive at a cardinal measurement of utility, for example, in terms of utils, fell into disfavor (e.g., Fisher 1892), in spite of the fact that there were still some economists who continued to attempt to provide a measure of utility (see Ramsay 1931; von Neumann and Morgenstern 1944).

John Hicks developed and completed Pareto's indifference curve approach (1939). Diminishing marginal utility disappeared with utility as such, to be replaced by the idea of a diminishing marginal rate of substitution. The theorem of value was restated as the marginal rate of substitution between two classes of goods to equate to the ratio of prices in equilibrium. The entire theory of rational consumer behavior was shown to be deducible from ordinally interpreted indifference functions alone. In other words, fewer metaphysical assumptions were required in the premises to draw the same logical conclusions. Further development along this line was undertaken by Samuelson who, anxious to rid the theory of any remaining subjective connotations of value and disturbed by the growth of a welfare economics based upon utility, made vigorous attempts to introduce purely behavioral hypotheses that would be sufficient to establish the existence of the utility function (1948).

All these developments unwittingly altered the original problem, which was to fortify the foundation of subjective value theory. Instead what these developments led to was the emergence of the logic of choice, a project that finally purged the subjective theory of value of its subjective content. In addition, to enable the logic of choice to be vigorous and self-contained, it was necessary to introduce formal assumptions, such as consistency, completeness, and transitivity. These assumptions are, of course, unreal and (ironically), by the standards of positivism, metaphysical statements. The crucial question, therefore, centered upon whether or not such a logical approach is defensible and, if so, on what grounds. The defense, it turned out, was relatively easy. One most powerful and convincing statement was made by Lionel Robbins.

> The foundation of the theory of value is the assumption that the different things that the individual wants to do have different importance to him, and can be arranged therefore in a certain order. This notion can be expressed in various ways and with varying degrees of precision, from the simple want systems of Menger and the early Austrians to the more

> refined scales of relative valuations of Wicksteed and Schonfeld and the indifference systems of Pareto and Messrs Hicks and Allen. But in the last analysis it reduces to this, that we can judge whether different possible experiences are of equivalent or greater or less importance to us. From this elementary fact of experience we can derive the idea of the substitutability of different goods, of the demand for one good in terms of another, of an equilibrium distribution of goods between different uses, of equilibrium of exchange and of the formation of prices. (1935, 75)

The defense could be carried further. Since we need to draw a line between discourses in psychology and discourses in economics, what we should do is to begin with an assumption with a minimum psychological content so that economic theorizing (as a separate discipline) could be rendered independent of developments in psychology. The substitution of the logic of choice for the approach that broadens the subjective base means that, provided the first axioms are correct, there is no need henceforth to subject the fate of economics to the discovery of new facts and theories in psychology. With respect to positing unreal formal assumptions, one could easily defend this step from an instrumental stance. Completeness, consistency, transitivity, and so on are not the core part of the neoclassical theory.[4] These subsidiary assumptions are posited for the purpose of logical clarification and can, therefore, be divorced from the core axioms of neoclassical theory as formulated by Robbins. Hence, their unreality is irrelevant to the validity of neoclassical theory.

Logical Ordinalism versus Cognitive Cardinalism

All this sounds plausible and makes good methodological sense at a glance. But many neoclassical theorists failed to make one subtle distinction. The way the economist represents how the consumer valuates or should valuate his or her preferences might not faithfully reflect how the consumer actually valuates his or her preference.[5] This may sound tautologous, but the failure to make such a distinction does underlie much of the controversy over the cardinal versus the ordinal approach to utility. From the viewpoint of the economist's representation of how a consumer valuates his or her preferences, the ordinal approach is no doubt a superior one. Part of the subsequent development of neoclassical value theory, as we have seen, is grounded upon the success of this approach. But this success did not go entirely un-

4. Of course, not all neoclassical economists agree to this.

5. Some economists, e.g., Friedman and Machlup, do recognize this distinction.

challenged. Katouzian, for instance, showed that the ordinal approach subtly and implicitly depends on some mode of calibrating utility. Even in the two-commodity case, he showed that one cannot ultimately avoid invoking the cardinal concept of utility (1980, 62). This poses a serious threat to the purely ordinal concept, for it means that the ordinal approach to consumer theory could not escape the problem of absolute valuation of utility or preference, no matter how it is presented. In addition, Katouzian is able to show that the techniques employed by the neoclassical economist to measure utility involve assumptions that are either logically circular or that are empirically untestable (64–67). To these challenges, the neoclassical theorist might adopt a different line of defense. He or she might contend that even if the ordinal approach is not completely free of cardinal elements, it is still superior to the cardinal approach from the perspective of theory choice. The ordinal approach is still a more powerful one in that it is possible to derive the same set of results from fewer premises (i.e., satisfying the rule of Occam's razor) and, therefore, is to be preferred on rational grounds.

Katouzian's arguments, however, bring to light the subtle distinction I have just mentioned. The ordinal approach cannot be entirely free of cardinal elements because at the level of valuating preferences, the consumer is actually employing the cardinal approach. This should not surprise us on second thought, for the real-life consumer cannot be a logical machine operating in a value-free society. The devices and criteria he or she uses in valuating utility inescapably partake the properties of his or her cognitive apparatus as well as the value system he or she has incorporated. The cardinal approach is extensively employed in the real-life valuation of utilities because the cardinal measurement of subjective preferences is a more efficient and, thereby, more powerful valuational device to the consumer as a cognizing agent. It is efficient because it not only ranks preferences, but also ranks them by their intensities. This is to be expected, because it would be absurd to expect the consumer, as an efficient economic actor, to perform two operations to accomplish what he or she could do in one. In contrast, the ordinal approach is a weak one for the consumer valuating real-life situations because it does not give him or her a ranking of preferences by intensities in one operation.

Thus, we seem to come to a paradox. As a logical theory of consumer preferences, the ordinal approach is clearly superior. The superiority of the approach lies in that, in a logical representation, we give more credit to that theory that posits fewer axioms for the same logical contents or results. But a better theory in terms of parsimony in logical representation need not be able to command the same descriptive or explanatory power of reality. In purging the cardinal elements in real-life valuational processes, in refining and justifying an ordinal approach, and in pursuit of more powerful logical representations beyond the ordinal type, the neoclassical subjective theory of value unwittingly changed its problem and its status to that of a pure, logical theory. It is no longer concerned about how consumers actually valuate preferences and how such valuation might affect price formation in the real world. In this regard, Georgescu-Roegen's remarks are insightful.

> Neoclassical economists have criticized Marx's theory of value because it reduces concrete kinds of labour to an abstract notion—general labour. Yet neoclassicalists have done the same; they have reduced concrete wants to the general and abstract want: utility. However, it is on concrete want, not on the general want, that an individual bases economic choices. (1982, 940)

To this challenge, one might retort that, in the process of theory construction, one has no way but to abstract the most crucial factors from the multiplicity of factors and their interactions in the real world. Otherwise, we would forever be stuck at the level of description. Even if we choose to stay at the level of description, we might never be sure whether or not we had ever reached a complete description of reality. Theoretical progress, on the other hand, is founded upon our deliberately ignoring some less important real-world factors in the process of theory construction and accepting that some kind of descriptive distortion is necessary. In this view, the ordinal approach can still be seen to be making important theoretical advances, notwithstanding its omission of certain cognitive factors.

The Logicalism of Neo-neoclassical Economics

The drawback of the ordinal approach is not that it has a more powerful representation to offer. The problem arises only when, after that representation was made, it was considered no longer necessary to deal with the subjective factors either in their own right or in relation to the objective measures that they were supposed to lend support to. In other words, an implicit finality was imposed on the subject after the first logical representation was made. It was no longer considered necessary to review whether or not the first extraction was appropriate, or whether or not some crucial factors that might be relevant to building a richer consumer theory were omitted. Naturally more anxious to formalize the link between subjective factors and the law of demand than in developing a theory of subjective value per se, neoclassical theorists unwittingly changed their focus to the formal aspects of choice soon after they were convinced that the law of demand had been firmly "proven." With hindsight, one could then say that what went wrong is not that the ordinal approach involves an unreal abstraction, for abstraction of this kind is tolerable, if it is to be viewed as a first step in the building of a broader framework capable of assimilating reality at a later stage. What went wrong is that the thesis of ordinal valuation was taken as a first step toward the enterprise of building a logical theory of choice, a theory that puts logical aims ahead of the realist's aim of explaining the real-world.

In this new orientation, what essentially had been a causal theory of value (i.e., explaining market prices on the basis of subjective states) was transformed into a logical theory of choice and optimization (i.e., finding equilibrium values and studying the possibility and the nature of optimal solutions under different assumptions and by different logical devices). Of epistemic significance is the fact that the change was too subtle to be easily detected. Nor could the process be reversed in any simple way. Since the basic epistemic aim of a logical theory is simplicity and generality, sweeping, simplifying assumptions have to be introduced into the logical system for the deductions to follow logically from the premises. Unreal assumptions, such as perfect knowledge of preferences, consistency in ranking preferences, or transparency of market information, were first introduced with an instrumental purpose. At that early stage, when the meaning and purpose of such assumptions were clearly understood and adequately allowed for in the interpretation of their logical deductions, they were harmless. Indeed, one might say that, to some extent, they constituted positive progress from the perspective of knowledge representation.

What caused trouble is that, as the logical deductions began to build up, these original instrumental assumptions changed their status imperceptibly. They were gradually taken to be the standard "ontological furniture" of the logical system and were not meant to be removed or to have allowances made for their meanings. Because logical theorems of the second or third generation have to rest on logical theorems of the first generation, and because one too easily assumes that the latter are proven theorems and, therefore, their ontology can be taken for granted, it was seldom considered problematic to apply freely the logical theorems of the first generation in the derivation of the second- and third-generation theorems. By the time a sophisticated logical system is built up, it is no longer easy to relax these originally *instrumental* but now *ontological* assumptions on an one-by-one basis, because the relaxed assumptions (even those of a more realist kind), still have to be blended into the rest of the system in order to derive new theorems. Thus, the system can hardly escape being contaminated by the unreal ontology unwittingly formed in the rest of the system, an ontology that no longer has any conceivable counterpart in reality (compare Kaldor 1972). Simply put, once one sets out to theorize under the dictates of logicalism, its demand for "pure" results as well as for generality and simplicity will produce a heuristic of its own. In time, it will transform the very nature of the inquiry and the questions to be formulated. From then on, there is no any easy way of turning back.

Thus, it turned out that neoclassical value theory, having undergone such a metamorphosis, was finally emptied of the subjective elements that it initially possessed. When the idea of marginal utility was finally discarded in the technical literature that subsequently ensued, one could say that it no longer enjoyed the status of a subjective theory, for it had severed the very causal link between the subjective factors that govern preference ranking and price formation. As it grew into a full-fledged, logical theory, its inquiry began to center on how the price system works as an interdependent system rather than how the price system works in relation to the very nature and structure of our subjective preferences. Its original subjective insights are no longer considered essential or important. With such development, one could say that the demarcation of what we conventionally label as neoclassical economics into the finer divisions of neoclassical economics and neo-neoclassical economics (Hennings 1986) gets additional justification. Neo-neoclassical economics is, simply put, the logicalist transformation of neoclassical theory.

The consequences of the dominance of the "logicalist" neo-neoclassical economics are well-known and need not be dealt with in any more detail here. If suffices to say that, equipped with a sophisticated logical structure and armed with a universal optimization principle, neo-neoclassical theory can, in principle, deal with any problem by virtue of its generality, interpreting any real-world economic situation as an equilibrium problem. But many aspects of the human world are too far from equilibrium to be captured by the equilibrium concept. The human situation, characterized by inadequate information, could incapacitate even the most consistent application of the optimization strategy. The idea of optimization, powerful as it is, cannot adequately explain the phenomenon of increasing returns and the phenomenon of growth. Human agents, with their many cognitive weaknesses, cannot always withstand social influences that can sway them into accepting suboptimal values and positions. These are just two examples of the kind of difficulties that a logical theory is clearly not able to handle.

A scrupulous critic might go further. He or she might question how good the neoclassical value theory is as a bona fide subjective theory in its original state. For, as we know only too well, there are important subjective factors that were clearly omitted from neoclassical value theory. Consumers are often less-than-fully consistent decision makers. They make mistakes in their choices and regret their decisions. Especially over objects or services of a lasting nature, the payments for which have to be made in the beginning, consumers generally seem to be less well placed to make a correct judgment. The neoclassical subjective theory of value was silent on these important exceptions and on the conditions that bring them about. While the law of diminishing marginal utility is sound and important, it seems to be restricted largely to consumption of a "sequential" type. Some types of consumption activities, for example, music listening or sports, seem to interest the players over a long period, as long as the enjoyment is not continuous. All these are important phenomena that fall outside the scope of neoclassical subjective theory. Whereas the relationship between these "facts" and price formation are by no means obvious, they cannot simply be dismissed or ignored on such obscurantist grounds. But, on the other hand, if these "aberrations" are to be taken seriously by neoclassical value theory, they will pose remarkable difficulties. To develop a richer subjective theory of value that could bridge knowledge of our mental order and the prices that prevail in an economy, we clearly cannot depend on neoclassical theory, even in its prelogicalist form.

CHAPTER 3

The Drawbacks of Existing Alternatives and the Criteria for a Tenable Theory of Value

Austrian Subjectivism

The subjectivism that was first espoused in the marginal formulation and that was subsequently ignored in the development of neoclassical economics was preserved by the Austrian tradition and well revived in neo-Austrian economics. Menger, one of the pioneers of the marginal revolution and the subjective theory of value, was a staunch proponent of the idea of subjectivity in analyzing economic behavior. Like Jevons, he defined utility in a relative sense, that is, as the ability of a thing to be put into a causal relationship with a want. But unlike Jevons, he strongly emphasized the subjective character of consumption and the complexity of human wants. He defined value as "the significance which concrete goods or quantities of goods obtain for us from the fact that we are aware that the satisfaction of our wants is dependent upon our disposing of these goods" (Menger 1934, 78). Value to the individual of any portion of the available quantity of goods, arising from the limitations of goods in relation to our wants, is equal to the significance attached to the least satisfaction made possible by a single portion of the total available quantity. From this, Menger showed how exchange takes place and the point at which exchange will cease. Whereas Menger conceded that each individual will, when the occasion for exchange arises, formulate some quantitatively determinate ratio in which he or she is willing to exchange and that this ratio will reflect the ratio of his or her subjective values, he held that the subjective values themselves cannot be conceived of as determinate quantities. It is at this point that Menger parted company with the neoclassical economists, as he insisted on the thoroughly subjective character of utility and on the impossibility of finding an objective measure of utility for comparing or adding together levels of subjective welfare among individuals. As such, subjective values will determine the limits of exchange and the limits of price but not directly the prices themselves, because equations of exchange indicate states where no exchange takes place rather than where exchanges take place.

This subjectivist insight was refined and enriched by subsequent Austrian economists. In the view of Mises, subjective means that different people pursue different ends. With Hayek, subjectivism was expanded to mean the different possessions of knowledge by different economic players. From these insights, important tenets characteristic of the Austrian school emerged. First, cost acquired a subjective meaning. It is not the observable money expenditure required to produce a commodity, but the value of foregone output from an alternative use of the same resources. Second, prices are seen to be signals that guide individual actions. As a result, a competitive market order could be viewed as an information system, transmitting information to economic actors automatically through the signals carried by prices. As such, it is also an ordering mechanism that enables economic actors to utilize widely dispersed information about the significance of circumstances of which they are mostly ignorant. In this view, the aim of the market order is to cope with the economic actor's inevitable ignorance of most of the particular facts that determine this order. Third, competition could be seen as a discovery procedure in which economic actors learn to improve their well-being through a process of trial and error. Because the market process is one of discovery, it stands in stark contrast to the kind of equilibrium characteristic of the neoclassical perfect information model, in spite of the fact that the market does tend toward equilibrium through the coordination of individual plans by the price system.

All these ideas sound very plausible. As a matter of fact, when compared with its neoclassical counterpart this account is a far superior one in terms of its ability to explain real-word phenomena, for example, entrepreneurship. It is also a powerful account in the elucidation of the subjective character of individual valuation, especially in terms of knowledge acquisition and expectation formation. Notwithstanding these superior features, the Austrian framework is not without its drawbacks and limitations. While many of its basic theses are true in outline, it leaves out of its account of value theory the important, more detailed processes through which individual valuations jointly interact to form prices and what kind of causal mechanisms are involved in these processes. Also objectionable is the fact that, within the Austrian framework, one cannot find a theory of value formation, that is, how consumers acquire the kind of preferences they hold. Although Menger emphasized the creation of new economic goods through the increase of knowledge, and Hayek implicitly implied that the knowledge and preferences of economic actors adjust spontaneously to changes in the market order, it is not unfair to say that, in general, Austrian economics did not pay much attention to those systematic factors in the economy that might shape individual preferences. This is not surprising, because the Austrian thesis of consumer sovereignty, based on their strong thesis of subjectivity in human judgment, naturally accords consumers almost complete autonomy in their judgments to the extent that, although not infallible, they are their own masters insofar as the kinds of values they are prepared to accept or reject.

These direct criticisms of its value theory aside, Austrian subjectivism is not without some general difficulties of its own. Within the Austrian school, one can discern different strands of thought that stand in tension with one another. At one pole, there is the radical position espoused by some neo-Austrians.[1] These radical subjectivists appeal either to the idiosyncracies of the individual or the general indeterminacy of the human condition. They subscribe, in general, to different degrees of methodological individualism. While theirs are refreshing insights, they generally stop at pointing out the difficulties of objectifying subjective phenomena, as the hard core of their doctrine consists largely of "negative" statements, for example, the impossibility of perfect information, the vagaries of consumer tastes and preferences, the impossibility of mechanistic predictions of human behavior, the impossibility of perfect knowledge, and so on. As a result, they might be accused of nihilistic tendencies, ignoring "the way in which the behaviour of individuals is shaped, selectively, by the reactions of other people, and by the situations in which individuals act" (Shearmur 1983, 80).

At the other pole, there are neo-Austrians who follow the footsteps of Mises. Not all of them endorse Mises's view that the first premises he posited for theory building are self-evident truths. But they generally believe, as Mises did, that it is not necessary for economics to interface with psychology. Such a belief arises either because these neo-Austrian theorists fear that attempts to interface economics with psychology would mean that the autonomy of economics has to be surrendered to the vicissitudes of discoveries of new psychological truths or because they are skeptical of applying fragmented and low-level findings in psychology to economics. Instead, they look to more abstract propositions pertaining to the general human condition with regard to, say, choice or scarcity as the basic axioms of their frameworks. One can call this position "praxeological subjectivism."

Occupying the middle ground is Hayek's position, which one might call "natural subjectivism." Although Hayek fully subscribed to the subjectivity thesis in the Austrian tradition, he did not, especially in his later days, find himself in agreement with the extreme views of either radical or praxeological subjectivism. Influenced by Popper, Hayek considered social phenomena to be merely a subset of complex phenomena in general. Like all other complex phenomena in the physical sphere, social phenomena are, in principle, capable of being studied by the same scientific method that we use in the physical sciences. The only methodological difference between the study of

1. See, for example, Addleson 1986.

the social sciences and that of the physical sciences, or more correctly, between the study of complex phenomena and that of "not-so-complex" phenomena, is that predictions in the social sciences are predictions in principle but not predictions in detail. Theories in the social sciences do not describe concrete individual occurrences in our daily life. They constitute the broad frameworks within which individual occurrences happen.

Other Alternative Solutions to the Problem of Value: Theories of Choice

Austrian subjectivism is not the only kind of subjectivism upheld by economists interested in the question of value. As the spell of the reigning neoclassical orthodoxy fades and as the idea of subjectivism acquires a wider meaning, economists who are influenced by the Austrians but do not feel obliged to accept its other tenets look to subjectivity as a source of inspiration (see Coats 1983). To some economists, subjectivism has come to include any theory that "takes private experience to be the sole foundation of factual knowledge, even if it admits that objective knowledge can be derived from this subjective base" (Shand 1980). Characteristic of these non-Austrian subjectivists is their view that it is necessary to rebuild a link between economics and psychology and to take the latter into account in offering economic hypotheses to explain real-world events, in particular in tackling problems of consumer choice and firm behavior (see Earl 1986; Loasby 1976; Wiseman 1983).[2] Earl, for example, takes the theories of personality developed by George Kelly, a U.S. psychologist, and Kelly's proposal to analyze human beings as scientists in order to analyze the behaviors of consumers and their reactions to different real-world situations. In this view, consumers attempting to cope with the complex world are similar to normal scientists, that is, they form theories about the world and test whether or not those theories fit. With this conceptual foundation, Earl attempts to explain various consumption phenomena, such as "keeping up with the Joneses," the nature of clashes in tastes, and sudden shifts in consumer durable purchases, that one has difficulty in handling with neoclassical theory. In order to distinguish this approach from the various brands of Austrian subjectivism, we might call it "scientific subjectivism." Although this is a budding development and much remains to be done to integrate plausible theories of psychology with theories about price formation, it is clearly a progressive research program in the

2. For a succinct account of the relations between economics and psychology, see A. W. Coats: "Economics and Psychology: the Death and Resurrection of a Research Programme" pp. 43–64 of Latsis 1976, as well as "Economics and Psychology: A Resurrection Story" in Earl 1987.

Lakatosian sense. It is progressive because, by Lakatos's standards, it is capable of yielding novel explanations of existing phenomena and of spurring a multiplicity of theories to compete among themselves. However, such a position is not without its weaknesses, the most outstanding one being that it faces the difficulty of selecting and determining, among the seemingly extensive repertory of psychological theories, what particular one should be the most pertinent and fundamental to building a theory of value. And since these theories of psychology exist on different levels of abstraction, there is the additional difficulty of determining the level of abstraction that is necessary and proper in the formulation of economic theories. In contrast, the praxeological subjectivist could claim an advantage in that, because they confine their importation of psychological theories to the most abstract level, they can avoid the problems involved in testing theories comprising propositions of different levels of abstraction.

The non-Austrian subjectivists are not alone in their attempts to advance new theories about consumer behavior and consumer choice. Both the limitations of the neoclassical model in explaining many aspects of consumer behavior and interest in empirical measurements of demand have also attracted many theorists from the neoclassical camp to improve upon the standard model by adding new behavioral postulates. Lancaster, for example, proposes that consumers should be seen as wanting commodities not for the sake of possessing them as commodities, but for the characteristics of which they believe them to be comprised (1966). There are expectancy value compensatory choice models (e.g., Fishbein 1963; Rosenberg 1956) that postulate the consumer as choosing a scheme of action with the highest total expected value among a range of possible schemes, each scheme being evaluated separately with regard to all the attributes or characteristics that are considered to be relevant. In competition with these models are the lexicographic choice models (e.g., Georgescu-Roegen 1954; Tversky 1969), that postulate that the consumer, while considering all of the possible schemes of action, centers on one single attribute at a time. The common problem with such models, which are built on the neoclassical framework, is their common implicit assumption that the information-processing capacity of the consumer is at once efficient and nonexhaustible, although lexicographic models of the behavioral type are designed to overcome such a problem. In a sense, some of these models are even weaker from the epistemic viewpoint than the standard neoclassical model. While the neoclassical model can defend its unreal assumptions by resorting solely to instrumental arguments, these attempts to inject some realism into the neoclassical model find new difficulty in blending or reconciling its proposed modifications (which are realist) with the remaining unreal assumptions in the framework that are supposedly to be justified on instrumental grounds. As in the case of theories put forward by the scientific subjectivists, these neoclassical appendages face the same problem of selecting, out of a large number of possible alternatives, the most appropriate revisions. Even granted that these problems can be overcome, there is still the problem of how to employ the revisions to explain the phenomenon of price formation so they can be qualified as value theories. Given such inherent difficulties, it is not surprising to find Mishan so cynical about these improvements on the neoclassical model.

> After all the display of technical virtuosity associated with such theorems, there is nothing that the practising economist can take away with him to help him come to grips with the real world. Indeed, he would be no worse off if he remained ignorant of all theories of consumer behaviour, accepting the obviously indispensable Law of Demand on trust. (1961, 1)

In recognition of the possible complementarity between neoclassical economics and Austrian economics, there are eclectic efforts to reconcile these two positions (e.g., Moss 1987).[3] Accepting the neoclassical model of constrained maximization as useful as a metaphoric device for modeling certain types of rule-driven behavior, Moss sees the opportunity for this position to be substantiated and improved "through the expedient of Austrian analysis." In his view, the Austrian framework, for all its brilliant insights into the economic condition (e.g., uncertainty, the creativity of the economic actor, and the importance of learning), is far from an adequate replacement for the neoclassical framework. Nor is it capable of providing a workable theory to account for price formation. On the other hand, the neoclassical framework, in spite of its unreal premises, commands considerable explanatory power, in particular with respect to price formation. Moss's view is an interesting one, but it is inadequate in two respects. First, it fails to make the distinction between the neoclassical model espoused by Marshall (with substantial realism and potential to explain particular cases of price formation) and the neoclassical model of the logical type that no longer considers it necessary to explain the price formation of particular products. Second, for all his electic claims, Moss has not shown a way of mending the neoclassical framework by injecting Austrian insights.

A Methodological Critique of Existing Theories of Value: Causal Depth versus Causal Breadth

Theories of value are causal theories, that is, are meant in the ultimate analysis to explain the phenomena of price formation. By this standard, logical

3. Moss calls his approach "refined subjectivism."

theories of the neo-neoclassical type have to be disqualified. Thus, regardless of the interactional and interdependent character of the general equilibrium theories, which represent the most sophisticated logical species, their essentially logical character deprives them of the status of causal theories. Hence the general equilibrium theories have to be ruled out as genuine value theories, notwithstanding that they are founded upon the brilliant insight that the price of a commodity depends on those of all other commodities.[4]

Cost-of-production theories of value are generally causal theories. In terms of their time frame and level of discourse, they possess a considerable causal breadth. They are ruled out as tenable value theories because they invariably lack causal depth, that is, their level of discourse is far above, if not entirely ignoring, the level of human valuation. Without causal depth, the mere search for causal breadth becomes a futile, if not altogether hazardous, enterprise. As I have noted, there is an inherent tension within the overall framework of all strictly objective theories of value. On the one hand, they acknowledge the vagaries of economic conditions and changes in the modern capitalist economy. That is why they set out to search after either a common measure or a source of value. But they fail to realize that it is exactly because the capitalist economy is growing in complexity that it will render price formation increasingly subject to and interdependent on a multiplicity of emerging socioeconomic factors that will inescapably affect the human valuating agent, the ultimate source of value, in multifarious ways. Without causal depth, these theories cannot reach the level of explaining changes in the valuating agents caused by changes in socioeconomic conditions. Hence, they are bound to be superficial, if not entirely off the mark.

In contrast, the Austrian theory of value possesses substantial causal depth but lacks causal breadth. Its causal depth is derived from its recognition of the fact that value must spring from the human mind and the fact that valuation is nothing but the mental weighing of alternatives. Not only is value subjective, but cost, an allegedly objective factor, is essentially a subjective phenomenon in the sense of opportunity foregone in the eyes of the valuating agent. In spite of its apparent causal depth, the Austrian theory of value suffers from two major flaws. Insisting on the thoroughgoing subjectivity of human action, it ignores the crucial fact that, behind what seems to be personally idiosyncratic and unique valuations, there exist (at the level of the human mind) systematic laws that govern our cognition, for example, our information-processing capacity and our receptivity to ideas that could give rise to and account for patterns to such apparent idiosyncrasies. In other words, in terms of causal depth, Austrian subjectivism has, probably contrary

4. Both Frank Hahn and Kenneth Arrow deny that general equilibrium theories have anything to tell us about real economies, but they insist that they remain a serious and valuable part of economics [General Competition Analysis (San Francisco, Holden Day, 1971) pp. vi–viii].

to popular belief, not gone far enough. Again, insisting on the thoroughgoing subjectivity of the human agent and, hence, emphasizing uncompromisingly the sovereignty of the economic actor, it has unwittingly assumed that the value system of the economic actor is formed entirely within his or her conscious resources and on his or her own terms. By implication, he or she must be immune from the power and persuasion of social agents and institutions. As a result, the Austrian theory of value is not well placed to develop any causal breadth in the sense of taking into account systematic factors in society that goad economic actors toward certain patterns of value consciously or unconsciously. As a corollary, it has no theory of value formation to offer, that is, a theory positing objective factors that guide economic actors to adopt of valuational tools or principles. In other words, it is not an "interactionist" theory in the sense of being able to integrate both subjective and objective dimensions across the microscopic and macroscopic levels and across different time frames.

By the standards of this methodological schema, the marginalists and early neoclassical theorists have done reasonably well. From the concept of utility and the law of diminishing marginal utility, they are able to derive the law of demand. With the same set of tools, they are able to analyze different cases of price formation under different market structures and be able to make predictions about price changes. In other words, the neoclassical theory (of the Marshallian type) is able to achieve, in a limited way, some degree of causal depth and breadth. Subsequent developments, under the spell of logical positivism (as I have shown in chap. 2), have suffocated the search for more causal depth. Cut off from developing more causal depth, it has, as a result, few fruitful alternative routes to choose from. The pursuit of a logicalist enterprise, seen in this way, is a logical development.

Scientific subjectivists come closer to the requirements of causal depth and breadth. Acknowledging the importance of the limits and limitations of the information-processing capacity of the human agent, their theories of choice employ postulates that recognize the shortcomings (but the important regularities) of the human mind. Recognizing the importance of social forces, they place the consumer in the broader setting of different social contexts (see Earl 1986). All these are efforts in the right direction. What seems to be lacking are the synthesis of such depths and breadths into a more unified theoretical framework and the choice of the right kind of variables and the proper level of abstraction for their postulates.

A New Causal Scheme of Value and Price Formation

In recognition of the methodological need for causal depth and breadth, a tenable theory of value has to meet two important criteria. For causal depth, it must be based on human cognition. For causal breadth, it must posit multidirectional causality in the sense that the objective patterns we posit for the human mind must be relatable to the objective patterns we posit for society in general. By implication, value and price are no longer unidirectional phenomena. The first point needs no elaboration at the moment, although I will return to it in a later section. The second point, however, requires some elaboration. The original problem of value is to explain the formation of prices. Consistently formulated in this manner, it becomes an entrenched idea in economics (but not necessarily in our common sense) that it is either human value or cost of production that governs price formation. Seldom do we theorize the other way round, namely, how does a set of existing prices of commodities affect our conception of value or our mental valuation of these commodities. If a set of existing prices have causal effects in this direction, could we then posit that this existing set of prices, being partly responsible for the generation or sharpening of the valuational mechanism in our mind, will affect the price structure of the same type of commodities in a second period via this mediating mechanism? Similarly, could we posit that any set of existing prices will have causal effects on the supplier's conception of the market or of the pattern of wants of the consumers, as well as of his or her own perception of his or her ability to fill the needs of the market? If so, would the existing set of prices lead these suppliers to develop new cost structures, which, in turn, might alter the market structure and affect price formation in subsequent rounds? Could we also presume that, from the existing pattern of prices, suppliers could infer some kind of pattern about the potential wants of the consumer and thereby develop novel items or modify old items to satisfy such potential wants, with the effect of altering the existing prices and market structure in a second period? These presumptions do not, of course, say that each and every set of existing prices will have these effects or have them to the same extent. But it would be inconceivable that such prices fail to impinge on the perceptional and motivational structure of the consumer and the supplier in one way or another. Before I contrast this new scheme with existing theories, let us first examine the nature of these causal directions.

Existing Prices as Guide to Cost Changes

The idea that existing prices can alter cost structures is not new. Austrian economists were fully aware of this direction of causation. In saying that prices are signals of opportunities or that prices are guides to action or that the market process is a discovery process or that entrepreneurship is an indispensable part of the market process, the Austrian position is highly congenial to what is being posited here. This is lucidly put by Hayek.

> Neoclassical economics never clearly brought out what I call the "guide" or "signal function" of prices. That was due to the survival of the simple

> causal explanation of values and prices, assuming that values and prices were determined by what had been done before rather than as a signal of what people ought to do. We can only fit certain phenomena into our scientific concept of the structure of the world if we give up the aim of explaining events by a single cause. We have now learned that frequently the behaviour of the individual is determined by his success in maintaining himself as part of a certain system within which it is not a single cause but the whole system of which he has adapted that determines his behaviour. For this reason, value cannot be explained by a single cause, but can only be understood as the determinant of what people must do to maintain the overall structures. (1983, 36)

What the Austrians have not done, however, is to elaborate these insightful perceptions into a coherent causal framework. Why they stop short of providing such a coherent framework may be attributed to their continual harping on the subjective character of individual action, which bars them from embarking on a systematic search for lawful regularities. In addition, they have not gone as far as asserting that having influenced the supplier or entrepreneurs in their decisions, the existing stock of prices will therefore causally affect prices in the second round via the mediation of these actors. Failing to see the connecting links between prices in a preceding period and prices in the subsequent period, they are naturally not interested in studying how these connecting links and their causal effects vary under different socioeconomic conditions (e.g., under what socioeconomic institutions entrepreneurship will thrive or be suffocated).

I will leave a more elaborate discussion of this thesis to part 2. For my purpose here, I offer a formulation in outline. I presume that a rational supplier in the real world accepts uncertainty and takes this into account in his or her production and marketing plans. To play safe, he or she would ordinarily prefer to be a price taker, that is, he or she would take current market prices as given, unless he or she envisages the power to alter the market structure. Whether or not he or she would enter the market would depend on how far he or she is able to work out a level of cost that permits him or her to reap a target profit margin. Input costs in the factor market appear, in general, to be well fixed and hardly alterable. But the entrepreneur who is differently endowed in respect to knowledge and insight and who is keenly motivated is often in a position to change his or her cost structure. He or she might seek to develop an indigenous method of production that can more effectively utilize his or her inputs even if the general state of technology remains unchanged. He or she might exert efforts to exploit market imperfections and secure some inputs at below-market prices. He or she might test cheaper substitutes to replace commonly used inputs, if he or she has the potential expertise to explore the value of these substitutes. Predictably, the more motivated and knowledgeable the entrepreneur is, the more chance he or she stands in coming up with a favorable cost structure and in supplying to the market either at the prevailing market price or at a lower price than the current market. Under competitive market conditions, his or her actions might lead to a round of price cuts made by other suppliers, resulting in a new set of prices for existing products in the next round.

Not all suppliers take prevailing prices as strictly given. Under monopoly conditions, a supplier has room to slightly change an existing price if he or she is confident that the improvements injected into an existing item would create (in the eyes of the consumer) a subjective gain that is large enough to justify the increased price the consumer is asked to pay. In this case, the supplier is in a position to alter both the existing cost and price structure with relative ease. The result, again, will be a chain of reactions in the market, leading to new price structures in a subsequent period. Even in the case of new products, a supplier does not operate in a vacuum. He or she surely needs to refer to the existing prices of relevant goods or commodities in order to adequately take into account what consumers would view as reasonable or tolerable prices. Rarely does a supplier base prices entirely on his or her own cost considerations and set prices by straightforwardly adding the costs of production onto his or her target profit without any reference to existing market prices. These arguments do not, of course, belittle the importance of costs in affecting price formation. In the final analysis, prices have to be realistically rooted in cost structures and no set of market prices can be indefinitely sustained without reference to basic costs. But it would be wrong to suppose, as some classical theories of value did, that because market prices must be ultimately based on the bedrock of costs, the former have to be causally determined by the latter in the long run.

Prices are, of course, not the only set of factors that matter in the supplier's decisions to supply. But they do give him or her the most important information to work with. From existing selling prices, together with nonprice data such as quality and services, he or she might infer, aside from how his or her competitors are performing, how his or her would-be consumers perceive value and therefore, have a glimpse into their patterns of want. From existing input prices, he or she could guess roughly whether or not a new venture will be a profitable proposition. However, it needs to be pointed out that not all prices will transmit the right kind of information to the supplier. Some prices can be systematically misleading, if the market structure is such that there are only a few players and that they collectively decide to bar entry. Thus, the usefulness of prices would depend on the existing market structure, which in turn would depend on factors such as government regulation or, more generally, on the rules set up or permitted by a particular socioeconomic system.

Prices in a socialist regime, for example, are obviously of little use to a potential supplier.

Existing Prices as a Guide to Preference Formation

I have said that the Austrians do not have a theory of value formation. This does not mean that they conceive the consumer, as their neoclassical counterparts do, to be a mechanical calculator of utility. On the contrary, the Austrian consumer is seen as a self-conscious, creative, sovereign economic actor. The implication of this image is that regardless of what social influence may exist, in the final analysis the consumer remains a sane being, capable of independent judgment of his or her best interests across different socioeconomic systems. How he or she acquires knowledge of his or her wants or knowledge of the want-satisfying potential of a commodity is not relevant because he or she will be able to act in his or her best interest all the same. As a result, value formation need not be a crucial part of a value or price theory.

Contrary to this position, I posit that a theory of value formation is an indispensable part of a general theory of value. I say this because any set of existing prices cannot fail to impinge on the pattern of value of the consumer, that is, his or her ranking of relative worths in relation to his or her existing or projected purchasing power. Such patterns will inevitably affect price formation in subsequent rounds, just as the supplier will base decisions, at least in part, on how he or she perceives the value pattern of the consumer and as the consumer will bring to bear his or her existing valuational framework to appraise prices, new or existing, offered by the supplier in the market.

Consider a hypothetical case. A girl who has never heard of or seen a diamond can hardly be expected to possess any idea of the utility or marginal utility of a diamond. If one would start to acquaint her with this commodity and its price, first in the context of other consumer goods and their prices, then in the narrow context of personal decorative items, and finally in the even narrower context of different grades of diamonds, one would expect that in time she will become more sensitive to the value of different grades of diamonds in terms of say, the cut, color, and defects and be able to appraise its utility with some subtlety when she finally confronts a choice situation. Alternately put, her idea of value and her capacity in appraising utility are critically dependent on a prior stock of product and price information to which she has been exposed in the market. As Townshend dramatically put it, if we woke up with amnesia and all prices stickers were gone, we would find it very hard to decide what things were worth (1937).[5]

Diamonds are, of course, an extreme example, but to different degrees the social stock of price information of various commodities does act as a

5. I am indebted to Peter Earl for this point.

guide to how the consumer ranks preferences and appraises expected utilities of different commodities. It enables him or her to acquire "theoretical" knowledge of utilities over the universe of commodities within his or her potential grasp. In other words, it is the network of existing relative prices that provides the lens through which consumers learn to "see" utility in respective commodities.

Needless to say, the consumer will test and apply the hypotheses of utilities contained in his or her mental map in actual cases of consumption. In some cases, he or she will find that the actual satisfaction that is derived from the consumption is well matched to his or her expected utility. In other cases, he or she might experience remorse, should the gap between the expected utility based on his or her mental knowledge of utility-price ratios and the satisfaction he or she derives from actual consumption turn out to be very much out of proportion. This is particularly typical of purchases that spread consumption over a long time (e.g., a club membership). In some cases, it will take some time before the consumer comes to fully appreciate the kind of utility promised tacitly by the price he or she has paid (e.g., an unskilled player might experience disutilities in the first tennis lessons). In most cases, he or she will, regardless of initial skepticism, gradually bend to the social convention of accepting the utility-price relations implicit within the prevailing set of prices. There are, of course, also cases of genuine misfits. On the whole, we can say that the consumer will gradually adjust his or her mental map of utilities as his or her experiences of actual consumption evolve. The totality of these small refinements and adjustments among different consumers will collectively and continually alter an existing regime of market prices. These changes will, in turn, educate old and new consumers alike about how they should see value in the universe of commodities offered by suppliers.

The upshot of this argument is: whereas prices do indicate relative scarcities, some of these scarcities are not real scarcities. They are socially imposed scarcities or scarcities generated out of social convention, that is, we see scarcity because we are socialized into believing that certain commodities have true worths. Alternately, a set of prices might be open to two different interpretations. In many cases, it is clear that a specific price indicates the level of relative scarcity. On the other hand, the price of a particular commodity seems, in some cases, to reflect merely the level of value that social convention confers on that commodity, regardless of whether or not the individual agrees with its implicit price-utility relationship. There is the old story of the grocer who took the same tea and divided it into three parts, one to be sold for a low price, one for a medium price, and one at a high price and found a market for all three.[6]

This line of argument is not entirely new. Sociologists have long been

6. I am indebted to K. Boulding for this point.

telling us how social values have come to infiltrate the interior world of the individual. In the founding days of sociology, Durkheim held that social facts represent the causal source of individual actions (1938). The recent rebirth of interest in macrostructural theory led by Robert Merton (1957), William Goode (1978), and Peter Blau (1977), among others, tends very much to emphasize the penetrability of the individual mind by social processes and social structures (e.g., the differentiation and interrelations of social positions). In the economics literature, how prices or price setters come to indoctrinate consumer preferences is not altogether neglected, especially among economists who work in the Marxist tradition (e.g., Baran and Sweezy) or who see much of modern consumption as the result of capitalists' manipulation (e.g., Galbraith). Leibenstein's concepts such as the bandwagon, snob, and Veblen effects (1950) are clearly related to the question of value formation, an area that neoclassical theory unwittingly neglects. From the cognitive viewpoint, the idea of existing prices serving as a crude guide to the relative value of different goods to the consumer is transparent. This is well put by Katouzian in his criticism of the ordinalist position.

> Suppose *x* is "a house" and *y* is "a motorcar." Let us assume that the consumer owns neither of these two "commodities." Normally, a house is more expensive than a car, though not always. Now on this assumption the consumer may prefer a house to a motorcar. But how can he say by how much he would prefer the one to the other unless he already knows the relative price of the two commodities in question? Ask anyone whether or not he would just prefer (let alone by how much) a house to a car, and he would tell you "it depends"—on what: on their market values? If he already knows the relative values of the two goods, then his "weighting" is no more than a reproduction of the relative market prices—i.e., it is not he who is "weighting"; they have already been weighted for him. . . . And, unless they [the consumers] are morons or they have just descended from outer space, they themselves have a pretty good idea of the relative market valuation of these commodities. Therefore, they are going to reproduce these relative prices in their so-called independent weightings. (1980, 65–67)

The Epistemic Status of the Proposed Value Theory

My proposal for a new theory of value will consist of four parts: (*a*) a theory of value formation, explaining how socially accepted values in the form of prices infiltrate the mental space of the consumer, how consumers acquire the valuational "software" that they possess, as well as how the peculiarities of their valuational "hardware," that is, their cognitive apparatus, affects the formation of their valuational "software," that is, their system of preferences; (*b*) a theory of consumer choice analyzing how consumers apply their valuational software to process their decisions in a choice situation; (*c*) a theory of cost formation analyzing how suppliers valuate an existing set of prices offered in the market with a view to altering their own cost structure in order to improve their sales or profit, to gain a larger market share, or to launch a new product; and (*d*) a theory of consumer-supplier interaction studying how consumers and suppliers stimulate each other into developing new modes of enjoyment and new products. From these positive interactions, new prices that represent mutual adjustments made by suppliers and consumers will emerge. A more detailed treatment of this theory will be given in part 2; at this point, I will confine my discussion to the elucidation of the epistemic properties of this new theory.

Similiar to a neoclassical theory of the Marshallian type, my theory is an "interactional" theory, exploring both the utility and cost aspects of price formation. But unlike neoclassical theory, mine has more causal depth and breadth. Its causal depth is reflected in the theory's basis in the properties of human cognition (i.e., the valuational hardware), and its positing how such cognitive weaknesses and strengths affect the formation of value within the mental framework (i.e., the valuational software). The causal breadth of the theory consists in its taking into account both real time and macroscopic socioeconomic variables such as institutional factors, size of organization, and market structures in the formation of cost and in the pricing policies adopted by suppliers. These two dimensions interact when the theory posits how suppliers can manipulate the valuational apparatus of consumers through different marketing devices and through the medium of the existing stock of price information.

Being interactional in nature, the theory naturally posits the interdependence between its different components. This interdependence, however, is very different from the kind of interdependence characteristic of general equilibrium theory. In the latter, the interdependence is entirely logical; without causal depth nor breadth, it cannot explain how an economy actually behaves or how an equilibrium position is actually arrived at. This latter question, in fact, never ceases to haunt the general equilibrium theorist (see Hahn 1973 and 1980). This position, as can be seen easily, is the logical result of the general equilibrium theorist taking the perceptional and motivational framework of the economic actor, as well as changes in socioeconomic institutions over time, as a black box.

There are, in addition, other important differences between general equilibrium theory and the presently proposed theory. In the proposed theory, human convention plays an important part. What is of value to the consumer is something that the consumer learns through the process of socialization, and such value is largely the product of social convention. Even on something as basic as food, different societies might have very different ideas about what should normally be eaten and what should not. If human convention plays such a crucial role, one should expect that, with the intense development of communication in the modern economy, these conventions are likely to propagate at a more rapid rate. In consequence, a certain set of conventions is more likely to be superseded by another at a faster rate. General equilibrium theory clearly cannot tell us about changes of this kind.

Because time is essential to causal processes, no simultaneous adjustments can be (or will be) presumed in my theory, as is the case of the general equilibrium framework. Since human motivation and human ingenuity are necessary ingredients in my framework, there is no a priori reason why the system I posit will necessarily move toward a state of equilibrium. Indeed, every act of an economic actor to alter the existing cost structure or to modify the existing price by way of, say, injecting new "perceived utility" into existing brands of goods and commodities amounts to a potentially disruptive force that might move the system away from equilibrium. On the other hand, every act of socialization that persuades consumers to accept the received interpretation of values of existing goods and commodities tends to move the system toward some kind of equilibrium. If equilibrium need not be the ultimate steady state of our theory, the idea of equilibrium is no longer an indispensable concept, although the idea of equilibrium as a metaphor does offer some extra insight. With human convention expected to play a larger role, there is necessarily a high degree of indeterminacy in the price system. Given such indeterminacy, any apparent similarity one might originally perceive between my theory and general equilibrium theory should now be dismissed.

The Appropriate Level of Causal Formulations for a Tenable Theory of Value

Positing interaction and multidirectional causality in my proposed framework means we need to admit that objective factors will penetrate into the subjective order of individuals, and, conversely, the subjective valuations of individuals will collectively affect an existing pattern of objective conditions. This brings us naturally to the question of what should the appropriate level of discourse for a theory of value be, if that theory of value were to possess sufficient causal depth and causal breadth. My thesis that existing prices infiltrate the mental framework of economic actors and affect either their utility expectations (as consumers) or their intentions to investigate the possibilities of altering the existing cost structures (as suppliers) clearly suggests that more than one level of discourse will be involved. Given such a plurality, what should the most appropriate level for a first formulation of the theory be and what ultimately will turn out to be the most important level of discourse? For causal depth, it seems that we have no choice but to concentrate, in the first instance, on the level of our mental framework, for, regardless of what other causal factors may be involved, they have to be linked with or converge at the level of people's interpretative and motivational framework. This is because our mental framework, being an interpretative mechanism, will select and absorb only those parts of external reality that it deems relevant and because only that part of the data that is internalized will have the causal effects of triggering certain decisions and actions or of forming part of the screening mechanism by which we permit the entry of new data.

But if a tenable theory of value must be causally formulated first at the level of people's interpretative and motivational framework, then is it not the case that we have come full circle to some kind of subjectivism? If so, are we not back to the same problems that haunt different subjectivist positions we have analyzed, such as the need to choose, for example, between the logic of human action (praxeological subjectivism) or the psychology of choice (scientific subjectivism)? This reasoning is mistaken. To posit causal relations at the level of people's interpretative and motivational framework does not mean that all the causal factors themselves have to spring from the realm of the subjective, as many subjectivists, in particular the radical subjectivists, would have us believe. Because a prevailing network of prices embodies socially endorsed values or constitutes signals of objective opportunities, facts at the social level inevitably penetrate the realm of the subjective. Hence, subjectivism in the narrow sense is inappropriate.

But the question of whether or not the causal statements we would accept as properly characterizing the discourse at the level of people's interpretative and motivational framework should be scientific ones, metaphysical ones, or some combination of both remains. In other words, the epistemological questions that plague different subjectivist theories are still with us, and indeed with every version of interactionism that one might posit. The remaining approaches open to us would be the praxeological approach and the scientific approach. Obviously, there are merits and drawbacks in each of them. The raw answer is, of course, that we should exploit the advantages of both the praxeological and scientific approaches while avoiding their respective drawbacks. But it remains to be seen whether or not this is, in principle, a feasible position, and, if so, how we should go about the job.

My proposal is inescapably an eclectic one because the relevant causal statements include statements at both the level of the empirical and the metaphysical. But the eclecticism is a sophisticated one that is characterized by several features. First, the metaphysics to be adopted, instead of being a set of loosely related statements, needs to be part of a coherent and systematic account of the fundamental, structural properties of human cognition. Second, a systematic metaphysics thus formulated will form the core of the causal statements for our value theory, with empirical statements and observations playing the role of falsifying or supplementing the former. Third, while such a metaphysical regime should preferably be well corroborated by established findings in cognitive science and cognitive psychology as well as being compatible with findings at the "subterranean" levels of neurophysiology and biology, it is more important that it is not shown to be inconsistent or falsified by the latter. In other words, we demand maximal realism of the metaphysical and cognitive assumptions we make with respect to any theory of value to be posited.

Such a "metacognitive" regime should, among other things, posit basic assumptions related to the following areas: (*a*) the nature of human cognition in the broader context of neurophysiology and of the cognitive resources of living organisms, (*b*) the structure of human cognition in relation to the human purpose and the constraints imposed by our environment, (*c*) the cognitive mechanisms by which people build upon their strengths or make up for their deficiencies, and (*d*) the development of people's cognitive resources from the viewpoint of evolution and evolutionary epistemology (see, e.g., Vollmer 1984). While new findings at the scientific level will gradually compel the revision of a particular metaphysical regime, we expect that, between such wholesale changes, a particular regime should be "functionally stable" for the purpose of formulating a value theory.

It is not the purpose of this book to justify the choice of the level of metaphysics rather than the level of the empirical as the appropriate level of discourse in the realm of social science theories. Without going into any detail and at the risk of oversimplification, several reasons for preferring the metaphysical level can be mentioned here (see Woo n.d.). First, it can be demonstrated that metaphysical assumptions govern, to no small extent, the choice of epistemic values (and, accordingly, the aims of science). As a result, they govern the choice of methods that in turn, will affect the selection of theories. This means that an explicit and systematic metaphysics open to revision plays a crucial role in predefining the proper terms of reference and context for any scientific study, as well as in alerting us to any systematic bias toward a particular set of methods and, by implication, a particular set of theories. Second, scientific findings in the realm of psychology or cognitive science are invariably formulated at the "molecular" or, at most, the "molar" level (see Gardner 1985). They might well complement, but cannot totally substitute for, the fundamental and global assertions that we tacitly employ in the course of scientific discourse and that can only be formulated at the metaphysical level. Third, no amount of scientific findings at the molecular or molar level can hope to exhaust the ideas we employ in metaphysical and global discourse. For example, no amount of empirical research can give us, say, a complete theory about the trade-off relations between our different cognitive capacities, for the idea of trade-off itself cannot be exhausted by findings at the empirical level. Conversely, these empirical findings can only be given a full expression of their meanings and, hence, their significance in the broader context of the idea of trade-off. That is to say, they need to be interpreted at the level of metaphysics in order for their significance to be fully appreciated.

Any particular metaphysical regime is fallible. While it is not possible to conclusively refute a metaphysical regime via the empirical route (because of the level of abstraction at which metaphysical statements are formulated), it is plausible for us to replace it by another regime, if it is plain that the "epistemic opportunity cost" of accepting the former is too high to be justified (see Woo 1990). In other words, it is possible for us to weigh the epistemic gains and losses of accepting a particular regime. In this view, the acceptance of any regime can be interpreted to consist in either the compulsory rejection of certain well-corroborated facts and theories or the compulsory acceptance of certain undesirable logical and empirical consequences, or both. Since metaphysical regimes are to be judged and "costed" on a "wholesale scale," "retail" changes at the empirical, scientific level will have little short-term effect on our choice of these regimes. Therefore, there is no need to immediately revise a regime with every new discovery of scientific truth at the empirical level. Thus, the justified worry of the praxeological subjectivist is removed. However, it should be pointed out that this is different than the kind of a priori position advocated by Mises. The metaphysical regime I adopt is merely a set of hypotheses capable of refutation even though they may appear to be self-evident truths.

Part 2
A General Theory of Value

CHAPTER 4

The Consumer in Choice Situations and the Question of Consumer Rationality

Part 2 of this book elucidates the different conceptual building blocks of an alternative theory of value (in the generalized sense I have defined), in the context of which a theory of value in the narrower sense (i.e., a theory of price determination) becomes possible and meaningful. This part is divided into four chapters, the first three will deal with different aspects of value formation and consumer choice, while the last chapter offers a new framework to formulate and to analyze different aspects of price determination. It needs to be pointed out that, whereas these chapters offer novel perspectives on the analysis of different aspects of a general value theory and try to be as encompassing as possible, the results of the analysis are likely to yield the first outline of a general theory of value rather than a comprehensive theory.

The neoclassical theory deals with price determination first through the study of consumer choice, followed by an analysis of the relationship between supply and demand conditions. On the question of consumer choice, my account differs from the former in that it distinguishes two realms of discourse in consumer choice. Besides dealing with consumer choice in actual choice situations, it deals with the consumer's preference or value formation in the prechoice stage. In this chapter, I will first deal with the way consumers process data and make decisions in choice situations. In chapters 5 and 6, I will address the question of value or preference formation. I will show how the "laws" of value formation affect consumer behavior and supplier behavior. The discussion of price determination in chapter 7 draws on my discussion of the different variables in these realms and their complex interactions.

The Fallacy of the Neoclassical "Idealistic Innatism"

As far as neoclassical theory is concerned, the question of value or preference formation is deemed either irrelevant or unnecessary. This is because what neoclassical theory posits is essentially a thesis of "idealistic innateness," that is, the consumer is considered to be perfectly endowed with a complete and well-defined set of preferences.[1] As far as consumer choice is concerned, neoclassical theory can be interpreted as postulating a strictly computational model that states that the consumers are equipped with the tools of marginal analysis. By virtue of their prewired program of utilities, they are supposed to calibrate (in an effortless manner) the marginal utilities of their intended consumptions or purchases and compare them with their respective prices in a choice situation. Given that consumers know innately how to maximize utility subject to a budget constraint, they will reach a state of equilibrium when, for the commodities they set out to purchase, the respective marginal utilities divided by the corresponding prices are equated.

Here the neoclassical model runs into difficulty. Consumers are supposed to be endowed with a prewired program of preferences. In a choice situation, they are supposed to apply this program errorlessly in computing the respective marginal utilities of the commodities they want to purchase and consume. Because the program is predetermined, consumers act in a way no different than a perfect utility-calculating machine. But we also know that neoclassical theory claims to be a subjective theory precisely because it takes consumers' immediate judgment of marginal utility to be the ultimate bedrock of their choices. Since some of these immediate judgments may be just whims of the moment, it is natural and often the case that consumers regret their choice and deplore their impulsive act after the event. Thus, we are faced with the following problem, namely, should we take consumers' preference maps to be unalterable master blueprints or should we allow consumers' moment-to-moment fancies to alter these given preference maps? This dilemma is not acknowledged by neoclassical theory, but it is only too obvious that any adequate value theory will have to take into account, if not successfully resolve, this dilemma in the formulation of its cognitive foundation.[2]

To save the theory from this dilemma, one thing the neoclassical theorist can do is to remove the assumption of the prewired program of preferences on the part of the consumer. For it might seem tenable to use a weaker thesis, namely, at any particular moment, consumers are in the best position to define their best interests and, correspondingly, to confirm the status of the utility or

1. This challenge might be met by the neoclassical economist on the grounds that such an assumption is not meant to be a real one. It is taken merely as a logical device for drawing deductive conclusions. The criticism made here, therefore, has to be understood from a realist stance.

2. This is similar to Sen's observation, i.e., neoclassical theory has too little structure: "A person is given one preference ordering, and as and when the need arises this is supposed to reflect his interests, represent his welfare, summarize his idea of what should be done, and describe his actual choices and behaviour. Can one preference ordering do all these things?" (1976, 102). In this regard, Sen suggests injecting some structures on top of the neoclassical model. Unlike Sen, I believe it necessary to inject new structures from the "bottom," which amounts to replacing the neoclassical model with a more realistic one.

the expected utility of the objects of their consumption. Whereas this is a sound argument in its own right, it amounts to accepting tacitly the moment-to-moment judgments of consumers as the ultimate authoritative account of value. If one were to accept this, one would have to give up the beautiful idea of absolute consistency that characterizes the neoclassical assumption of rational choice and rationality. If one were to give up the idea of absolute consistency, one has to give up, by implication, the idea that one could predict consumer behavior and consumer equilibrium beyond the realm of the immediate. But then, there is no more guarantee that these judgments made in different moments will necessarily be consistent among themselves because what is in the best interest in one moment may clash what is best in another.

Accepting less-than-consistent choices raises another problem for the neoclassical economist. This means that possibilities are now open for us to study patterns of less-than-consistent preferences and how they come to be formed. Taken out of the neoclassical context, the study of these patterns can be fruitful research and would be welcomed by anyone interested in real-life consumer behaviors. But since the neoclassical theory is fundamentally logical instead of empirical, it cannot accept open-ended empirical statements into its set of axioms; they would immediately weaken the logical force of its framework. To preserve its logical power, it is necessary for neoclassical value theory to stick to the idea of a complete, consistent master program of preferences,[3] regardless of the "epistemic opportunity cost" that has to be incurred by making this assumption.

The Relativity of the Significance of Choice Situations

The consequence of accepting the supposition that each time consumers make a choice they will bring to bear the same master program of preferences is serious. Choice situations vary in their relative importance. There is obviously a qualitative difference in a choice situation in which consumers spend one dollar from one in which they spend a million dollars. One would suppose that, in the latter situation, consumers will be more cautious and will take into account more considerations than if they were to spend just one dollar. The upshot is this: in every choice situation, consumers actually make two sets of decisions. The first decision is related to the relative significance of the choice situation that is, in part, reflected by the size of the transaction.[4] If a choice situation is deemed to be significant by the consumer, he or she might consciously or unconsciously exert more search effort to gather relevant informa-

3. Sen calls this the one, all-purpose preference ordering (1976, 102).

4. The significance is only partial because the size of the transaction is not the only determining variable. It can, however, be used to indicate crudely the relative significance of a choice situation.

tion, or put in qualitatively better effort to develop the appropriate criteria of choice. On the other hand, if the purchase is a trivial one, if the choice situation is so pressing that it does not permit a search, or if the return of searching or careful weighing of alternatives is highly uncertain, then it is only natural for consumers to avoid investing too much before making a decision.

In other words, every actual choice made by a consumer is preceded by a prior decision about the relative significance of the choice situation itself and, by implication, the extent to which he or she is prepared to invest effort and tolerate errors. This decision is generally made at an unconscious level. It is made explicit only under highly structured situations with well-defined properties,[5] situations that might have serious consequences for the interests of the consumer, or situations that involve the explicit interests of parties whom the consumer cannot ignore. Recognition of this level of prior decision is important, because it is the neglect of this level that creates an irredeemable difficulty for neoclassical theory. Simply put, neoclassical theory has either to accept this level of analysis or assume it away. If it assumes it away (as it actually does), then it has to suppose that consumers will tackle each situation with the same level of attention. This position would immediately mean that consumers do not optimally distribute their efforts, for, by the logic of the neoclassical optimization principle, they should allocate their mental resources in such a way that the marginal efforts of decision making equate to the marginal importance of different choice situations. If consumers choose not to apply this rule, then they must assume that effort is available in unlimited supply and there is no need to distribute it efficiently, or else they have to assume that all decisions are effortless. The first assumption contradicts the very idea of efficiency espoused by the neoclassical model, whereas the second assumption is simply false. In light of these considerations, we might safely assert that any adequate theory of consumer choice, and by implication, any value theory needs to delineate this level of prior decision and take it into account in formulating theories of consumer behavior.

If the neoclassical model were to accommodate this particular level of prior decision in consumer choice, the innateness it tacitly embodies might compel it to posit that consumers do possess another innate mechanism that can optimally distribute their efforts or attention to various choice situations. Whereas this further assumption enables neoclassical theory to solve the problem thus raised, it nonetheless leads it into another difficulty. Whereas it is plausible for us to speak of innate preferences, it would be senseless or even ridiculous to speak of having an innate map of relative significance of choice situations that have yet to be realized, or to speak of knowing a priori the level of effort that may be required to tackle an unforeseen choice situation. In this

5. This is often the case in business situations.

connection, the remark made by Kahneman and Tversky regarding the general flaws of the theory of rational choice is insightful.

> The descriptive study of preferences also presents challenges to the theory of rational choice because it is often far from clear whether the effects of decision weights, reference points, framing, and regret should be treated as errors or biases or whether they should be accepted as valid elements of human experience. (Kahneman and Tversky 1982, 171)

Cognitive Strategies and Processes in Choice Situations

Subjective judgments of the significance of choice situations inevitably relativize the processing procedures an economic actor adopts in choice situations. In these situations, we might follow Kahneman and Tversky (1982) in positing consumers who are guided largely by the principle of representativeness. This principle permits us to make different postulates for different choice situations. For example, when consumers face a specific choice situation that they deem largely insignificant, they may follow, say, one of the following courses of action depending on the degree of significance attached to the situation. Over transactions that are considered trivial, they may simply follow the dictates of convenience and take up an option on a first-come-first-served basis. Where they feel compelled to make some effort before making a decision, they would retrieve from memory a specific concrete case encountered in the past that best approximates the current situation and follow that case accordingly. In the absence of a concrete case, they may conjecture a "prototype" that matches (in its broad outline) the options available in the current situation. The prototype can be viewed as a configuration of price and quality relations typical of the standard product or commodity in the mind of the consumer. These processes are likely to occur almost instantaneously. Once consumers gain access to a concrete case or a prototype that even vaguely matches an option available in the situation, they would usually stop pursuing the matter and make a choice. Such expediency is well justified. In such trivial choice situations, it clearly is not worth the consumer's effort to search for the best value for the price for the simple reason that a conscious search usually incurs disutility. In this regard, the crude neoclassical idea of optimization, manifested in this particular case by equalizing the marginal utilities of different choices with respect to the marginal efforts incurred, is warranted, but for a different reason.

In choice situations that consumers regard as nontrivial, they may adopt the following processing procedures, again largely in an unconscious way. The product offered and an offering price will trigger the memory of a corresponding or comparable mental prototype. If the actual price offered is more or less identical with the price data contained in the mental prototype, the consumer will check if there is any difference between the actual quality offered and the quality data contained in his or her mental prototype. The reverse also holds, namely, if there is not much difference between the quality offered and the quality data contained in his or her prototype, he or she will direct his or her attention to checking the price difference. Complications will arise when there are simultaneous quality and price differences. Further complications will arise when there is more than one item offered with variations in both prices and qualities. In the case where only price difference prevails, the problem facing consumers is whether or not they will accept the difference and, if so, how much more or less of the product or commodity they are going to take. In other words, the decision will be based on quantity. This particular case fits nicely with the neoclassical model. In the case where the comparison is focused upon quality differences, consumers may carry out some mental calculation of the additional expected utility promised by the improved quality or by the extra features contained in the product offered or, conversely, of the reduction of expected utility caused by the lower quality or by the missing features in the product offered. In either case, the consumer would probably make some kind of very simple cardinal comparison of utility between the product offered and the prototype in his or her mind.

Whereas it would be a relatively simple mental exercise to convert a difference in quality into a difference in expected utility, the mental calculation involved would become much more complex if price differences and quality differences have to be taken into account at the same time. The complexity would escalate if more than one product with even more variations in features and prices were to be involved. Given the fact that the consumer in an actual choice situation finds many decisions relatively effortless and painless, we might conjecture that he or she actually adopts decision rules with far greater simplifying power than the subtle conversion of quality differences into differences in expected utilities. I suspect that consumers might skip the conversion process in these more complex cases. I also suspect that they will simply concentrate on the more relevant quality aspects of the product offered, compare them with a counterpart in their mental prototype, and check if the difference is justified by the price difference, if any. If the differences are moderate, consumers would settle the deal without further ado, provided that the price difference falls within their tolerance limits and is intuitively justified by the moderate difference in quality. If the differences are substantial, consumers would simply drop some of the less crucial quality aspects and concentrate on the more prominent one instead of going through the process of utility conversion. Or they may conjecture another relevant prototype, if one were available, and make a fresh comparison. Or they might look at the quality differences again and decide upon a particular quality feature that matters most before making another comparison. Whatever they do, it seems that consumers will try to avoid, as far as possible, the meticulous process of utility conversion and valuation, especially where they have more than one offer to choose from. In a nutshell, the strategy adopted is one of simplifying, relaxing, or changing standards until the differences between the candidates become sufficiently prominent and the proper choice becomes transparent.[6] Such a strategy is particularly required when the consumer is "indifferent" to the choice situation. In our present view, a state of indifference is not the "end state" that reveals a consumer's equilibrium. It is, instead, an indication of a state of indecision and mental tension resulting from the consumer initially adopting a set of decision criteria that are too tight to allow a decision.[7]

This account does not attempt to give an accurate description of the complex cognitive processes and strategies involved in decision making. Much of this research has to be left to cognitive scientists. Rather, I want to bring out some broad cognitive principles (or metafacts) involved in such processes. I hope that, by clearly stating some of these principles, the flaws of the neoclassical framework will become more transparent. One cardinal principle is that, in a choice situation, consumers freely apply their previously acquired mental prototypes. Many decisions are arrived at not by comparing the price ratios of different products with the ratios of marginal utilities, but by the much more simple device of comparing, in very broad outline, offers with standard mental prototypes or by contrasting only the most outstanding differences between the offers and these prototypes. Here, the same criticism leveled against ordinalism is applicable. The theory of consumer equilibrium (beyond the sequential case) in the generalized form is a logical theory. It is not a cognitive theory. In a cognitive theory, we would posit that, as a problem-solving animal, man will invariably adopt different types of simplifying devices to facilitate decision making in complex situations. Hence, we can expect consumers to employ a multitude of methods to simplify their decision making in different situations rather than to follow the universal method of utility computation across situations.

Another basic principle that must be acknowledged is that a large part of the consumer's decision making is conducted at an unconscious level. I have already mentioned that the decision of the relative significance of a choice situation is usually made at the level of the unconscious and that the triggering of different mental prototypes is more or less automatic. Besides these, I should mention that our mental switching to different criteria in the process of

6. In this connection, the irrelevance of the Baynesian model of decision making to real-life decisions is obvious.

7. Such a dramatic difference in interpretation reveals, once again, the epistemic difference between a logical theory and an empirical theory.

decision making is often made at an unconscious level. So are decisions with respect to how far we should tolerate errors. The latter govern the extent to which we tighten or relax our decision criteria. With a large part of our decision making in a choice situation being handled at an unconscious level, it is necessary to advance some explanation of why this is the case. I will return to this point later.

If the preceding thesis holds, then, conversely, we have to take seriously another basic principle, namely, that our conscious information-processing capacity is highly restricted and we reach the limit of this capacity rather quickly. This thesis, first advanced by Miller, is well corroborated by findings in cognitive science (see Miller 1956).[8] A law of increasing effort cum decreasing returns seems to be at work when we attempt to increase the load in the course of information processing, for example, by adding more variables into a framework under consideration or by positing additional interrelations among existing variables. Not only does it become, beyond a point, abruptly more difficult for us to hold data simultaneously in our mind, but the possibility of error may increase at an exponential rate. If this is true,the computational model of choice implicit in neoclassical theory breaks down completely. For if consumers are taken to be typical representatives of the computational model, they would have to possess a cognitive capacity far beyond that possessed by ordinary people. Here again, as in the case of ordinalism, the theorist is either confusing a logical theory with a cognitive theory or he or she wrongly believes that it is possible to do away with a cognitive theory in developing a tenable theory of consumer choice.

The Flaws of the Neoclassical Concept of Consumer Rationality

The preceding analysis has important bearings on the question of consumer rationality. According to neoclassical theory, consumer rationality consists in either the idea of consistency of choice or the idea that the consumer maximizes his or her satisfaction or utility or both.[9] The idea of consistency of choice could be conceived in a different manner. A set of choices can be

8. Miller's classic statement is: "There seems to be some limitation built into us either by learning or by the design of our nervous system, a limit that keeps our channel capacities in this general range. On the basis of the present evidence it seems safe to say that we possess a finite and rather small capacity for making such . . . (judgments) and this capacity does not vary a great deal from one simple sensory attribute to another" (1956, 86).

9. Elster contrasts rational man with economic man (1983). The former involves only consistent preferences and consistent plans. The latter is a much better endowed creature, with preferences that are not only consistent but also complete, continuous, and selfish. I take economic man to be a rational being in the broad sense.

considered internally consistent if it satisfies certain binary relations, some of these being more demanding than others (see Hansson 1968; Richter 1971; Sen 1971). But consistency, by itself, cannot be a sufficient condition for rationality. As Sen cogently puts it,

> if a person does exactly the opposite of what would help achieving what he or she would want to achieve, and does this with flawless internal consistency (always choosing exactly the opposite of what will enhance the occurrence of things he or she wants and values), the person can scarcely be seen as rational, even if that dogged consistency inspires some kind of an astonished admiration on the part of the observer. Rational choice must demand something at least about the correspondence between what one tries to achieve and how one goes about it. (1987, 13)

Indeed, even the very idea of pure internal consistency, in Sen's view, is not cogent, since what we regard as consistent in a set of observed choices must depend on the interpretation of those choices and on some features external to choice as such (e.g., the nature of our preferences, aims, values, or motivations).

In the cognitive sense, one might interpret consistency to consist in the idea that the consumer is in possession of a consistent master map of preferences instead of attaining the necessary consistency in his or her choices in all situations, although the two interpretations yield logically equivalent consequences under normal circumstances. In a way, one might say that neoclassical theory tacitly commits to both interpretations. But, as I have contended, this cognitive idea of consistency is not tenable. The existence of a level of decision concerning the relative significance of a choice situation prior to the act of choice suggests that the consumers' possession of a consistent map of preferences runs against the idea of rationality. An all-consistent map would logically require that it be complete. An indiscriminate application of a complete, consistent map across all choice situations entails, as I have shown, a misallocation of mental resources on the part of the consumer.

If consistency is not an inadequate or tenable idea, what about the idea of maximization of self-interest, utility, or satisfaction? In this case, the distinction between intention and result is of great relevance. Whereas one can agree with the idea of maximization of satisfaction as an intention, the same idea based on achieved results has many difficulties. As far as actual behaviors go, we have ample reason to contend that the consumer does not always behave in an entirely rational manner. Overindulgence to the point of yielding disutility and regret, such as getting drunk at a party, overeating at a sumptuous buffet, or staying out late to the point of exhaustion cannot be accepted as entirely rational behavior or defended as compulsions.[10] As I have pointed out, the ability of the consumer to maximize his or her satisfaction can be called into question once he or she steps beyond the realm of immediate acts of consumption. Even for the most alert and sharp consumer, a gap between the initially expected utility and finally realized utility always exists and is, more often than not, a variable. When intertemporal utility relations are considered and taken seriously, one can find some consumers actually adopting the strategy of satisficing rather than maximizing. Briefly, satisficing is the strategy or balancing or trading off multiple, conflicting, or not easily definable objectives. In addition, it needs to be pointed out that maximizing one's immediate satisfaction is not always tantamount to maximizing one's overall interest: cigarette smoking is a classical example in this regard.

On the whole, the fruitful adoption of a maximizing strategy presupposes some crucial conditions that might or might not be fulfilled in a particular choice situation. In the first instance, the goals of the actor need to be univocally defined. In the case of consumers, this is generally not problematic, although there are cases where consumers do have conflicting goals to serve or where they have an imprecise idea of what they really want. In addition, such maximizing acts should have no, or comparatively little, negative repercussion on the future good or potential gains in subsequent time frames. As far as consumption is concerned, this might require consumers to exercise self-discipline to achieve the best results, but that may not always be forthcoming. For consumption that extends into the future, consumers are characteristically seen to be impulsive at their point of commitment. They are invariably over-optimistic in their projection of future utility.

Another condition for the fruitful adoption of the maximizing strategy is that the effectiveness of the means to attain the goals must be well established or well tested. Such effectiveness clearly depends, in certain cases, on the consumers' particular knowledge and skills, for example, in monitoring certain instruments as well as on the availability of certain required information. Apart from clear-cut cases, consumers who are in doubt and who wonder whether or not they should step up their search effort to acquire more relevant information or whether of not they should give special attention to a particular choice situation in order to better define their position are invariably haunted by a sense of uncertainty over the effectiveness of the search effort or attention they will invest. Because of the existence of such uncertainty, consumers are often hesitant to devote resources that are commensurate with the perceived importance of a choice situation. Although such underinvestment is not unjustifiable in many instances, the tendency to form a habit and to universalize such a habit is not uncommon among consumers.

---

10. However, Becker and Murphy (1987) argue that some compulsive behaviors can be defended on rational grounds.

Situational Rationality

If the maximizing strategy does not entail the necessity of achieving desired results because of an inadequate knowledge of future wants or of means to realize those wants, should we not simply confine the idea of rationality to the bounds of an immediate choice situation. Because all decisions are realized within the context of a situation, the rationality that we display in different choice situations might still yield the best results we can hope for and enable us to make a virtue out of our limitations. That is, can we say that a choice situation alone, by virtue of its special characteristics (e.g., clarity of objectives and constraints), imposes sufficient conditions for rational choice on the consumer? In other words, can we legitimately speak of a situational rationality?

Situations are generally structure conferring, and choice situation is one that can be categorically classified as well structured. Thus, we can expect that, given the well-structured property of any choice situation, the rationality of the actor will prevail. Under such conditions, the human actor, willing or not, is somehow "forced" into some kind of rationality. This thesis is similar to Popper's position.

> There are good reasons, . . . for the belief that concrete social situations are in general less complicated than concrete physical situations. For in most social situations, if not in all, there is an element of rationality. Admittedly, human beings hardly ever act quite rationally (i.e., as they would if they could make the optimal use of all available information for the attainment of whatever ends they may have), but they act, none the less, more or less rationally; and this makes it possible to construct comparatively simple models of their actions and interactions, and to use these models as approximations. (1960, 142)

There are, of course, ill-structured or open-ended situations. In these situations, the number of variables is difficult to specify, perhaps far too many to track down and far too difficult for the human actor to hold and appraise simultaneously. But choice situations are, as a rule, well-defined. Hence, it is possible for us to speak of the idea of situational rationality in the realm of consumption and to employ it in support of the neoclassical thesis.

This argument, however, faces a number of difficulties. First of all, not all choice situations are equally well structured. Surely a large number of choice situations are well structured with clear-cut goals and with well-defined constraints. For example, a thirsty consumer in a place where there are only two kinds of drinks to offer is in a well-defined situation. But one can easily envisage oneself to be in a situation where one is not altogether sure whether or not one is really thirsty and whether or not one wants any particular drink, even though plenty of options are available. Indeed, as a society becomes more affluent and as our command of material goods extend far beyond our daily needs, we are more likely to be at a loss about what we truly want in some situations where we are confronted with offers and expected to make a choice. Our goals become diffused.

Nor does a well-structured situation of necessity force an economic actor into rationality. Some situations drag an economic actor into making decisions that he or she need not have to face. For example, a woman in the company of extravagant friends ends up buying more luxury goods than she would have bought by herself and, in doing so, she has to forgo many essential items that normally yield higher utilities to her. Department stores are especially skillful in creating situations where shoppers psychologically feel compelled to buy something because they are pressed either by a sense of urgency or by the fear of loss that is implicitly or explicitly manipulated by the sales situation. In cases of this kind, an external factor, imposed by the situation, pushes the human actor toward less-than-rational behavior. Part of the tyranny of the situation arises, too, from the fact that, in certain situations, even if the actor refrains from making a decision, his or her indecision together with the passage of that situation means, in effect, that an implicit choice has been imposed on him or her. For example, a person may blame himself or herself for his or her indecision in buying an apartment that turns out, after the event, to have been a good value for the price. In the same vein, many addictive actions are not correctable because of the existence of an external tyranny imposed by recurring situations.

Notwithstanding these difficulties, one might suggest that we can perhaps retain a weaker form of consumer rationality if we combine the idea of maximization with the idea of a well-defined situation. Because a choice situation is structure giving in the sense that the goals and the constraints are well defined, we may, perhaps, speak of rational choice in the sense that, under normal circumstances, the actor will make the best out of a situation, regardless of whether or not what he or she maximizes in that situation is consistent with his or her overall preferences and values. That is to say, an actor can still be considered to be rational in terms of his or her given aims and resources within the context and the terms of the situation. In this weaker sense, what rationality is displayed by consumers is, of course, restricted to their concept of the parameters of the situation and to the limited resources they can exploit within the situation. This does not mean that the rationality thus displayed will be sustained beyond that single situation. For example, an articulate man manages to get a very good discount in a purchase in a particular situation and, hence, can be said to be rational in the context of that situation, although it may turn out that his purchase is largely prompted by impulse and that, upon reflection, he has no real need for such an item. His action is, therefore, less than rational in view of his overall interest.

This weaker thesis, apparently not bearing much content, is capable of refinement. To render the thesis somewhat more meaningful, consumer rationality can perhaps be extended to cover situations where the consumer does take into account, as far as possible, his or her broader needs within the parameters and resources of the choice situation, although there is no guarantee of attaining desired results or of the absolute consistency of choice. Consumers become less than rational only when they face more extreme situations where they are compelled to bypass their broader interests and concentrate completely on the interests of the particular situation. Such more extreme situations are generally characterized by the fact that the goal of the immediate situation is in conflict with a consumer's overall interest, but that the consumer has decided (consciously or unconsciously) to ignore the latter for the time being. Another plausible situation that leads to the exclusion of considering broader interests is that the consumer has difficulty in defining the relationship between his or her immediate and broader interest. Part of the difficulty arises from the fact that a large part of the relevant parameters and variables relevant to a proper compromise decision lies beyond either his or her present knowledge or capacity to gather such knowledge. In part, such a difficulty could be attributed to the existence of trade-off relations between trying to gather information with the risk of being unable to make good use of it and sticking with the limited amount of information that one can manage reliably (Heiner 1986).[11] Thus, we might be in situations where we spend much more time worrying about the few extra dollars when we buy a car radio than we do when buying a car (Thaler 1980).[12] But on the whole, it is seldom the case that we entirely ignore our interests beyond the immediate when we are making a choice in a particular situation. There is, in other words, a deep concern to choose, as far as possible, in a way that is consistent with our broader interest. With the idea of consistency posited in this manner, perhaps we could intelligently speak of consumer rationality in a pragmatic sense.

The Idea of "Naturalized" Rationality

There is yet another sense in which we can speak of "pragmatic" rationality. My analysis of the prior level of decision with respect to the perceived significance of a situation suggests that the economic actor has greater rationality than is usually posited. Indeed, the rule of equimarginality and its underlying idea of optimization, to which neoclassical economists subscribe, have far more applications than they first recognized. It has been shown, notably by Becker, that a wide range of social behaviors (e.g., criminal behavior, marriage, or child-rearing), display an admirable degree of rationality (see Becker

11. I am indebted to Peter Earl for this point.
12. I am indebted to Peter Earl for this point.

1976). Even in extreme cases such as addictions, which would normally be viewed as the antithesis of rational behavior, Becker and Murphy (1987) are still able to sustain a claim of rationality. They demonstrate that addictions, even strong ones, are usually rational in the sense of involving forward-looking maximization with stable preferences. They show that, in contradistinction to other approaches, a theory of rational addiction better explains well-known features of addictions and appears to have a rich set of additional implications about addictive behavior.

Becker and Murphy, however, do not attempt to generalize their findings to a theory of rationality. As a result, they have not inquired about the deeper foundations upon which their broadened rationality framework rests. Had they done so, they might have discovered that, beyond the subtleties of rational calibration made by the economic actor that they uncovered, there must exist another stratum of unconscious processes and mechanisms that yield such subtly rational behaviors. As I have shown, the economic actor is generally able to judge the relative significance of different choice situations at the level of the unconscious with reasonable accuracy. Indeed, insofar as the intuitive ability to allocate mental resources is concerned, an economic actor's performance must be considered amazingly satisfactory. As I have also shown, an economic actor's judgments and decisions in a choice situation are actually guided by some kind of intuitive yet highly efficient tools and strategies (e.g., the extensive use of imagistic prototypes). In other words, the rationality of the economic actor can be said to be deeply rooted in his or her cognitive makeup and manifested in the delicate and subtle manner in which he or she balances various deep and sometimes conflicting factors and considerations in different situations. Formulated in this way, the rationality of the economic actor can be said to go far beyond what he or she is actually conscious of. As such, rationality can be characterized as "naturalized."[13] Rooted in the funda-

---

13. This idea, emphasizing the biological root of our rationality, might help to dispel some of the current concerns in cognitive science over its present incapacity to capture the less-than-rational states of man. These worries were well put by Gardner.

> As one moves to more complex and belief-tainted processes such as classification of ontological domains or judgments concerning rival courses of action, the computational model becomes less adequate. Human beings apparently do not approach these tasks in a manner that can be characterized as logical or rational or that entail step-by-step symbolic processing. Rather, they employ heuristics, strategies, biases, images, and other vague and approximate approaches. The kind of symbol-manipulation models invoked by Newell, Simon, and others in the first generation of cognitivists do not seem optimal for describing such central human capacities. . . . Human thought emerges as messy, intuitive, subject to subjective representations—not as pure and immaculate calculation. . . . Innovation of the computer leads naturally to a concentration on logical problem solving (à la Newell and Simon) or on orderly, highly rule-governed analysis (à la Chomsky). But evidence from neuropsychological and developmental studies of mental processes has indicated that our concepts of cognition need to be considerably broadened. (1985, 385–86)

mentals of biology and cognition, such naturalized rationality represents nothing less than the result of man's highly successful adaptation to changing environments over millions of years of evolution.

That man has to be rational without being conscious of being so is only natural. Consciousness is probably only a relatively recent invention of man (Jaynes 1976). Over a much longer period and before such an invention, pressures for survival demanded that man had to make immediate, sound judgments and quick responses in most situations. To generate efficiently a sound response in any situation requires tapping our instinctual resources, because the conscious apparatus is by no means competitive in terms of speed, although it does excel in other areas (e.g., accuracy in representation and ability to deal with time frames beyond the immediate). In this naturalized view, the idea of rationality goes far beyond what we are capable of articulating in terms of logical analysis, consistency, or maximization. The instinctive mechanisms we unconsciously employ in decision making are bound to be more subtle than they first appear to be, and the subtleties involved in them clearly remain to be discovered and articulated.

"Cultured" Rationality: "Scientific" and "Procedural" Rationality

Whereas the idea of naturalized rationality is powerful and remains to be fully articulated, it is also obvious that, in our particular path of cultural evolution, we have acquired abilities beyond naturalized rationality. There are two important aspects to this development. The first aspect is related to the emergence and development of the conscious mind. The specific origin of this part of the human mind, of course, remains highly speculative. Jaynes contends that human consciousness does not begin in the ancient prehistory of animal evolution, but is likely to be a learned process brought into being out of a later (about 3,000 years ago), hallucinatory mentality by cataclysm and catastrophe and is still developing. While we need not agree with Jaynes in his more detailed conjectures, we can argue that because the flowering of the individuated human order presupposes individual consciousness and would seem to require the extensive use of language, the rise of the human consciousness might well correlate with the emergence of human language and, thereby, can have only a relatively short history.

The development of human language hand in hand with human consciousness means that intellect (i.e., concepts and logic) gradually replaces, in part, our instincts as a causal source of human action. It also means that the structural properties of language (e.g., the canons of logic, notion of consistency, rules of syntax, and the compressive power of concepts) begin to govern the way we construct more precise as well as broader representations of reality, upon which our conscious judgments are based. With this development, human rationality goes beyond the naturalized sense in which we act instinctively in a well-balanced and judicious way in a particular situation. The open-ended structure of language, offering wide possibilities of competing representations and necessitating the emergence of higher order criteria to eliminate less desirable representations, coupled with the fact that knowledge is dispersed among different individuals enable human thoughts to be systematically added, cumulatively refined, and corrected. Scientific knowledge in the sense we now understand it is possible.

Scientific progress is not the only manifestation of the rational side of the cultural order of man. Progress on another side is manifested in man's continuing experiments with new forms of socioeconomic organization in order to achieve higher levels of production and new breakthroughs in technology. Rationality is thus displayed in the way people organize themselves into production units and permit decision making to follow impartial procedures laid down by these organizations. When the technical side of decision making is given a scientific underpinning and is applied to the formation of impartial rules and procedures for organizational decision making, we come close to the idea of procedural rationality espoused by Simon.

Simon characterizes the rationality held by neoclassical theory as "substantive" rationality. To Simon, the neoclassical position represents a false ideal. We can expect substantive rationality only in situations that are sufficiently simple as to be transparent to our mind (1976). As an alternative, Simon proposes the notion of "procedural" rationality. In his view, it is more fruitful to concentrate on the rational processes that economic actors use to cope with uncertainty or to manage risk. Behavior is therefore procedurally rational when it is the outcome of appropriate deliberation, and its procedural rationality depends on the process that generates it. Procedural rationality, being concerned with finding efficient procedures for computing actual solutions to concrete problems, is essentially a cultural phenomenon. As such, it prevails largely within clear-cut and well-defined situations (e.g., chess playing, business decision making, or public policy administration). Simon also claims that, because this concept is rooted in and takes into account the limits of human information-processing capabilities, procedural rationality works well in psychology.

The notion of procedural rationality formulated by Simon is crucially tied to the idea of computability and the idea of computational efficiency. In this view, it can be interpreted to consist in our positive efforts to improve the "degree of structuredness" of our situations and, thereby, in promoting the intensity of our awareness in dealing with the pragmatics of economic life. Naturally, procedural rationality prevails in those realms of the modern economy where we have more successfully organized ourselves in well-structured situations, in particular in production. Formulated in this way, procedural rationality can be further seen as the rational response of the economic actor or the economic organization to the complexities of the modern corporate economy, with the goal of injecting more order into economic life. In this interpretation, procedural rationality, which adds a new competence in dealing with our affairs, is both the cause and result of our rapidly developing business civilization.

Cultured "Irrationality": The Plurality and Conventionality of Human Values

With improved decision-making procedures, one would perhaps say that our cultural evolution seems to enable us to go a long way toward reaching that stage where we can say that the rationality we display meets the requirements of what Sen (1987) calls "correspondent" rationality wherein choices correspond with aims. This, however, does not turn out to be the case in many realms of human behavior. Although man could be said to be conceptually rational in scientific inquiries,[14] the ordinary person does not always find themself in the kind of well-structured situation that the scientist finds himself or herself in in the scientific world, where truth seeking is the dominant and almost undisputed value.[15] Nor is the ordinary person like the "organization man" who subscribes to clear-cut organizational goals and standard procedures. He or she resides in a "life world" where values are pluralistic and often in conflict with one another. As we passed the phase of bare subsistence, what we see as important is no longer merely dictated by raw biological needs. What we come to treasure through cultural transmission and by virtue of the process of socialization are more pluralistic. Thus, whereas most of our behaviors could still be justified from the perspective of situational or naturalized rationality, one might contend that an increasing part of our behavior falls into the realm of the "less than rational" from the perspective of our socially acquired goals and interests.

Because cultural values are human inventions, (although they are bounded by the ultimate biological value of survival for both the individual and the species), their formation is subject to contingent factors that one cannot describe on an a priori basis. One might conjecture, on the basis of Jaynes's research, that in the early phases of human history, where only collective values matter or where individual values are largely subjugated to collective values, individual rationality and group rationality may converge

14. This is, of course, a gross generalization. For some conflicting views, see Feyerabend 1975; Kuhn 1970.

15. Not all philosophers agree with this view. See Rorty 1979 and such hermeneutic philosophers as Ricoeur (1978).

toward each other. Under such circumstances, individual rationality would almost guarantee the attainment of rationality at the collective level. But with the development of man toward an individuated order and beyond the mere biological value of survival in both in the individual and collective sense, modern man has woven an intricate network of cultural and individual values that are plastic and in a state of flux. Therein lies the source of our less-than-rational behavior.

The complexity of cultural values, be they individual or collective ones, can be further characterized by the following features. Generally, cultural values are more or less hierarchically organized. In spite of their hierarchal structures, priorities among these values are not always clear-cut for the individual. There are plenty of gray areas where one has to weigh individual values and make arbitrary judgments. In addition, since different values invariably spread over different time frames, the cognizing agent is faced with different possible trade-offs and suboptima. At the risk of oversimplification, one could say that the plurality of values is partially rooted in the plurality of time frames that is characteristic of our vision of future. In a sense, the development of human values can be said to be the product of the evolution of our capacity to visualize the future. Such a capacity, in turn, is rooted in the development of a more fundamental capacity, namely, an imagination that permits us to form images independent of our immediate reality (Taylor 1983). As can be expected, these different values need not be consistent among themselves. Certain individual values clearly do not contribute to the overall good of the individual and some values in a particular time frame are often in conflict with values in another. Furthermore, because cultural values are largely conventions, their respective relevance to our basic biological survival, both for ourselves and our species, is difficult to appraise, especially when such values come in packages.

Whereas people are competent, in a computational sense, to work out a rational course of action under a set of given or well-articulated values, it is not always the case that they are able to competently manage their value system and arrive at an "optimal dose" of their value combinations in a particular situation. Moreover, as Arrow has shown in his "impossibility theorem" (1963), it is impossible to combine a number of plausible-looking value judgments in deriving social choice on the basis of individual preferences. For example, a set of four innocuous-looking conditions for social choice would yield an "impossibility" in the sense that they cannot all be fulfilled at once (1963). Many apparently transparent value judgments, therefore, turn out to have opaque and, thereby, surprising implications, especially when they are jointly considered. The complexities involved in managing value issues and considerations are further multiplied in situations where conflicting values reign, where means-end relationships are blurred, or where multiple trade-offs between values and action plans are possible. Under these circumstances, the human actor is not always well placed, given the limitations of his or her conscious mental operations, to make decisions in his or her best interests in any consistent manner.

Consumer Rationality Revisited

The conventionality of most values in the real world means that they are bound, to no small extent, to the spirit of the time or the social ethos of a particular place. Values, at the level of culture, are therefore always in flux. In the sphere of consumption, what to consume or not to consume clearly falls within the realm of the conventional in many instances. The kind of options that we now confront are very subtle ones (e.g., choice among different brands). Consumers, unlike producers, are not organization men who are obliged to follow certain procedures designed to meet certain standards of rationality. They are still very much individuals in the realm of consumption, because they usually do not have to account for their behavior except to themselves. They are always free to follow their instincts, because there is no absolute standards to go by in the realm of conventions. As a result, consumers can fall prey to interest groups who come to discover that consumer values are actually highly malleable and can easily be spurred to impulsive action.

Should we despair? Before we arrive at any conclusion, there is an important aspect of consumer rationality that I have yet to explore, namely, that consumers, like other economic actors, do seem to be able, within certain limits, to learn from their decisions and mistakes. I will return to this important subject in chapter 6.

CHAPTER 5

A Theory of Value Formation and Supplier Manipulation

Value Formation and Neoclassical Theory

Invariably, a social science theory that purports to study human behavior or human action has to take a position, in one way or another, about what people's basic or dominant cognitive characteristics are. It would be inconceivable for people to think or act in isolation from the characteristics of their cognitive apparatus. Even those parts of their actions that are seemingly driven by instinct have cognitive content and are inspired by some kind of cognition of their external or internal realities. The fatal drawback of subjective theories of value in general, and that of the neoclassical theory in particular, consists in their holding metaphysical presuppositions of human cognition that contradict accounts of human cognition put forward by findings in cognitive science, evolutionary biology, and evolutionary epistemology. This is particularly the case in respect to the theory of value formation, which inescapably involves assumptions about human cognition. In this chapter, I will first construct an account of value formation that takes into consideration established facts and theories of cognition. As we go along, I will contrast this account with the cognitive presuppositions espoused by existing subjective theories of value.

I have shown that, in choice situations, consumer rationality in different senses can be said to prevail, for example, in the allocation of attention or search effort or in switching to a different set of decision criteria. Such a display of rationality generally requires the presence of a well-structured situation. At the level of value formation, consumers are, however, no longer blessed with the benefits of this kind of situation. On the contrary, we have reason to surmise that consumers exposed to different channels of value formation are very different than consumers acting under well-defined choice situations. In the informal or loosely structured situations characteristic of the channels of value formation, value transmission takes place largely through the unconscious stratum of the mind. In these processes, consumers are seldom aware of unsubstantiated claims, unfounded authority, or even gossip of different kinds. We find them indiscriminately taking in unfiltered data, mal-represented concepts, unqualified generalizations, and even false information. In short, our value norms are nurtured largely where we are most unguarded. However, it needs to be pointed out that although the unconscious mind is involved in both the process of value formation and in choice situations, this involvement has entirely different consequences for consumers. In choice situations, it serves to efficiently discharge much of the consumer's decision-making load. But the same efficiency means that the contents stored in the unconscious mind would be responsible for dominating the preconceptions of the individual about what is important and what is not, that is, his or her pattern of values.

As I have previously pointed out, the question of value or preference formation is deemed either irrelevant or unnecessary by neoclassical theory. As a logical theory, it is compelled to accept assumptions that, altogether, amount to asserting the position of "idealistic innateness." Consumers are considered to be perfectly endowed with complete and consistent sets of preferences. As a consequence, they are capable of ranking any combination of goods in order of preference and, by corollary, are able to specify all possible combinations of goods among which they are indifferent as well as all combinations of goods that are preferred or not preferred. In a nutshell, consumers are in command of perfect self-knowledge insofar as their preferences are concerned. By all accounts, these are odd assumptions.[1] What is more surprising is that these assumptions have always been considered to be perfectly compatible with the idea of marginal utility and as necessary to infer the state of consumer equilibrium. But the very idea of marginal utility and, by extension, marginalism in general can be interpreted as showing a deep cognitive presupposition opposed to the assumption of perfect preference ordering. In a cognitive interpretation, marginal valuation can be seen as a natural strategy of the human actor to make up for one of his or her fundamental cognitive defects, namely, his or her limited attention span. Given such a limitation, it is natural for consumers to restrict their attention to their most immediate state of satisfaction or to comparing the expected satisfaction of a particular item of consumption (which they should know best) with the marginal value of their money at that particular moment. Hence, marginal appraisal or valuation is a sound cognitive strategy. But this interpretation clearly contradicts the cognitive interpretation of the implicit "perfect endowment" thesis of neoclassical theory. Once again, this speaks of the fundamental schism between a logical theory and a cognitive theory, each governed by a different set of epistemic considerations. The former is very much concerned with making minimal assumptions for maximal logical content, whereas the latter is chiefly concerned with maximizing empirical content within certain logical constraints.

1. See chap. 4, n. 1.

Value and Scarcity

Before I develop a theory of value or preference formation, I should clarify the idea of value by distinguishing different meanings of the word *value*. Before I start, I should point out that, while I subscribe to the idea of value in the broad sense of the word and will apply this broad meaning throughout my discussion, my subject matter confines the realm of discourse largely to utilitarian values related to material consumption or consumption that requires the aid of some material good, however minimal the material side may be. From the crude idea of "true worth," we can refine the idea of value by discerning four levels of meaning. First, we can take value to mean what is of true worth to people in the broad context of the well-being and survival of individuals and, by extension, of the species as a whole. Since it is conceivable that what is crucial to an individual's well-being or survival might not be known to him or her readily (for instance, certain kinds of vitamins), what is of value in this sense is bound to differ in many ways from his or her subjective perceptions. It is, however, plausible that, with the advance of knowledge, this gap can be slowly narrowed. Second, we can take value to mean what a society collectively sees as important and worthy of individual pursuits (e.g., in contemporary Western society, a house, a car, or a club membership) regardless of whether or not such highly valued objects of consumption really contribute to his or her well-being. As we might expect, individuals of any particular society tend to conform to some commonly held desires or goals. The degree of infiltration of "social" values into the particular "value map" of an individual depends, of course, upon the overall social ethos, the type of education, the process of mass communication, the distribution of social or economic classes, and so on that prevail in a particular society.

Third, we take value at the level of the individual to refer to what the individual holds to be worthwhile to possess, to strive or exchange for. With due allowance for individual idiosyncracies, the pattern of values held by the individual typically reflects those held by the society as a whole. In this regard, we can further distinguish two categories of value. The first category consists of divisible, discrete objects of consumption that the individual attaches importance to. The second category is of a less divisible, "wholesale" kind. It can be conceived to consist in a conglomeration of objects of consumption that collectively constitute or define a life theme or life-style that an individual wants to participate in. Consumption objects that fall into this latter category can be seen as particular manifestations of an intangible life theme taken as a holistic system. Fourth, we can take value in the most concrete sense to refer to the amount of utility that consumers see as residing in a particular object and that they aim to maximize out of a particular act of buying or consuming.

In confining our discussion largely to the realm of economic activities, that is, to values that are somehow related to material consumption, our discussion of value is oriented toward values of the "exclusive" kind in contrast to values of a catholic kind (e.g., religious or moral values). As such, the concept of value is inescapably tied to the notion of scarcity. Similar to the notion of value, the idea of scarcity is a heterogeneous one and is, therefore, deceptively simple. Needless to say, all scarcities have to be "recognised" scarcities, namely, a perception of scarcity is a necessary condition for scarcity to occur. Beyond this necessary condition, we can, however, distinguish scarcities of different kinds. Certain scarcities are relative to the state of technology, namely, the scarcities are perceived to be scarcities as such and command the value they are perceived to possess because we have not yet reached that state of technology that enables us to produce them or produce them on a mass scale. Other scarcities are relative to social conventions, namely, they represent what society has persuaded people which goods or services command value, regardless of whether or not they do contribute to the well-being of an individual. As can be expected, such persuasions can be effected by suppliers, who are in a position to manipulate the preferences of individuals. (I will return to this point later in this chapter.) Still other scarcities exist because the consumers' power to appreciate or their skill in participating is limited to a certain state. Should they be able to expand their level of appreciation or skill in participation, such scarcities would be reduced. Because scarcities of this kind are contingent upon certain social factors and conventions or upon individual endowments, they are clearly subject to change with the development of new socioeconomic conditions and structures.

The Fragmentary Nature of Individuals' Mental Maps

What then is the significance of this analysis? First, because value must ultimately be perceived value, it is possible that, for the same material object, the value or utility perceived by an individual at one particular moment can be different from the value or utility perceived by the same individual at a different moment. There exists, therefore, room for analysis at the level of individual's perception of gaps in perceived values in the short term as well as value changes in the long term. Second, because individuals are strongly subject to socialization pressures and to the tyranny of certain choice situations, and because certain scarcities are relative to social conventions that are bound to change, a number of scarcities we perceive might turn out to be more apparent than real in the broader context of our overall and long-term interests. In other words, scarcities might be "manufactured," should some social agents want and have the power to do so. Because the perceived value of certain objects of consumption can be made to increase by reducing access (instead of arising from the true or intrinsic use value it may possess), it is, in principle, possible for some suppliers of certain types of manufactured goods to simulate the idea of exclusivity and to infiltrate this idea into the value map of the consumer. This means that perceived values can be manipulated by way of manufacturing apparent scarcities.[2] Third, since the level of value we attach to some objects of consumption depends upon our participatory skill or appreciative power, the way we build up or lose these powers will affect how we perceive value. Therefore, we need to study the cognitive structure of man and his value map in order to develop a theory of value formation that can account for how modern consumers acquire their value maps, which are imprinted with artificial scarcities.

This brings us to a major hypothesis, namely our mental maps are characteristically and inescapably fragmentary. First, there is much evidence to show that information in our neuronal network is deposited in a distributive manner and our brains operate at least in part via parallel distributed processing (see Rumelhart and McClelland 1986). This type of mental architecture naturally allows for the existence and development of compartmentalized value systems. Second, much of our storage and retrieval of data are largely "imagistic" in character (see Kosslyn 1980; Shepard and Metzeler 1971). This means that, in our minds, a lot of information cannot be reduced to a purely logical system of propositions or into an internally coherent system devoid of inconsistencies. Third, because inputs are fed into our system at different times, a continuous, overall reorganization of our mental data system to take these new inputs into account is either impossible or implies energy consumption that is not well spent.[3] Fourth, it is plausible to assume that, because much of our cognitive resources are emotion laden, the varying degrees or different qualities of emotions that are attached to the data we hold naturally fragment our mental maps into heterogeneous parts. This is supported by the fact that a part of our mental maps must consist of value norms founded upon personal experiences that are inseparably fused with emotions of different types and orders. Fifth, due to our limited retrieval capacity and the distributive deposit of data, it is not viable for us to simultaneously retrieve, in a perfectly smooth way, every detail we need and recast those details into a

---

2. The idea of manipulation espoused here is similar to, but fundamentally different than, the idea of rent seeking. Manipulation in my framework is formulated largely at the level of the perception and cognition of the economic actor. Starting from the level of cognition, manipulation, altering the very fabric of cost and price structures, can develop into socioeconomic structures that are self-perpetuating. Hence, manipulation can develop into runaway situations and therefore also needs to be studied from a historic-dynamic perspective. This is different than the idea of rent seeking, which is generally associated with either public choice literature (see, e.g., Buchanan, Tollison, and Tullock 1980) or with neoclassical political economy (see, e.g., Colander 1984) and is generally formulated with the aid of the equilibrium model.

3. The maintenance cost of our brain in terms of energy consumption is next to that of the liver, which consumes the highest amount among all human organs. See Granit 1982, 103.

coherent whole before final retrieval.[4] One can safely say that our mental maps are inescapably fragmentary, a thesis that is squarely opposed to the assumption of the perfect cognitive order implicitly espoused by neoclassical theory.

The fragmentary mode of mental organization described here must be disappointing to those who hold that people's mental organization, capable of wielding great powers, should be closer to the kind of architecture presupposed in the neoclassical model. What is not obvious to them is that, although we lost structural elegance in fragmented organization, we gained in terms of speed of access to data, in flexibility of organization, and in the volume of data that can be accommodated.[5] This is a plain truth, for what evolution has handed down to us is a mental system that at once takes into account economy of raw material and efficiency of operation and organization as well as maximal openness to adaptation, a system that must rank very high among the success stories of evolution. Indeed, only a system as plastic as our mental system can efficiently accommodate the heterogeneity and complexity of our inputs. Because data contained in our minds are distributively organized instead of being centralized, search time and processing time can be reduced. Because much of our storage and retrieval of mental representations are imagistic, the interrelations between the various variables and components in our mental images would require no further translation and, therefore, no intermediate organizational work is required to render the latter obvious to us.[6] Besides, the existence of a prior layer of decision about the relative importance of a situation means that our minds are able to reduce the extent of data retrieval and thereby control the economy of the retrieval. All in all, the system is extremely efficient in spite of, as well as because of, its plasticity.

Given this fragmentary mode of cognitive organization, what can we say about properties of our value maps and about value formation? First, the imagistic mode of organization means that what we store in our value maps are largely concrete experiences or messages. This means that the formation of value must be a long-term process, and each particular experience or situation can be presumed to deposit some imagistic materials in some corner of our mental maps. Second, because we posit distributive organization to take place with maximal plasticity and spontaneity within our mental "files," fusing distinct value themes with individual, concrete, imagistic storage of experiences, it is clear that we need not make special and conscious efforts to absorb value themes or to develop these themes within us. Hence, we can

4. If we had done so in every situation, our species would have faced the problem of elimination.

5. The structural complexity of our central nervous system is formidable if we take into account the connectional organization of the nervous system down to the synaptic level.

6. Not all cognitive scientists agree with this point; see Pylyshyn 1984.

safely posit that value formation consists in largely unconscious processes, a thesis I have already emphasized throughout my preceding discussion. Third, because our mental data are distributively deposited, the more concrete encounters and instances of the same theme we deposit into our memory, the more likely these materials will be organized into a wider network, accounting thereby for the sticky conceptions we develop for certain value themes. This explains why values related to life-styles, which are invariably formed over long periods, are at once deep and influential. Fourth, given the fragmentary nature of our mental organization, it is often the case that we carry in our different mental compartments conflicting themes of values. This is all the more likely because value formation generally takes place at the unconscious level and because value inputs penetrate at different times.

The fragmentary mode of cognitive organization also suggests that retrieval of data from our mental maps is not likely to be a mechanical process. One might surmise that, given the distributive nature of our mental organization, experiences or instances of the same theme that are deposited far and wide in our mental maps are more likely to be retrieved than those of other themes. Different than the organization of a mental map, the retrieval of data, however, is sequentially instead of distributively organized, probably for the reason that holding retrieved data simultaneously and in clearly defined relations is a conscious operation and, hence, requires an unjustifiably high expenditure of energy. As a result, only a small amount of data is retrieved in a sequential manner at any time. By virtue of the distributive nature of data storage, there is bound to exist some randomness in which data are retrieved. There is, therefore, always a possibility that, in a specific situation, an out-of-the-ordinary value norm that is inconsistent with the major value themes of an individual will be retrieved and will provide the dominant rationale for his or her actions at that particular moment. Were this the case, perfect rationality in the sense that the action of an individual is bound to be consistent with his or her dominant values can no longer be assumed.

The Question of Value Formation

We now come to the more specific question of how value and price norms are inculcated and changed in the mind of the consumer. By extension, we can also inquire about the factors that govern the formation of such norms. I have contended that the existing stock of prices in the market provides a broad guideline to the perceived values of different commodities. Being indices of relative scarcities, differences in the prices of these commodities are generally taken to reflect variations in the level of value. Cognitively speaking, this rule of proportionality is well justified: it is simple to follow and it makes good sense. Indeed the more an economy becomes monetized, the more such a working rule is useful to the consumer. This is particularly so with respect to those prices that are fairly sticky over time or that fluctuate within some steady or predictable range. Indeed, for certain goods whose prices remain stable for a long time, it is likely that such stable prices come to be viewed as "normal" prices and the value they stand for as standard values and are, therefore, expected to remain unchanged. Any departure from these sticky norms would be translated into moral judgments, for example, any increase in price beyond the acceptable limits of these norms might be considered as rampant profiteering on the part of the supplier. Perhaps this explains why inflation in its early phase is usually very much resented. Perhaps such a moral dimension of stable prices also explains why firms are generally reluctant to increase their prices during an early inflationary period, even if they suffer from a profit squeeze. One conventional explanation is that such restrained action is needed to preserve goodwill. In my present account, such action can be interpreted to reflect the prudence of the supplier, perhaps unwittingly, in avoiding moral reactions associated with price increases. The rational supplier who aims to minimize maximal loss might as well wait until other suppliers have tested consumers' reactions.

Consumers do not expect, of course, stable prices for all types of goods and commodities. Agricultural commodities, for example, are expected to fluctuate in accordance with weather changes and seasonal variations. For these commodities, prices are genuine indices of scarcities and neoclassical price theory is well placed to explain the question of price formation. What seem to pose problem for the conventional theory are cases where consumers accept considerably higher prices for goods that have only undergone different packaging that does not change their substantive use values. In other words, why is it that, for some differently packaged goods that have not changed in content, their newly set prices are taken seriously (by the consumer) as reflecting at least a proportional, if not a disproportionally higher, increase in value?

Differently put, we need to explain the paradox of why people sometimes resent very small increases in prices for certain goods, while they are willing to accept, in other instances, large price increases that are clearly not commensurate with changes in real worth to a wary outsider. The neoclassical theorist does not, of course, see this as a paradox, because the fact that consumers are willing to pay for the goods must already indicate that they have found their "consumer equilibrium," that is, the marginal utility they obtain from the latter purchase must have reached the point where spending their money is justified, namely, it equates the marginal utility of their money. The transaction would also be viewed in this manner by an Austrian economist. They would believe that the consumer would not have spent his or her money without seeing a subjective surplus.

I am willing to concede that the consumer must have seen something special in the differently packaged product that makes it appear qualitatively different than the original. We might follow up the issue by asking questions, such as, what is that something special that one sees, whether or not this something special is a lasting feature in the perception of the consumer, whether or not he or she would still see such a special feature and agree to pay for it after he or she has learned that the use value actually remains the same. The conventional economist could, of course, argue that discussions of this type are matters of psychology and, hence, fall outside the field of economics. These may be questions of psychology at the individual level, but if there are a sufficiently large number of consumers sharing such perceptual idiosyncracies, the latter are no longer idiosyncracies per se. They become, instead, social phenomena to be explained in terms of socioeconomic variables.

A slightly different formulation is this. For a consumer willing to pay a higher price for a differently packaged product, it is essential that he or she sees additional value in that newly packaged product. Since we presume that the extra value does not come from the end use, it must be attributed to some subjective creation on the part of the consumer. But consumers cannot create their subjective values without some raw material, and if a number of consumers should behave in the same manner, the raw material they draw from must come from some common source, that is, it must be social in character. This should not be surprising, because the kind of satisfaction we strive for is liable to become more social in character as we pass well beyond the stage of bare subsistence.

The consequences of consumption taking on a more social character and social meaning are manifold. One consequence is that we learn to consume not merely for the sake of consumption, but we also consume for the sake of demonstrating our ability to consume. On this phenomenon and the closely related phenomenon of conspicuous consumption, Veblen ([1899] 1953) and, to some extent, Leibenstein (1950) offer most interesting insights. Another consequence of the socialization of consumption is that we become more susceptible to the influence of agents or institutions that are in a position to systematically manipulate social values. Since our wants beyond the level of bare subsistence are partly what we ourselves define, they are less clear-cut than the satisfaction we would get at the level of subsistence. In societies where social values are diverse or are in a stage of transition or flux, we can expect that the individual's wants become more obscure and dissipated. The latter condition makes him or her susceptible to manipulation because the more he or she is uncertain of his or her wants, the more he or she needs an authority to tell them what he or she should see as important. Value formation, in this account, is contingent upon the type of society we live in and on the type of socioeconomic institutions that dominate that society.

Real Versus Apparent Value

Value manipulation can be a systematic enterprise. Before I go ahead with my analysis, let me develop a few conceptual tools. First, we need to follow up the thesis of the social character of consumption and to make the distinction between real and apparent value. This distinction, as I have pointed out, would not be possible or necessary in a theory that assumes either consumer infallibility (as in the case of neoclassical theory) or consumer sovereignty (as in the case of the Austrian school). In these theories, all perceived values are real values. Contrary to these positions, I posit that what we perceive as value prior to our act of consumption might turn out to be misleading. I will account for the existence of apparent values in a later section. Before that, let us first consider some demarcating criteria. One such criterion is that consumers are more likely to experience more real value out of a particular choice situation if they accept, as their working guide, that utility and price are inversely related. In contrast, consumers are more likely to experience more apparent value if they do not consistently apply to the inverse link between price and utility in a choice situation. As a result, a higher offer price than the one their mental prototype for the same product supplies might lead consumers to project more value onto the product in question and to see more utility out of it rather than to see less real value being offered.

Another method by which we propose to demarcate real value from apparent value is this: the more the expected utility approximates or is exceeded by the actual experienced utility of a consumer in an act of consumption, the more that purchase or consumption can be said to exhibit real value in the eyes of the consumer. Conversely, if the actual, experienced utility falls significantly short of the expected utility and on a recurrent basis, we can say that the consumer has come under some kind of illusion in his or her judgments of value. As a rule, the more consumers experience after-purchase remorse, the more they have permitted apparent value to dominate them in choice situations. In general, such remorse arises because there is a discrepancy between customers' momentary perceptions of utility of a consumption object in a choice situation and their broader interests. In other words, apparent values prevail if the decisions made by consumers in choice situations fail to take into account their broader or deeper preferences.

There is yet another indicator by which we might infer apparent value from real value. We can crudely say that the bigger the difference between the price of a product and its production cost, the further that particular product is removed from its real value. The reverse also holds, namely, the more closely the price of a product approximates its production cost, the more closely it stands in relation to its real value. A corresponding dynamic rule would be that the more the price of a product tends to gravitate toward its cost, the more real value it commands. On the other hand, the further its price drifts from its cost, the more apparent value it can be said to display. This formulation naturally reminds us of Smith's theory of value. Smith's theory, being an objective theory, was, however, not formulated at the level of individuals' cognition and motivation. In addition, whereas Smith was convinced that the capitalist economy is self-regulating and, therefore, market prices would tend toward value (i.e., natural prices), we have reason to believe that the modern capitalist economy seems to favor the development of factors that induce some prices to move away from their basic costs of production, that is, toward the formation of apparent value.

It needs to be pointed out that these operational rules, useful as they might be, do not serve as a justification for the concept of apparent value. Either the neoclassical theorist or the Austrian subjectivist can easily argue that any idea of apparent value that is defined with reference to external factors such as cost, or even after-purchase remorse, is irrelevant. As long as we accept the idea that consumers are always in the best position to tell where their true interests lie, all apparent values are still genuine values, that is, they still represent the best possible judgments in the choice situations in question. The Austrian subjectivist may agree with my ideas in broad outline, but I take the mistakes made by consumers more lightly and see them as providing opportunities for consumers to learn. It does not occur to either school that consumers might persistently come under the illusion of apparent value because of certain structural, socioeconomic factors that prevail at the macroscopic level. The ultimate justification of the distinction between real and apparent value must, therefore, rest upon the entire framework I have so far developed, not merely upon operational rules that have been proposed.

The Phenomenon of Cost Opaqueness

We can further refine the relationship between real and apparent value in terms of the extent to which the prices of products gravitate toward their basic production costs or move away from them. For this purpose, I introduce the idea of the cost transparency of a product, namely, the extent to which a typical or representative consumer is able to see through the actual cost of production required or embodied by the product in question.[7] A cost-transparent product, by definition, is one that a typical consumer can have either some rough idea of its overall basic cost or some sense of the proportion of the various components that make up the overall basic cost. In contrast, we may say that a product is cost opaque if the consumer finds it difficult to see through its cost structure. From the preceding discussion, we can posit that

7. This is very similar to Peter Earl's "rip-off" notion.

the more cost transparent a product is, the more likely a consumer is able to make accurate judgments about its real value. However, given the sophistication of the modern economy, one could say that most consumer products would be cost opaque to the consumer anyway. Even in less sophisticated products, it would be extremely difficult for the consumer to know the proportion of the respective cost components. So, why do we have to bother with a concept that seems to be irrelevant?

My argument goes like this: like the neoclassical theorist, I presume that the consumer is intent on maximizing his or her utility or overall interest. In addition, I assume that the typical consumer is inquisitive and is averse to making fallacious judgments about the expected level of utility of his or her consumption objects. Being inquisitive, he or she is naturally curious about the basic cost of the objects he or she pays for. Being protective of his or her position, he or she is naturally inclined, without overstraining his or her mental resources or affecting the efficiency of decision making, to bring to bear on choice situations as much relevant information as possible. Price, quality, and expected utility aside, he or she will not hesitate to employ a reasoned or intuitive idea of the possible cost of the object as an additional aid for his or her judgment. He or she will not, of course, go as far as actually trying to work out the costing of the object in question and will surely lack such actual data. But this does not prevent the consumer from making some rule-of-thumb surmises on the relative proportion of the basic cost in an offer price and, thereby, making some crude inferences about the level of the supplier's profit margin. Consumers will not have the expertise to work out the real costing, but they could always infer, from the different prices offered, some broad notion of what they believe, rightly or wrongly, the level of cost to be and take such a level as an input to their decision-making process as long as such inferences can be handled without conscious consumption of mental energy. And even if they are not able to form specific ideas about the level of cost for individual items, they could still make reasonable inferences about the overall margin set by different suppliers.

Alternatively formulated, I contend that, unlike neoclassical theory, the perceived utility-price relation of a consumption object would be altered a great deal if consumers were to make their judgments upon additional information or ideas about the cost structure of that object, regardless of whether or not that cost information or idea is merely conjectural or well reasoned. Were consumers to possess such cost ideas, they would either become more sensitive to the existing utility-price relation or, more probably, see a different utility-price relation altogether. Carrying this thesis further, I consider it reasonable to surmise that, other things being equal, had consumers possessed more specific ideas about price and cost, they would tend to purchase those items whose costs are closer to their offered prices, if only to minimize the risk of being shortchanged. In this view, consumers would resort to calibrating utility-price relations only in the case where costs are too opaque.

The modern economy can be said to be characterized by the following features that render most of its production cost opaque to the consumer: ever-increasing specialization, greater diversity of goods available, the availability of sophisticated consumer durables, the emergence of large corporations, the growing importance of the service sector, the growing size of government, as well as the intense development of marketing and advertising know-how. As a result of ever-increasing specialization, modern consumers are less and less dependent on home-made products and articles. They become increasingly dependent upon the supply of goods, the production of which they have little idea about or experience with. Hence, most of the items consumers buy and consume are no longer cost transparent. A greater diversity of consumer products, in a similar vein, renders the proportion of goods that consumers might have some cost ideas about relatively insignificant. As a result of the increased application of technology in production, more consumer items, in particular durable goods, tend to have a higher technological content. This naturally contributes to the cost opaqueness of these items. The rise of the service sector in the modern economy also contributes to the rising proportion of goods and services that are cost opaque, because services are generally appraised in terms of their quality, which is less subject to cost calculation. Furthermore, taxes, both direct or indirect, tend to render the cost structure of a commodity more opaque, especially in respect to luxury items such as tobacco, alcohol, and perfume.[8]

My thesis, however, extends beyond the realm of the consumer. Whereas we might concede that consumers seldom rely on their cost ideas as a criterion to judge a price offered because most costs are opaque and, hence, the concept of cost opaqueness is of little relevance to judgments of value,[9] the same cannot be said of modern producers who, I contend, are also becoming increasingly insensitive to their own cost structure. This is particularly true of the large, multiproduct firm or conglomerate. With a larger overhead to be spread over a multiplicity of products, it becomes increasingly difficult for a large firm to accurately allocate overhead cost to individual products. Indeed, owing to the enormous expansion of its internal coordination activities, the relationship between its basic production cost and its overhead cost becomes blurred. Even if the multiproduct firm has a clear idea of its overhead, the way it allocates its overhead to different products would still depend on the composition of its products, as well as its pricing policies in respect to its different products. Because multiproduct firms seldom have the same basket of prod-

8. I am indebted to Alan Wong for this point.

9. I am indebted to A. N. Rugina for this criticism.

ucts, it is natural for their allocation of overhead to individual items to vary significantly. Hence, there can be considerable differences in cost definitions even if the basic production costs of different suppliers are more or less the same. Increased government intervention and regulation, too, impose upon modern producers costs that are not immediately transparent, even to the producers. Furthermore, because the large firm, out of its inherent interest in perpetuating itself, secs a longer time-horizon in its business decisions than individual entrepreneurs or small firms, it tends to invest significant portions of its resources in long-range projects. Because prevailing market and cost data are disproportionately meager with regard to the overall amount of data needed to justify or support such projects, the margin of error in these cost projections is generally high and unpredictable. Taking into account these factors, we can reasonably say that, in spite of the fact that they all command large teams of cost accountants, the large, multiproduct firm in general has increasing difficulties in tracking down the real cost of a single product, in particular a product that requires a relatively long lead time. And if the average firm is becoming increasingly insensitive to its own cost structure at any particular time, small wonder the consumer finds it almost impossible to infer costs from the prices offered.

The Cognitive Foundation of Manipulation and Advertising

One consequence of increasing cost insensitivity on the part of the firm is that it will strive to maintain a sufficiently high margin to insure it against errors or to adopt measures that would enable it to sell as much as it produces. These measures are particularly required in the case of the large firm that invests heavily in the future. To make up for the wide margin of error that characterizes such investments, the large firm is inclined to resort to a wide range of manipulative techniques. These include lobbying for favorable government legislation and regulations, manipulating the market by way of advertising, controlling retail outlets, and so on. On the part of the consumer, his or her increased insensitivity to the cost of what is consumed as well as his or her seeking greater social satisfaction naturally provides favorable conditions for such manipulative activities.

Even for relatively cost-transparent products, consumers are open to manipulation. Their susceptibility to manipulation could be said to be rooted in their basic cognitive weakness. Of particular relevance is the fact that consumers are malleable at the level of their unconscious and in ill-structured situations where they are typically less vigilant. These defects can be further traced to the basic mode of our mental organization, in particular the fact that our mental maps are inescapably fragmented and our mode of information retrieval is linearly organized.

With fragmentary mental maps, individuals as cognizing agents are generally not able to synthesize values into a systematic whole and use this whole in making judgments in each and every choice situation. Such fragmentation, too, makes us unable to reconcile conflicting values easily. In addition, the asymmetry between our conscious and unconscious operations makes us all the more susceptible to socialization pressures. On the one hand, our unconscious structure is such that information could easily penetrate our memory system. On the other hand, our conscious operation being a highly constricted one, the retrieval of information has to be organized on a linear basis. Hence, in contrast to the vast reserve in our memory, only a meager amount of data is retrieved by consumers in their judgments in many choice situations. Needless to say, the more memory is dominated by repetitive messages, the more chances these repetitions stand of being retrieved. This means that if values that infiltrate the unconscious of the consumer become dominant, they will significantly govern what he or she chooses to value and predefine what would become a potential choice situation.

The emergence of manipulative factors leads, at least in part, to the dethroning of the sovereignty of the consumer, for no matter how vigilant consumers are, they can only be vigilant when in conscious choice situations. Manipulation is powerful because it attacks the initial section of the causal chain leading to final consumer decisions, namely, the deep, basic source of value and preference formation. It tacitly shapes what consumers consider to be important and predetermines (in some broad way) where their money should go. These unconscious decisions are, by nature, of a higher order than decisions made at the level of choice situations, not only because the latter are inevitably selected and constrained by the former, but also because they determine the amount of attention and search effort that consumers unconsciously allocate to different choice situations. Since the manipulative supplier is attacking consumers at the level of the unconscious mind, that is, where they are least prepared and least vigilant, it is difficult to see how consumers are able to defend themselves with their own "rational" resources. This is particularly so if their peers seem to gradually succumb to the subtle power of manipulation. The result is that, in spite of a consumer's first awareness of the gap between real and apparent values, such awareness will gradually be nullified by the repetitive messages of advertising. What possesses merely apparent value may in time become acceptable as something real, although in reflective moments, consumers may still question their conversion to such a state.

The upshot of this is that our cognitive characteristics provide the background conditions whereby we become susceptible to manipulation and accept the illusion of apparent values. The nature of this development can be interpreted as this: whereas our "naturalized" rationality is solidly constituted and time tested from the biological and evolutionary perspective, this rationality is increasingly challenged by changes in the very man-made environment that we have so successfully constructed. These changes, as I have shown, have the unintended effect of producing less-than-rational behaviors on a wholesale scale. This is because our long evolution, while preparing us to survive well in some communities, has obviously not prepared us for the kind of large-scale, mass communication society we now find ourselves in, a society so favorably constituted for mass social manipulation (see Dawkins 1986).

Strictly speaking, advertising, even of a purely informative kind, is difficult to fit into neoclassical theory, especially if we insist on perfect competition and its attendant Pareto optimality.[10] However, given its real-life importance, it is somehow accommodated in some liberal versions that attempt to relax the assumption of perfect information. In this connection, advertising and marketing efforts can be seen in a positive light. George Stigler, for example, says,

> Advertising is, among other things, a method of providing potential buyers with knowledge of the identity of sellers. It is clearly an immensely powerful instrument for the elimination of ignorance—comparable in force to the use of the book instead of oral discourse to communicate knowledge. (1961, 220)

Even if one were to accept such a liberal interpretation, it is clear that, in present-day circumstances, advertising has gone beyond the function of information dissemination into the realm of image making and value formation. This is well put by E. H. Chamberlin.

> An advertisement which merely displays the name of a particular trademark or manufacturer may convey no information; yet if this name is made more familiar to buyers they are led to ask for it in preference to unadvertised, unfamiliar brands. Similarly, selling methods which play upon the buyer's susceptibilities, which use against him laws of psychology with which he is unfamiliar and therefore against which he cannot defend himself, which frighten or flatter or disarm him—all of these have nothing to do with his knowledge. These are no informative, they are manipulative. They create a new scheme of wants by rearranging his motives. (1966, 119–20)[11]

The power of advertising lies in its usual strategy of persuading the consumer to accept higher priced products as standing for higher values. An

10. This point was brought to my attention by an anonymous reader.

11. I am indebted to Alan Wong for this citation.

effective strategy is to play on the consumers' imagination, helping them to associate the satisfaction they will obtain from consuming the goods advertised with that enjoyed by more successful people or people belonging to higher income classes. In effect, the supplier-advertiser, in advertising his or her products, is parceling out to consumers, on a "retail" basis, the indivisible life-style of the higher income class and the image of greater success. Alternatively put, the power of advertising is rooted in the advertisers' capacity to guide consumers to associate the products offered to them with something grander or something more meaningful that is worth paying for. By virtue of their cognitive make-up, consumers tend to retain vivid images and slogans as well as simplistic reasoning. In repeating messages, advertisers manage to fuse the images of their products with the preference space of consumers to the point that desires for these products gradually become unconscious or "innate." Because data retrieval operates in a linear and sequential mode, the more dominant a theme is in the overall mental space of consumers, the more chance it stands of being retrieved. Hence the power of advertising.

Advertising has another effect. In emphasizing the quality or the utility of a product, it diverts consumers' attention to the nonprice features of the products in question. In distracting consumers from price considerations, advertising manages to erode their vigilance to price increases. In other words, advertising has both the aim and effect of reducing the consumers' price sensitivity. I have said that the rule of proportionality between price and value is amply invoked in the process of value formation in consumers' minds. The same principle is exploited by the supplier-advertiser who is out to stir the deep desires of the consumer. Higher prices are to be inferred to imply higher value. If consumers fail to see this link in the first instance, it does not matter, for they can always be indoctrinated through repetitive advertising. After all, consumers are too inferior, because of their own economic inability to afford higher priced goods, to pass judgment on what society as a whole perceives as good value. Deep in us, our long-lost, bicameral mind is perhaps being reactivated when society (through the mass media) reaffirms its authority on us and challenges our individual ability to appraise value and make choices.

The Nature and Significance of Manipulative Cost

As the average firm becomes less cost sensitive and as the need for more manipulation is required, manipulation becomes second nature in the modern consumption economy. Advertising, packaging, and marketing thus become part and parcel of modern business in the realm of consumable goods. Because advertising or marketing costs are open-ended (in contrast to basic production costs), the addition of advertising and marketing costs onto the basic cost of a commodity means that the opaqueness of cost is further enhanced. The general acceptance, by modern consumers, that marketing or advertising costs are a normal cost that they have to absorb indicates not only that consumers are not only less concerned with the cost side of the products they are offered, but also that they will become less vigilant in appraising the price side of the products.[12] Given the fact that the relationship between the target price and the manipulative cost of an item is largely a fuzzy one, and given that the reactions of consumers, especially the first ones, to advertising are not easily predictable, the margin of error that must be allowed in a manipulative budget due to ineffectiveness has to be substantial. Hence, there is an inherent indeterminacy with regard to the actual manipulative cost that might finally be incurred. Needless to say, such unpredictability further contributes to the cost opaqueness of a product. As the manipulative cost grows and accounts for a disproportionately higher ratio in the overall cost of a product, whatever cost idea the consumer might initially have will become obscured.

The emergence of the manipulative cost as an important component of the overall cost adds a new dimension to the causal direction of price and cost. I have said that, in a free market, prices provide the guide to cost restructuring, provided potential suppliers are motivated and knowledgeable. With the inclusion of manipulative costs as an important component of the overall cost, the causation of price and cost is further complicated. Needless to say, the inclusion of manipulative costs affects price formation. But the opposite direction of causation is also at work. Suppliers who set out to manipulate the supposedly malleable consumer would be led to ask the following questions: how much advertising or marketing would be required in order to persuade target consumers to accept such and such a level of price; if they were to raise the price of a product by a certain margin without a substantial loss of sales, what amount of manipulative cost (e.g., new packaging cost, advertising cost, and so on) would be required to achieve this end. In formulating answers to these questions, one can see that the supplier's perception of the level of manipulative cost he or she is prepared to expend plays a dual role. On the one hand, being part of the overall cost by definition, the level of manipulative cost influences the level of price to be set by the supplier. But on the other hand, a target offer price conceived and adopted by a manipulative supplier often presupposes a budget that he or she is prepared to use for manipulative purposes. Prices set in this manner determine, to some extent, the level of costs. And as more prices presuppose some kind of manipulative costs, the direction of causation swings importantly toward prices as the determining

12. Consumers are sometimes seen to defend the costs incurred in advertising activities. Because advertising has the effect of expanding aggregate demand, cost per unit and, by extension, unit price can be lowered through the mechanisms of economies of scale. But this holds only in cases where few suppliers advertise.

variable in the modern economy. My earlier conjecture of the importance of this direction of causation is further confirmed.

The Fallacies of Existing Theories of Value Revisited

The preceding discussion should throw new light on the fallacies of objective theories of value in the strict sense, be they cost-of-production theories or labor theories, as well as their irrelevance to the modern consumption economy. Cost-of-production theories of value in general presume that prices are determined by costs in a straightforward manner. I have pointed out that this is not the case even in a competitive market economy, for existing prices serve as important indices of opportunities whereby present cost structures can be gradually altered, affecting prices to be set in the second round. With the advent of the modern firm, a growing share of the costs that were once classified as direct production costs becomes the overhead cost of the firm. This is particularly so with respect to labor. As a larger portion of the workers employed by the firm becomes salaried staff with long-term employment contracts and with a variety of fringe benefits, the simple idea of labor cost as a kind of direct cost is no longer valid. Besides, the larger a firm grows, the more products it makes, and the more it spends on research and development, the allocation of its overhead cost to the respective products it makes becomes more imprecise. The complexities involved are further enhanced as manipulative costs become an increasingly important component of the overall cost and because it is not always easy to properly allocate such costs to individual products.

The upshot of this is that the idea of cost is inseparably related to the structure and scale of the firm and to the socioeconomic institutions that have a bearing on such structures and scales. All these are variables in different socioeconomic settings. As the modern, multiproduct firm grows into a mammoth organization with complex structures and objectives, the idea of cost is expected to acquire new dimensions (see, for example, Cyert and March 1963; Strong and Waterson 1987). My discussion shows that the present-day concept of cost in the firm has developed complexities that clearly go far beyond the simple conceptions of the early cost-of-production theories of value, let alone the monistic labor theories. And if the apparently simple idea of cost proves so deceptive, it is no longer surprising that the relationship between price (which is an equally complex idea, as I have already shown) and cost can hardly be captured by any monistic theory.

For reasons different than these, neoclassical theory also fails to capture the subtle relationships between price and cost. At its subjective foundation, neoclassical theory ignores the cognitive malleability of the consumer. At the level of analysis where cost is involved, neoclassical theory collapses the two variables of price and cost through the postulate of perfect competition. As a result, the theory is in no position to offer dynamic explanations of the development of the modern economy and, by implication, to offer insightful analysis of the complexities of modern consumption. Indeed, as modern firms grow into mammoth organizations, expanding their investments into long ranging horizons and hence accepting more uncertainty as an unavoidable business condition, the gap between reality and the kind of timeless equilibrium assumed by the neoclassical model widens. In contrast, the nature of uncertainty in the real world can be better grasped by our present framework. In my view, the modern supplier, equipped with advanced manipulative technology and successfully goading the consumer into accepting certain preferred patterns of value, is able to reduce much of the apparent uncertainty in the business world. Such manipulative power thus functions to equilibrate supply and demand for a wide range of consumer products, but in a way very different than that conceived by the neoclassical model. In my view, equilibrium is often brought about not so much by price adjustments of these products, but by adjustments on the cost side, that is, by adjusting the level of the manipulation budgets.

These complexities, too, are not captured by different strands of subjectivism, in particular by the more radical versions of Austrian subjectivism. The idea of consumer sovereignty and the idea of the supremacy of subjective judgments embodied in Austrian subjectivism prevent their theories from accepting the idea of the consumer's malleability. In exclusively emphasizing subjective factors, they miss the whole array of objective conditions and developments that mold our subjective perceptions and our judgments of value, price, and cost, conditions such as those I have outlined here.

The Rise of the Distributor-Producer in the Manipulative Economy

As might be expected, manipulation, vesting the supplier with new power, becomes a permanent feature of modern consumption. With such a development, the role of the distributor or, to be more precise, the role of the distributive function gradually rises to dominance.[13] At the risk of oversimplification, I may perhaps conjecture that the economic history of the market economy seems to move from the phase of the sovereignty of the producer to the phase of the sovereignty of the consumer and, at the present time, gradually switching to the phase of the sovereignty of the distributor and the distributor-producer.[14] With this development, one might also say that the

13. This distinction is necessary because a firm can be both a producer and a distributor. When I use the word *distributor* in this section, I refer essentially to the function of distribution.

14. I employ this term to indicate the significance of the distribution function even when the distributor is also the producer, e.g., tobacco and soft drink suppliers.

factor of power comes of age in economic analysis. Economists such as Galbraith (1967) have long been aware of power's pervasiveness in modern capitalism. Unfortunately, earlier formulations, lacking the support of the right kind of cognitive theories, were not mature enough to capture the subtleties of the idea.[15] With the aid of cognitive theories, we are now in a position to give a deeper cognitive interpretation of the idea of economic power. One such interpretation I propose is to conceive power as either the capacity of an economic actor to deliberately make information that is required for rational judgment by other economic actors opaque, or the capacity on the part of an economic actor to generate misleading or confusing information to the extent that it distorts the sense of value held by other economic actors. In short, economic power is the capacity possessed by an economic actor first to generate, or to impose ignorance on, other economic actors and then to exploit such ignorance.

In this account, modern, large distributors or distributor-producers are in a distinct position to wield power over the consumer.[16] They are able to wield such power by virtue of the scale of their operations, by virtue of the "positional" advantages they enjoy, and, above all, by virtue of the manipulative technology they command. By building a supreme corporate image with distinct supplier "idiosyncracies," by controlling extensive retail outlets, by rendering credit more easily available, by exploiting the technical interdependence between related products, by eroding the sense of guilt some consumers may have in overspending, marketing conscious distributors or distributor-producers are in a position to realize all the potential power promised by their manipulation technology. Vested with such power, distributors are in a position to dominate producers who are their contractors or subcontractors and to drive a wedge between the consumer and the contractor-producers. Because marketing-oriented distributors are generally more concerned with total sales than the sales of specific items, and because their manipulative techniques and extensive networks of encountering the consumer enable them to sway consumer preferences and thereby to dictate the contents of production, they are generally able to dictate the terms in dealing with contractor-producers.

One might contend that interdistributor competition as well as competition between different contractors operating under a distributor would have the effect of reducing part of the undesirable monopolistic power of the distributor or distributor-producer. This is not to be denied, for competition will surely compel the manipulative supplier to create as much real value as apparent value. The most successful suppliers seem to be the ones who are able to do

15. James Tobin unjustifiably dismisses the importance of the concept of economic power on the grounds that no operational definition is possible.

16. This does not deny the important role and economic contribution of the distributor or the function of distribution. Part of the economic function of distribution is to make options amply available to consumers.

both well. However, interdistributor competition also tends to result in product differentiation, giving rise to mutual forbearance in the economy, as distributors are generally reluctant to enter into price competition among themselves, especially in an oligopolistic market (see Scherer 1980). They are more inclined to make strategic investments that will deter later competition (see, e.g., Schelling 1960). Furthermore, the conglomerate operations characteristic of these distributors as well as their predatory pricing will give rise to higher prices and profits (see, e.g., Scherer 1980; Utton 1979). In defense of nonproducing distributors, one can argue that the abnormal profit or rent they reap as a result of their domination over consumers and contractors will be channelled, in part, to sponsor long-range production plans or to foster product innovation. But on the other hand, one has good reasons to suspect that the large distributor laden with multiple management objectives and dominated by an administration-oriented staff would not be as vigilant as the smaller producer-contractors in employing their resources and in serving the best interests of consumers. Needless to say, distributors or distributor-producers who reap easy profits tend to breed an inefficient, "sheltered" sector within their organizations, where their managers may pursue objectives other than maximizing corporate growth and profits (see Amihud and Lev 1981; Marcus 1982). In turn, the growth of such a sheltered sector will prompt distributors or distributor-producers to further manipulate their consumers to accept, within certain limits, higher prices. Within some bounds, consumers are likely to pay more and more for apparent value. Consumers are probably subsidizing some inefficient firms that, in the next round, may ask for more.

CHAPTER 6

A Theory of Consumer Capital

Stigler and Becker's Idea of Consumption Capital

I said in chapter 4 that consumer rationality can be enhanced by consumers' acquired knowledge and skills gained through the learning or consumption process. We can call such acquired potential and power consumer capital. The idea espoused here is similar to Stigler and Becker's notion of consumption capital (1977),[1] although, as the subsequent discussion will show, the two ideas differ considerably in their details, their emphases, and their ramifications.

That consumers in the consumption process operate with some kind of capital is implicit in Marshall's work.

> There is an implicit condition in this law (of diminishing marginal utility) which should be made clear. It is that we do not suppose time to be allowed for any alteration in the character or tastes of the man himself. It is therefore no exception to the law that the more good music a man hears, the stronger is his taste for it likely to become. (1923, 94)

Marshall, however, did not pursue this observation much further. This is understandable because Marshall did not take the phenomenon of increasing competence in appreciating music to be an exception to the law of diminishing marginal utility. He merely attempted to restrict the field of applicability of the law to snapshot moments of consumption in order to take away any likely threat such phenomena might pose to the theory of demand and of consumer equilibrium grounded on the law in question.[2]

Stigler and Becker took an important further step. They found support for the proposition that one might usefully treat tastes as stable over time in the notion of "consumption capital" (1977), among other arguments. As far as neoclassical theory is concerned, this is a path-breaking approach. This is

1. I am indebted to Becker and Earl for their comments in this regard.

2. Although Marshall did not pursue this further, he did make many references to changing tastes, especially through changing environments. He even asserts that, over a long period, activities produce wants rather than the reverse. This was pointed out to me by an anonymous reader.

because orthodox neoclassical theory portrays the consumer as an automated, passive agent who, being always capable of telling precisely where his or her preferences lie, is not expected to be a creative actor capable of growth and development. In fact, he or she is too perfectly endowed in the first instance to need development and learning of the kind sought by real economic actors in the real world. Whether or not he or she will develop an increasing or decreasing interest in certain consumption activities or types of consumption over time naturally has no place in a model of this kind.

The thrust of Stigler and Becker's hypothesis is that widespread or persistent human behavior can be explained by a generalized calculus of utility-maximizing behavior without introducing the qualification of "tastes remaining the same" (1977, 76). Because tastes are learned by exposure to new experiences, individuals repeatedly exposed to a stimulus acquire, as it were, "consumption capital," a body of knowledge and attitudes that raises the "marginal productivity" of consumption of the goods in question, thus increasing demand for them. As a result, one no longer needs to avoid the question of taste or to take it as inscrutable within the analytical tools of economics. With the concept of consumption capital, Stigler and Becker try to explain some seemingly less-than-rational behaviors, such as addictive behavior, that traditionally fall outside the reach of neoclassical apparatus. By elucidating the time factor inherent in the concept, they have also been able to make interesting hypotheses about the accumulation and maintenance of such capital.

Interesting as these ideas are, the chief purpose of Stigler and Becker's analysis remains that of demonstrating the expandability of the explanatory power of the neoclassical apparatus. In doing so, they are, in effect, further exploring and exploiting the potential of the optimizing principle implicit in the neoclassical framework to explain real-world phenomena that had been considered to fall outside the purview of the traditional realm of neoclassical economics. The concept of consumption capital fits perfectly into this scheme because it enables the optimizing principle to be applied in more subtle ways than had been recognized. As such, the idea of consumption capital, notwithstanding the contribution made by its substantive contents, turns out to have great instrumental importance for a more powerful and encompassing neoclassical theory of consumer behavior. In contrast, I contend that the idea of consumer capital I present is central to any consumer theory. Therefore, it is of paramount importance to analyze the concept in detail and to deal with the first principles governing consumer capital formation entirely in its own right. The question of whether or not neoclassical theory can be expanded with the aid of this concept must be viewed as a matter of secondary importance.[3]

3. There is an unresolved, inherent tension between the idea of consumption capital and the neoclassical framework. Once conceived to be able to possess and accumulate capital,

The Components of Consumer Capital

I define consumer capital as the conglomeration of knowledge, skills, and interests that are embodied and sought by consumers for the purpose of present or future consumption. From this crude idea, it can be analyzed as comprising six facets: (*a*) the information and experience acquired and embodied by consumers with regard to various consumption objects and activities, including, for example, negative experiences in the past, (*b*) consumers' skills as well as interests in enjoying objects of consumption or participating more fruitfully in consumption activities, (*c*) consumers' propensities to try out new types of consumption and their power or willingness to search out and use new information, (*d*) the knowledge and skills accumulated and employed by consumers in bargaining and decision making in choice situations, (*e*) consumers' background knowledge and their stocks of information regarding how they should protect their interests as consumers, including how to best settle disputes, and (*f*) physical aids, equipment as well as amenities, that are required in the process of consumption.

Formulated in this way, the idea of consumer capital has much in common with that of producer capital, and is, in particular, similar to the idea of human capital. Just as producer capital is required for the production of goods and services, consumer capital facilitates the "production" of higher levels of utility by consumers, which would not be possible without the kind of knowledge, skills, or interests that they embodied. While these higher levels of utility are privately experienced and are, therefore, essentially subjective phenomena, their manifestations are nonetheless capable of being intersubjectively articulated or validated.

With this definition, we could proceed to show in what way consumers are induced to build up their capital, under what circumstances such capital will grow or degenerate, to what extent suppliers can augment the capability and willingness of consumers to build up their capital, and to what extent the actions of suppliers may dismantle such capital. The elucidation of these points should give us a better idea of the process of value formation. The analysis, too, will have important implications for our explanation of price determination, details of which I will leave to chapter 7. Such an analysis can also be recast into a dynamic one to shed light on the historical development of the consumption phenomenon in different economies or across different stages of an economy.

---

consumers are tacitly turned into active actors capable of development, as opposed to consumers in the neoclassical sense, who are passive, automated computing agents, an assumption upon which much of the neoclassical logical edifice is based. It is not clear whether Stigler and Becker go as far as abandoning this standard assumption and fully accept the ramifications of that abandonment.

Increasing Returns in Consumption and Consumer Capital Formation

As I have already pointed out, the principle of diminishing marginal utility is by no means the only mechanism that governs all consumption phenomena. In fact, the only case this principle never fails to hold is that of sequential or continuous consumption where diminishing returns clearly set in with additional units of consumption. In other realms, different principles seem to prevail. One can witness, for instance, some principle of constant utility at work with respect to consumers who are habituated to certain patterns of consumption (e.g., smoking a cigarette at specific hours of the day or dining out every weekend). With regard to the operation of the principle of increasing returns, examples in real life abound. Hobbies and sports, that is, activities that involve the active participation of the consumer and generally lead to the upgrading of the consumer's skills over time, are typical. Whereas it is true that consumers would experience diminishing marginal utility in a particular act of consumption or within a particular activity period (e.g., playing squash or reading beyond one's normal range of time), we could easily witness the upgrading of the level of interest and skill of a consumer over time. We could also gauge his or her growth of interest, which can be shown to correlate with his or her skill improvement. Once this is established, the failure of the neoclassical model in explaining a wide range of consumer activities becomes obvious. Its validity can be seen as restricted to one single period of activity or one single act of consumption[4] and is contingent on the presumption that a particular unit of consumption can be cut up into many small units that are incrementally consumed. The latter presumption is, as a matter of fact, guided by a mechanistic image of utility espoused by the early marginalists and their corresponding theory of value (e.g., Jevons [1871] 1970), an image in line with the intellectual ethos of the day. Clearly, these restrictive presumptions imposed by the neoclassical theory of value lead us to ignore the possibility that utility can spill over into different time frames (e.g., our fond memory of a past consumption event) or triggered without present consumption (e.g., music ringing in one's ears).

Specific examples of increasing returns to increased consumer capital are numerous. They include, among others, piano playing, stamp collecting, chess playing, singing, dancing, photography, mountain climbing, listening to classical music, and playing electronic games. Indeed, Marshall's example of music appreciation can be considered paradigmatic. Depending on the level of skill required to appreciate the utility of the hobby, a consumer who first takes on these activities as a hobby would generally experience disutility and frustration in the initial learning periods. As his or her skill develops, so the

4. Becker and Murphy's analysis represents attempts that transcend such restricted time frames.

consumer's interest is gradually stimulated. As can be expected, the interaction between these two mutually sustaining factors will foster the development of a habit, which alone might sustain the routine activities of certain consumers. Thereafter, these three factors, namely, skill, interest, and habit become interlocked with one another, providing the dynamics of the consumer's escalating involvement in the specific hobby.

Once a hobby becomes well formed, it is possible to predict the level of consumption activities that is related to the particular hobby and, correspondingly, the amount of material consumption related to these activities. In general, one can predict an acceleration of the level of consumer involvement and, correspondingly, of the necessary amount of material consumption related to these activities, until a plateau or a series of plateaus are reached that might continue or taper off gradually, depending on changes in the environment or circumstances of the consumer. After a consumer's skill has peaked, one might conjecture that the regular participation of the consumer is sustained more by the force of habit. And for the consumer whose skill in some specialized area has reached the level of a professional, his or her interest might be further sustained by the socioinstitutional incentives and stimuli that the profession endows upon him or her. He or she might even capitalize on the skill and turn the hobby into a source of income.

The social dimensions of consumer capital accumulation are no less interesting. Much of the increased enjoyment experienced by the consumers, apart from the sense of achievement they get from their improved skill, comes from the company they develop in these activities. Consumers' increased expertise may win them a growing reputation among their partners and friends, and the new company they keep may bring a heightened social status. Predictably, these developments will lead to the enhancement of the consumers' self-images and thereby to their willingness to further invest in consumer capital. Golfing is one example in this regard. In this view, Stigler's and Becker's strictly economistic approach (as exemplified by their analysis of the relative increase in consumption in respect to music appreciation) has seemingly missed the rich social dimensions behind the idea of consumer capital.[5]

Consumer Capital and Consumer Rationality: The Mutual Enhancement Model

Up to this point, my analysis of consumer capital agrees with that of Stigler and Becker in broad outline. But the formation of consumer capital, though conspicuously predominant in skill-laden hobbies or sports, is not restricted to these kinds of activities. Even an experienced shopper can be said to be

5. In this connection, Etzioni's case (1986) for a multiple-utility concept, taking into account moral and psychological dimensions, is interesting and important.

regularly building up his or her consumer capital. Since the idea of consumer capital presupposes that the individual mind is not a blank slate, one might say that one's stock of consumer capital is continually subject to alteration through acts of consumption. New consumption experiences, satisfying ones and unpleasant ones alike, naturally guide the consumer toward new patterns of consumption. Without much exaggeration, the process of consumer capital formation can be said to pervade much of our economic life, just as the process of human capital formation that takes place invisibly pervades a large part of an economy's production activities.

I have mentioned that consumers generally allocate their search efforts commensurate with the importance of a choice situation. With heightened consumer interest in the process of consumer capital accumulation, consumers are more prepared to expand their search efforts and attention, in defiance of the propensity to underinvest that I postulated earlier. Additional search efforts or attention are now justifiable from the viewpoint that they represent some kind of capital investment, the payoff of which might occur at some future date. Even more interesting, such efforts can be seen as utility creating under some circumstances. Just as a worker may derive, in the process of building up his or her human capital, special joy from a heightened sense of achievement, the interested consumer might also derive joy from his or her effort to build up consumer capital, regardless of whether or not such effort will eventually yield payoffs. Alternatively, consumer capital formation is utility generating in two aspects. Aside from generating an extra capability to produce utility for future consumption, the very process might be utility generating under certain circumstances.

One might further surmise that, within certain limits, the more information circulates in a market and the more options are open to consumer choice, the more chance consumers stand of building up their capital. A large part of consumer capital actually takes the form of mental prototypes in the minds of consumers. These prototypes can be analyzed, in part, as correlates between variations of price and variations of quality. The existence of a more sophisticated market means that the consumer is exposed to more chances to recognize finer co-relations between such variations. Within the limit of what consumers can cognitively grasp, such increased exposure and sophistication naturally equips them with a sharper sense of value, enabling them to see more subtleties in a particular choice situation and to gauge more accurately the real value of the goods they are interested in. In other words, increased consumer capital tends to enhance the rationality of the consumer in choice situations. Increased rationality on the part of the consumer, in turn, tends to foster more competition among suppliers in the production of real values. In developing ever sharper perceptions of the relations between quality and price, interested consumers unwittingly impose stricter standards upon production, permitting fair rewards to those suppliers who care to improve and eliminating those who perform less well.

Similar to our previous analysis, suppliers are not passively receiving signals from consumers in this framework. They anticipate consumers' interests and play a positive role in cultivating the latter's creativity in their consumption activities. As I have noted, imaginative suppliers perform the role of an educator, actively passing new curricula in the realms of their specializations to consumers to help them build up capital, in the hope that the latter may differentiate the suppliers' presumably superior products from the rest. For innovative and imaginative suppliers, this kind of supplier-consumer relationship must be seen as a positive one. They will no doubt face a population of more demanding consumers whom they help to educate, but they will also benefit from an expanding market. With a clientele commanding higher appreciative power, competition among suppliers will naturally center more on quality. Emphasis on quality, leading to a more segmented and differentiated market, in turn, provides the favorable condition for orderly competition among suppliers,[6] consumers, continually seeking more value through their capital accumulation, are generally tolerant, in an enlightened and subtle manner, of price increases and are prepared to reward better performers with higher margins. On the whole, a more responsive clientele tends to inspire more confidence on the part of suppliers and to encourage them to invest more in new innovations and, hence, in expanding the range of their products. Furthermore, the price flexibility these consumers give to suppliers enables them to reap healthier margins and to ride through recessionary periods less painfully.

Expanding this view, the development of capitalism can also be interpreted as being spurred by the dynamics of this kind of positive consumer-supplier interaction. Its market institution enables options to be made amply available, and with them, increased opportunities for consumers to develop their interests as well as their capital. As consumers expand their interests and capital, they will invariably generate more demand for suppliers. Incidentally, I might also say that my present framework, formulated at the level of cognitive and motivational structures, that is, at the level of psychology, can be seen as offering an additional perspective to justify the function of market.

The idea of consumer capital goes beyond the direct knowledge and experiences consumers build up about consumption objects and activities. Another important aspect of consumer capital consists in the knowledge consumers accumulate with respect to protecting their interests, that is, the knowledge related to how they should act to avoid being cheated in the first

6. It needs to be pointed out that the same emphasis may, in the hands of manipulative suppliers, become a strategy for manipulation.

instance and the legal knowledge to settle any subsequent disputes. Predictably, the overall level of disputes in the realm of consumption in an economy can be related to the level of its stock of consumer capital (in this particular sense). Increased "protective" knowledge and capital on the part of consumers would initially increase the number of disputes because enlightened consumers will use their newly gained weapons against fraudulent suppliers. But as suppliers gradually become accustomed to the behaviors of protection conscious consumers, they would act rationally to avert actions against them. In the long run, a more sophisticated community of consumers and suppliers will mutually adapt to each other, resulting in a lower overall level of disputes.

Negative Factors in Consumer Capital Formation

The preceding analysis deals with different aspects of consumer capital formation and their ramifications. We now come to factors that discourage the accumulation of consumer capital. As far as skill formation is concerned, Stigler and Becker postulate that age poses a negative factor. Besides this factor, we can posit a number of other factors that deter our conscious or unconscious efforts in building up our consumer capital. Some of these factors affect consumer capital in the substantive sense, that is, they relate to the specific contents of consumption. I have mentioned that the actual experiences of consumers are an important part of their consumer capital. But accumulated experience is useful only if goods in circulation in an economy are relatively stable. If new supplies and new items quickly displace old ones, whatever old experiences consumers have obtained will fast become obsolete. In this regard, one might draw a parallel between the destruction of producer's routines by the Schumpetarian entrepreneur, although there is a limit to the application of the metaphor.[7] If the displacement comes too fast, old experiences will become irrelevant, if not sometimes misleading. Similarly, increased information available to consumers, while generally useful, beyond a certain point becomes confusing.

Thus, depending on how fast an economy develops, the rate of formation of consumer capital in the substantive sense of specific knowledge or experience of consumption objects can be positive or negative. An enlarging market normally creates the dynamics for product innovation and is, therefore, conducive to consumer capital formation. But if product innovation comes too quickly, consumers may fear, especially for goods with considerable technical content, that it would take them too much time and effort to learn to enjoy the new product thoroughly. Consumers may fear that unless they pass a certain

7. This was pointed out to me by an anonymous reader.

threshold in their investments, the return on the investments might be uncertain. In other words, they may be frightened off by the apparent sophistication and the complementarity of such products. Similarly, too rapid changes may lead to "dropouts" among consumers who feel that they can no longer cope, thereby depleting part of the existing stock of consumer capital in use. In other words, technological development in any field does not necessarily create consumer capital formation at the same rate among different segments of the target consumer population.

Interestingly, the advent of technology has another impact on the formation of consumer capital. In addition to opening up new possibilities for enjoyment and thereby compelling consumers to alter their existing stock of information, some new inventions also enable consumers to improve their skills or to step up their power of appreciation, as in the case of the introduction of certain electronic gadgets. But reliance on technology for consumption surely would reduce some of our incentives to enjoy those activities that require serious learning efforts or that erode the capital we have accumulated by rendering both our skills and our existing aids or amenities obsolete. For example, television takes away some of our time for reading, and pop music, which requires little mental investment, tends to discourage us from investing efforts in appreciating classical music. Electronic games, too, while endowing us with some new capabilities, also strip us of some of our interest in and our ability to play traditional games such as chess.

An economy dominated by manipulation, as may be expected, poses barriers to consumer capital formation. As I have shown at some length, the organized economic manipulation we witness today is capable of producing confusion on a mass scale in the realm of consumption. The goal of manipulation is numbing our sense of value and our sense of judgment. The more successful these manipulative activities are, the more degenerative the quality of consumer decisions will become and the less consumers will rely on their original resources to make their judgments. This explains why more consumers are prepared to pay a premium for guaranteed quality and to patronize higher priced brands that consistently offer value for money. In short, manipulation, benumbing consumer sensitivity and reducing consumers' self-reliance, might render ineffective the capital consumers have accumulated in the past, and, by extension, make them less inclined to make the effort to build up new capital.

This development should not surprise us. As I have mentioned, more and more goods consumed in an affluent economy do not arise from our biological needs. We acquire a propensity to consume them because we learn that they are desirable through the process of socialization. As more consumption falls into this category, consumers depend more on what society tells them is preferable. Whereas we are all very sharp in appreciating value that is related to our basic biological needs, we are much more ambivalent in appraising consumption of a social type. We need confirmation from others, for example, our friends and our neighbors, that something we consume is of value. We are anxious to follow what those whom we regard as leaders in society tell or persuade us to consume and advertiser-suppliers are quick to fill this role. Once the authority of these manipulative actors is well established, consumer capital formation (beyond the sense of "protective" knowledge and skill development), in the sense of the pursuit and build-up of independent resources for judgment, will inevitably slow down.

Consumers in the modern economy have the benefit of the service of organizations that are devoted to their protection. Consumer organizations, sponsored either by the government or by consumers themselves, whether charitable or profit making, are important agents that help to create consumer capital by providing and disseminating reliable information and useful advice to consumers. But, on the other hand, they also have the unintended consequence of reducing consumers' self-reliance to some extent. Since information provided by these organizations cannot always take into account individual circumstances and backgrounds, overreliance on information of this general kind might subtly reduce the propensity of consumers to exercise their best judgments and to maximize their exposure, as well as to apply the lessons they might have learned through their own particular exposures and experiences.

In sum, the modern economy at once induces and discourages consumer capital formation. In the realm of sophisticated products, in skill-intensive consumption such as sports and hobbies, and in protective knowledge, it is clear that, by and large, the impact of the modern economy on consumer capital formation is positive. The same, however, cannot be said of skills that are easily rendered obsolete by technological development and of knowledge of consumption objects that are quickly replaced by novel items. With respect to luxury goods and consumption of a social character, consumer capital formation is adversely affected with the advent of mass manipulation. Apart from negatively affecting the incentives of consumers toward capital investment by way of mastering the subtle contents of consumption objects, manipulation has a negative impact on the quality of consumer decisions as a whole. And as we move toward more socially guided consumption, and as manipulation joins forces with rapid product innovation, we can no longer be optimistic that consumers will be willing to invest more for judicious consumption.

CHAPTER 7

Toward a New Framework of Price Determination

The Epistemic Relation Between Price Theory and Value Theory

In the preceding chapters, I have spelled out the relationships between different aspects of consumer value formation, consumer capital, and consumer rationality. Whereas these analyses have clear implications for price formation, the conventional economist would be inclined to skip these basic questions and choose to deal with the question of price determination in a more straightforward way. But as I have shown, there cannot be an adequate theory of value (in the sense of a "pure" theory of price determination) without a theory of value in the broader sense, including, inter alia, how value norms come to be formed in the minds of consumers and how they affect the way consumers respond to products offered to them. In this connection, we posit that there exists an epistemic causal relation between a theory of value in the broader sense and a theory of price. Together, these elements as well as their interrelations constitute a generalized theory of value. Acceptance of this new formulation of the problem of value means that, without having an adequate theory of value in the broader sense, there is no way we can fully understand the phenomena of price and price determination.

I have already tried to explain why we have only a theory of price instead of a broader theory of value in present-day economics. I have pointed out that, in spite of the marginal revolution in the 1870s settling for a subjective foundation of value, subsequent developments, guided by positivist thinking, were steered by the conviction that economics as a science should avoid being overburdened by subjective elements and that there is a need to strip that foundation (as far as possible) of psychological theories. Complementary to this development was the attempt to chart an independent realm of discourse for economics by way of dealing with economic phenomena on their own terms and resources. This was achieved by explaining economic phenomena either by invoking solely economic variables or by positing a logic of human action that required minimal psychological assumptions. Seen from this stance, the subjective foundation in which modern economics is said to be rooted (i.e., the maximization of subjective utility) is a mere starting instrument, a kind of intellectual ladder that must be pushed into the background as soon as we arrive at some apparently secure objective ground that enables theorems to be formulated by using economic variables alone. The result of this tacit epistemic strategy is that the economic theorist generally tends to settle on a minimal subjective framework that is just sufficient for an objective base to be built and then to freeze this subjective foundation as if the problem of subjectivity has been solved once and for all, or as if that subjective foundation need no longer or cannot be further refined. Viewed this way, one might interpret subsequent developments as constituting, in effect, a counterrevolution to the marginal revolution. This counterrevolution has its basis in the problem of searching for a subjective foundation for a theory of value as an alternative to the cost-of-production theory.

The freezing of the subjective foundation and the subsequent attention given to building a price theory that is free of subjective elements (hence, free of theories of psychology) mean that instead of reexamining the validity of the cognitive assumptions tacitly embodied by that subjective foundation, subsequent economic theorists are compelled to inject more and more unreal assumptions into their framework in order to sustain the increasing sophistication of their logical edifice on instrumentalist grounds. Even assumptions that are plainly absurd from the viewpoint of common sense, such as perfect preference ordering, gradually come to be accepted by some economists as if they were an indispensable and integral core of the neoclassical framework.

In other words, starting from the motive of building a price theory independent of psychology, economists produce, through a series of steps, a pure logical theory of price cast in the general equilibrium framework. Whereas many economists are not unaware of the fact that they are actually building a logical theory of price, they are nonetheless convinced that a general equilibrium price theory significantly adds to our understanding of economics by providing us the most rigorous and encompassing framework, in particular by defining the conditions whereby general equilibrium is to take place. Some defenders even assert that general equilibrium theory represents a fruitful approach to our orderly understanding of reality (i.e., its empirical progressiveness; see Weintraub 1985). The general equilibrium model, being a broad analogue to a competitive economy, is bridgeable to reality in principle, provided we are able to develop the right analytical techniques. Or, to say the least, a general equilibrium theory would give us the theoretical reassurance that we are on the right track in seeking an adequate general economic theory (Hausman 1981).

If what economists actually strive for is building a logical theory of price, then it should no longer surprise us that they do not need a theory of value (in our broad sense). As a matter of fact, a theory of value in our broad sense, bound to embody realistic cognitive assumptions, would stand in the way of building a pure, logical theory of price because the former assumptions would be very different from those required by the latter. Indeed, as soon as we are able to make the distinction in terms of epistemic aims and status between a pure, logical theory of price and a theory of value based upon realistic cognitive assumptions, we can readily see that a theory of price determination that sets out to explain real-life phenomena cannot exist independently of a broader theory of value rooted in the study of the cognitive apparatus that we use for utility valuation as well as the study of the cognitive process of value formation. The "epistemic opportunity cost" of doing away with the latter would be that we have to accept theories that no longer command important, real-world explanatory power.

The Approach to Price Determination: The Partial Equilibrium versus the General Equilibrium Approach

The marginal, subjective theory of value, in spite of its limitations, does not necessarily lead to the development of an unreal theory of price determination as manifested in the subsequent general equilibrium theories. Marshall's formulation of the theory of value, representing one major direction of subsequent developments, involves a technique that can be said to be derived from three closely connected goals: comprehensiveness, realism, and significance for economic policy (see Roll 1953). The forces behind both supply and demand, according to Marshall, determine value. They are to be conceived of as the two blades of a pair of scissors and it is useless to ask which does the cutting. Behind demand is marginal utility, reflected in the demand prices of buyers, while behind supply is marginal effort and sacrifice, reflected in supply prices. Marshall's analysis of market equilibrium thus seeks to describe the determination of the market price and the quantity bought and sold. The equilibrium price-quantity combination is determined by supply and demand, and the equality of supply and demand ensures the consistency of buyers' and sellers' desires. By applying a partial equilibrium approach and by distinguishing different time periods over which the forces tending to establish equilibrium are conceived to be operating, Marshall is able to develop an elaborate framework for the analysis of price formation and adjustment and apply it to concrete problems.

One can clearly discern a great amount of realism in this approach. Indeed, the wisdom contained therein becomes the standard basis for much work in fundamental economic analysis and for handling a lot of applied work in economics. Such realism is gradually lost, however, as subsequent economic theorizing, in search of more rigor and systematicity, turns away from the Marshallian approach, preferring instead the Walrasian mode of general equilibrium theorizing. But the idea of equilibrium can be both a realist and logical concept, depending on how it is treated. The way it is employed by Marshall is fundamentally a realist application. It is a far cry from the purely logical concept of equilibrium as espoused by general equilibrium theories. In the former approach, the problem is fundamentally that of analyzing real-life equilibrating forces and the adjustment processes at work within a definite time frame and within a well-defined situation with clear-cut constraints. In this approach, realism is preserved in three ways. First, the problem to be solved is itself a real one. Second, the way an economic situation is formulated bears a sufficient analogue with reality. Third, in spite of aggregation, the cognitive roles of the economic actors in question and their perceptions of the situation constitute the basic point of reference and remain in the background of the analysis. In contrast, the problem of general equilibrium theorizing in the Walrasian tradition is essentially a representational problem, one of finding a unique solution to a mathematical representation. Subsequent developments of price theory, in the false belief that general equilibrium theorizing is either a logical extension of partial equilibrium analysis or is a higher order intellectual activity to be justified in its own right, gradually turn to the general equilibrium approach as a new point of departure. As a result, emphasis is given to exploring new modes of mathematically representing the economy in equilibrium with minimal axioms and to explicating the mathematical properties (e.g., the stability or determinacy) of such mathematical systems. The standard problems confronting economic theorists become ones involving the proof of the existence of an equilibrium and the determination of equilibrium prices in the system. In this way, price theory in the general equilibrium framework becomes elevated to a pure, logical theory bearing little relationship to the real-life processes of price determination operating at the level of the perceptions and expectations of economic actors.

To sum up, general equilibrium price theory, being a pure, logical theory, is a pseudotheory of price determination. It is not an empirical, causal theory that is able to explain the real-life processes of price determination. To the latter end, we have to go back to the level of the economic actors' motivations, perceptions, and expectations in the context of specific market situations. This means that a realist theory of price determination has to be formulated at the level of partial equilibrium. One cannot be sure whether or not such a partial analysis can be knitted neatly into a broader framework or ultimately be expanded into a general theory, but it is clear that any general theory that eventually emerges will be very different from the general equilibrium price theories we now have.

But the way our present framework approaches the question of price determination still differs substantially from the Marshallian approach. Whereas Marshall concentrated chiefly on manipulating economic variables, keeping some relatively simplistic cognitive assumptions in the background, I emphasize cognitive variables as much as economic variables in my approach. Another difference lies in the choice of the level of realism that should be preserved in the inevitable process of abstraction. In my case, realism must be preserved down to the level of people's cognitions and motivations, whereas in Marshall's view, the proper level of economic discourse can be independently and legitimately conducted at the level of economic variables (e.g., aggregate supply and aggregate demand).

The task in this chapter, then, is to relate the different theories I have developed in the preceding chapters to the question of price determination. Considering the complexities I will be injecting, the resulting framework will be broader in scope but more segmented than existing price theories and, expectedly, will also be considerably less precise in its formulation. Although this framework is going to be more encompassing, it can hardly reach a level of generality similar to that of general equilibrium theory, partly because of the real-life complexities involved and partly because of its epistemic rule of preserving realism down to the level of human cognition. My approach in formulating this framework will be as follows. I will first concentrate on the different facets of price sensitivity and price acceptance on the part of consumers and will afterwards analyze in each case its implications with respect to price setting or pricing on the part of suppliers. Structurally speaking, this approach is an analogue to the supply and demand framework and involves, to some extent, the idea of equilibrium. As I will show in the exposition, however, the idea of equilibrium has only a secondary role to play in the framework. In addition, it needs to be pointed out that the framework presented is a very coarse structure and is by no means meant to be a comprehensive one. My goal is merely to provide a first outline for further research.

An Alternative Framework of Analysis: Price Acceptance and Price Sensitivity

I will begin with the question of price acceptance, because each purchase made by consumers represents their voluntary acceptance of the price offered, with or without going through any bargaining. Each purchase made by consumers or each deal concluded between them and suppliers also presumes that consumers have, to different degrees, exercised their "best" judgments and, by extension, their vigilance. In some cases, consumers may find it very easy to accept a price offered. In other cases, they may have to overcome some psychological barriers and may have to justify why they have chosen to spend their money one way instead of another. From the viewpoint of suppliers, an offer will be unrealistic if an important number of their target buyers refrain from purchasing. To suppliers, each offer they make constitutes a potential test of whether or not the price that they set is acceptable and each purchase made by buyers means that they have passed this test. A theory of price determination, in this view, seeks to study, in the first place, the conditions under which a sufficiently large number of buyers accept offers made by suppliers to warrant the latter enough revenue to sustain their businesses, and then how suppliers, taking into account the conditions of price acceptance on the part of their buyers, go about setting prices in the belief that they will come to be accepted by the target buyers. In experimental economics, considerable work has been done in discovering how buyers come to accept prices offered, especially under conditions of uncertainty.[1] However, with neoclassical price theory standing in the way of this research, a more theoretical but realistic treatment of price acceptance is not available.

I posit that the notion of price sensitivity is central to the analysis of price acceptance. There are two aspects to this notion. From a static viewpoint, it can be defined as the measure of the importance of the price factor relative to other relevant factors such as quality or convenience. The dynamic counterpart of this notion measures the extent to which price changes alter consumers' perceptions of the importance of the price factor relative to other considerations in making decisions. The notion of price sensitivity leads us to ask several sets of questions. First, in what types of consumption objects or activities would consumers generally show more concern over the price aspects of offers and, by corollary, over price changes? Second, what types of situations would sensitize consumers to the price aspect of an offer rather than other aspects of it and, by extension, sensitize them to price changes? Third, to what extent can such a sensitivity be augmented or reduced by consumers themselves or by suppliers? Answers to these questions are clearly important in analyzing issues of price determination and, by implication, the issue of price setting on the part of suppliers, for altogether they amount to offering some kind of systematic framework for studying the different conditions that govern consumer choice.

From the epistemic viewpoint, the framework of price sensitivity can be said to be superior to the neoclassical framework. There are two aspects to such superiority. The first is related to how the respective frameworks view utility maximization. In the neoclassical framework, the intention of the consumer to maximize utility unwittingly collapses with the end of utility maximization. Taking utility maximization as a necessarily attainable fact means that the consumer will no longer have to bother with any intervening factors in the real world that might prevent the actualization of the end-state. As a result, the logicalist variant of neoclassical theory is led to formulate its problem as one of determining the formal conditions of consumer equilibrium. In turn, this implies that neoclassical theory is inescapably involved in questions of

1. This was pointed out to me by an anonymous reader.

utility measurement and of the choice between the cardinal and ordinal approach, questions that involve enormous conceptual difficulties. In contrast, my framework is able to avoid these difficulties, for it takes the motive of utility maximization as only the indisputable intention of the consumer that may or may not be fully realized. While to some extent it accepts the idea that consumers strive to move toward some kind of equilibrium, the considerations involved go beyond the simple calculus of price and utility. It recognizes, instead, that there are a multitude of intervening factors that consumers take into account in allocating their budgets and in appraising offers. One central goal of this approach is studying the various conditions under which consumers accept different offers made by suppliers. The adoption of this approach, by corollary, means that the main thrust of studying price determination is examining the various conditions that sensitize consumers to the price factor and to changes in this factor in relation to other factors in their decision-making processes.

From the epistemic point of view, the present framework is also superior to the neoclassical one in that the notions of price acceptance and price sensitivity that it takes as primary are more encompassing notions. They are more encompassing because they cover cognitive as well as economic variables. Potentially richer in content, they are not only useful complements to purely economic concepts such as the price elasticity of demand, but they also leave the question of price determination sufficiently open for it to be causally related to psychological and cognitive factors. Building upon concepts that might serve to bridge economics and psychology, we thus come closer to our enterprise of relating the theory of price determination to the broader theory of value. What conventional economics takes as background parameters are now turned into variables that need to be addressed within this framework.

The epistemic significance of this proposed method is far-reaching. Economists who had long hoped for a return to realism by relaxing, one by one, the existing unreal assumptions built into the neoclassical framework must have been frustrated by the difficulties of the task. This is because the "neoclassical scaffolding," as Kaldor (1972) called it, has become so thick and impenetrable with every successive reformulation of neoclassical theory that no relaxation of any one of its unreal assumptions would be able to yield any transparent measure of how far we are removed from reality. In contrast, my framework is free of this difficulty. My framework, by virtue of its causal depth and flexibility of discourse, is open enough to allow the interchange of status between parameters and variables even in subsequent stages of development. As a result, true empirical progressiveness in a piecemeal manner is achievable in principle. Another merit of the proposed framework is this: when we need to study objective conditions that govern consumers' price sensitivities, we can enrich our analysis by taking macroscopic parameters (e.g., real time or sociocultural institutions) into account. As a result, the potential exists for developing a macrodynamic theory of consumer choice, that is, for studying changes of consumer behavior in various types of economies or over different phases of economic development.

In order to demonstrate the relationships between factors that govern price sensitivity and price acceptance by consumers and, by implication, the price-setting behaviors of suppliers, I will select a few areas that I believe can help illustrate the kind of approach one might fruitfully adopt. Needless to say, my choice is arbitrary, for the areas that will be discussed are not meant to be exhaustive. Nor can the subsequent discussion be in-depth, for my goal is merely to sketch an alternative approach rather than to offer detailed, substantive theories of price determination. Thus, while what I outline here will be helpful as a point of departure of future research, rigorous treatment of substantive content lies outside the scope of this book.

Price Sensitivity and Budgetary Constraint

According to neoclassical consumer theory, maximization of utility by consumers is subject to a budget constraint that is a mathematical expression of limited income. Given the budget constraint, the ratio of the marginal utilities of say, two products, can be shown to be equal to their price ratio for a maximum. However, in positing fragmentary mental maps on the part of consumers and in positing the thesis of mental efficiency, an overall consumer equilibrium can no longer be guaranteed in each of every act of consumer choice. It would be unrealistic and even counterproductive to expect consumers to retrieve and compare the marginal utilities of all other goods in each situation.[2] As an alternative, I assume that consumers generally preallocate, consciously or unconsciously, their disposable incomes into a hierarchy of different budgets and subbudgets to cover different categories of goods in a functional way.[3] How rigidly their overall income is subdivided and how flexibly these subbudgets are applied affect, to no small extent, their price sensitivities in general and their sensitivities to price changes in particular.

Broadly speaking, we can distinguish two conceptual poles, namely a fixed-budget regime and a flexible- or flex-budget regime. The former condition generally prevails over consumers who receive low, fixed incomes and are almost entirely dependent on such incomes for their consumption ac-

2. A shortcut would be to measure the marginal utility of a product with the marginal utility of money for the consumer. But this would require the assumption that the marginal utility of money remains consistent for consumers. Otherwise, the overall preference pattern of the consumer in question will be jeopardized.

3. This allocation serves partly to simplify decisions and partly to cope with uncertainties in the endowment (cf. Earl 1983).

tivities. The fixed-budget regime can be characterized by the following features. First, the allocation of the income into budgets and subbudgets is usually very detailed. For example, one might have a fixed transportation budget to cover the number of journeys one makes during a week, or the number of meals one takes during working days. Second, the flexibility of transferring funds between different subbudgets is limited. Third, the residual, uncommitted portion of that income is typically small or negligible.

As one might expect, consumers under fixed-budget regimes are highly sensitive to any change in price. With a considerable part of their consumption more related to basic needs, a price increase in such items is likely to have a negative effect, given that the demand for these items is generally inelastic (e.g., the number of journeys to the workplace). As a result, such consumers will be compelled either to trade down the quality of their consumption or else go into deficit spending through borrowing unless the increase in prices is compensated by an increase in income, or unless they can dip into other subbudgets or the residual, uncommitted category that may exist for contingencies of this kind. Although one would generally expect that rational consumers in such a predicament would first reset their overall priorities and revise their budget allocations before going into debt, it often happens that, depending on the social ethos of the time, many real-world consumers are reluctant to alter their ongoing habits and prefer to borrow in order to maintain their existing life-styles.[4] Clearly, this is an area where psychological, social, and cultural factors play an important role.

One cannot, of course, tell beforehand whether or not price decreases in certain commodities will lead consumers operating with rigid subbudgets to increase their consumption of the commodities in question (a substitution effect) or to apply the savings to another subbudget (an income effect), although one would be inclined to think that the former is more likely to be the case. Whereas one would expect perfectly rational consumers to reset their subbudgets each and every time such income effects come about in order to optimize their overall levels of utility, this clearly would involve too much change in the consumers' mental framework to be workable in reality, except in cases where the positive income effects are sizeable. Thus, it often happens that some price declines in items that are demand elastic lead more to substitution effects (e.g., more alcohol consumption if the price of alcohol should go down regardless of the fact that the person in question is badly in need of the money for other areas).[5] On the surface, such a switch does not necessarily represent the most optimal allocation from a global viewpoint. However, if we

4. In this case, the marginal utility of the borrowed spending exceeds the marginal disutility of the debt incurred.

5. This problem does not arise in the neoclassical framework that assumes a perfect ordering of preferences.

take into account factors such as convenience or expediency, the optimality of such an allocation may nonetheless be justified.

At the other pole, we have consumers who operate under a flexible-budget or even nonbudget regime. Such consumers either receive large regular incomes or they do not have to take their current levels of income into account in determining the size and patterns of their overall spending. The latter is possible if the consumer can always draw or expect to draw upon reserve assets. In this situation, price increases or decreases in certain consumption objects, while having potential substitution effects and income effects on the consumer, is of little relevance to the pattern of consumption. The income effects may, in fact, not even be noticeable. As a result, the overall cognitive sensitivities of such consumers to price changes are likely to be moderate, if not insignificant. There are, of course, different degrees in the flexibility of the budgets for different consumers in this category. In reality, few consumers operate entirely without budgetary constraints. The majority probably operate with flexible budgets with certain ceilings, supported perhaps by a residual budget with no predetermined amount. Given that the relative income effects resulting from price decreases are small or negligible for this category of consumers and given that the pattern of consumption of these consumers is not sensitive to price changes, there is little need for suppliers in this realm to compete by way of price cutting, especially for those types of consumption where demand is relatively inelastic. In this connection, it would be counterproductive for the supplier to cut prices, because price cutting would be easily associated with the inherent inferiority of the items supplied.

A case that is similar to the flex-budget regime is trivial or convenience consumption (e.g., a scratch pad). But in this case, consumers tend to pass over both the price and quality aspects of an offer. They would seldom query the quality and still less the price; they would buy whatever happens to be available at the moment. The implication for suppliers is that there is generally no motivation to upgrade quality or to give special attention to cost and price reductions. Since convenience and access become the crucial criteria of consumer choice, availability of supply and, by implication, the breadth of the distribution network represents the prominent area for successful suppliers to direct their attention.

The modern economy, moving toward higher levels of affluence, is increasingly populated by consumers who operate under a relatively flexible budget regime. This is reinforced, to no small extent, by the greater sense of security accorded by present-day social and welfare programs practiced in many industrialized countries. The greater sense of security inculcated by these welfare programs means that consumers become less restrained in their spending and are more prepared, on the spur of the moment, to dip into the residual, uncommitted category of income (savings). In a similar vein, the development of an economy toward a more affluent state inevitably leads to a continuing redefinition of what constitutes inferior goods or trivial consumption by its consumers. As affluence grows, much of what was previously considered to be necessary consumption is reduced to the category of inferior goods or of trivial consumption. Consumers' increasing affluence naturally leads them to reject what they had subjectively considered to be inferior consumption or consumption that is associated with a low status. Price reductions for this category of goods, instead of pushing up sales, might have the negative effect of rapidly reducing to the status of low-grade consumption. In this circumstance, the price sensitivity of consumers works in the direction of dampening their demand for these goods. In short, life-styles matter significantly in governing the price sensitivities of consumers, and this, in turn, has important implications for pricing behaviors (see Earl 1983 and 1986).

Price Sensitivity and Price Stability

Another interesting framework that offers insights into consumer behavior is to contrast consumers' price sensitivities under the respective regimes of price stability and price instability. There is a group of products (e.g., agricultural products), the prices of which are subject to wide fluctuations. With regard to this category of products, consumers are accustomed to price fluctuations, although they do hold specific ideas about what the normal ranges of fluctuation should be. As I mentioned previously, the neoclassical model is generally applicable to the analysis of price determination for this category of products. Consider consumers who have a certain budget for some product, say fruit. Subject to their constraints (which can be flexible within some limits), they will maximize utility by buying seasonal fruits that are in abundant supply and, hence, represent a better value for money. Should certain types of fruit become more expensive because of restricted supply, consumers will switch to those types that they subjectively believe are the closest substitutes for what they want and that are more abundant and, thereby, less expensive. Clearly, the law of diminishing marginal utility works in such situations and consumer rationality is well maintained. Since consumers are psychologically accustomed to the price fluctuations of these products, suppliers usually set prices by way of a simple cost-plus formula.[6] Suppliers would add to their basic costs some conventional margins and modify them in light of their particular structures and overheads. These rather standard margins can be shown to be jointly determined, apart from some historical, contingent factors, by the

6. There are, of course, many other reasons for adopting the cost-plus formula, e.g., administrative convenience.

level of suppliers' overhead and risk factors peculiar to the trade. Where fluctuations in costs become considerable, suppliers might flexibly adjust their margins in order to maintain certain sales levels.

In contrast, there is another category of products, especially manufactured goods and services, over which consumers hold sticky expectations (to different degrees) about how prices are to be set. I have previously pointed out the moral dimensions behind such stickiness in extreme cases and explained why suppliers in general tend to avoid raising prices, especially at a time when inflation is negligible. In a stable price regime, an asymmetry between price and quality from the perception of the consumer can be discerned, namely, the consumer is more sensitive to changes in price than to changes in quality. As a result, competition usually takes the form of cost and price reductions, and, even when costs go up, suppliers tend to maintain selling prices as far as possible. Suppliers who are capable of reducing their prices even by small amounts are almost sure to win a larger share of the market. To aggressive suppliers, price reductions represent a sound strategy, provided that they are not constrained in the expansion of their capacity and provided that they are not afraid of retaliation. Indeed, it may not be an unsound business proposition to reduce costs and, hence, prices by way of trading down in quality, provided that the quality decrease is not seen to be conspicuous. For those industries where cost reductions are difficult to achieve due perhaps to technological stagnation or to inflation, the need to maintain old prices might, over time, force suppliers who survive the profit squeeze to gradually trade down the quality of their products. In these cases, we might witness a decline in quality over time unless new technological breakthroughs emerge (reducing costs) or new marketing methods are successfully adopted by the market leaders (which alter the basic value norms of consumers).

As might be expected, any price offered that deviates from the normal price held stickily by consumers in a stable price regime, even for products or services that are capable of some differentiation, will be resisted. Such sticky expectations are natural. From the cognitive viewpoint, a concept once formed in our mental framework tends to persist even when there is evidence against its empirical relevance. It is in our own interest to protect the core beliefs we happen to hold about reality. This might be attributed to the fact that too abrupt a change may negatively affect our self-confidence about understanding the external world or that frequent reorganizations of our mental order is too costly (in terms of energy expenditure) to be maintained. In the extreme, our egos tend to look upon ideas and knowledge we happen to enlist as part of our innate and defining characteristics that need to be preserved at almost any cost.

Charged with emotions of this kind, it is not surprising that the consumer might, in response to a price increase, act in a less-than-rational manner (e.g., changing his or her existing supplier even if it means that he or she might sacrifice convenience). Such less-than-rational actions are understandable because price increases are indeed capable of stirring deep emotional reactions. Price increases of a wholesale kind, especially when accompanied by huge negative income effects, have the effect of injecting uncertainty into the mental horizons of consumers and stirs their deep fears of loss. As the regime of stable prices is challenged, consumers' fears go beyond their immediate economic interests, and they are suddenly stirred into new levels of alertness. Consumers are made painfully aware of the fact that their mental pictures of the future and, accordingly, their overall patterns of spending must be reformed to cope with the vagaries of the new regime. By corollary, protective actions and strategies must be adopted to cope not only with the loss of real income but also with the loss of wealth. In short, in the wake of dawning inflation, the individual economic actor is compelled to reorganize his or her mental order to accept a radical change in his or her conception of the economic reality and, unwillingly, to move into a state of mental hypersensitivity. Given such deep emotional underpinning, it is no wonder that consumers tend to respond negatively and emotionally to even small price changes in the beginning of an inflationary era. Needless to say, once inflation starts to reign, a chain of protective moves will be unleashed by different economic actors and groups. On the whole, the economic actor who becomes typically hypersensitive tends to make a linear projection of the future, anticipating future price increases before they actually take place. Collective actions of this kind, left unchecked, will pave the way for a phase of runaway inflation. Since it is not the purpose of this work to study the mechanisms and effects of inflation, I will confine my analysis to the relative sensitivities of the consumer to the price factor versus other factors in his or her decisions under the respective regimes in question.

I have pointed out that, in a stable price regime, consumers are highly sensitive to any price changes. I have also pointed out that, other things being equal, suppliers tend to compete with each other over price reductions and tend to avoid initiating price increases. In an unstable price regime, in particular during inflation, consumers are hypersensitive to price increases to the extent that they may even anticipate them. Under this regime, consumers experience a sudden expansion of price information. They are liable to become overloaded and confused, for prices no longer serve the function of signaling value in the usually reliable manner. For their part, suppliers are quick to exploit such a situation and profit on the distorted senses of value held by consumers. The royal road to profit is therefore manipulation. Actions to improve quality become, if no longer profitable propositions, at least secondary concerns. As a result, attention to quality or competition through quality improvements will suffer under an inflationary regime. Pricing on the part of suppliers, taking into account the consumers' expectations and fears as well as future movements of suppliers' costs (which are also rising), becomes a complex issue and a battleground of wits between different economic actors.

Thus, neither a stable price regime nor a highly unstable one favors competition in terms of quality: such competition is best pursued in a regime somewhere in the middle range, especially in a regime of creeping inflation. Under this regime, consumers have expectations of steady price increases. As might be expected, an additional quality improvement that accompanies a price increase will give consumers a good reason (or even an excuse) to justify the new offer, although they might still be prepared to accept a price increase in any case. On the other hand, suppliers who lower their prices, though welcomed by consumers, might invite some kind of skepticism. On balance, it is clearly a more profitable strategy for suppliers to follow the general trend of price increases, at the same time giving consumers conspicuously better value for their money. Hence, quality improvements seem to be most feasible and favored under such a regime. However, it needs to be pointed out that with rapidly changing technology, among other factors, the range of goods that fall under the stable price regime should diminish in proportion to the overall goods circulating in the economy.

Price Sensitivity, Consumer Capital and Competition

The idea of cognitive asymmetry between price and quality as an analytical device does not find a place in neoclassical economics. This is to be expected because it is considerably more convenient to ignore price as a quality indicator. Implicit in the basic postulate of conventional demand theory is that consumers have complete and correct information about all prices and the utility of any conceivable bundle of commodities. Hence, price as an indicator of quality becomes redundant (Gabor and Granger 1966).[7] Besides, conventional demand theory chooses to deal largely with goods of a homogeneous nature. Because quality differences do not exist among such goods by definition, a "perfect" cognitive asymmetry can be said to prevail between price and quality from the perception of the consumer. In other words, consumers are assumed either to be unable or to choose not to appreciate quality differences. Hence, competition becomes de facto price competition.

In addition to the assumptions of the perfect ordering of preferences as well as that of the homogeneity of goods, the neoclassical theory of price determination is also rooted in the assumption of a perfectly competitive market. By way of logic, it would appear that, under such ideal conditions, the "law of one price" will hold. Economists since Jevons (who gave the theorem only a verbal elaboration) have taken it for granted that a single price

7. I am indebted to Peter Earl for this point.

prevails in a perfectly competitive market. But as Fusfeld shows, there is no rigorous proof of this one-price theorem in the entire literature of modern price theory (1990). According to Fusfeld, even in perfectly competitive markets, an original distribution of bids and offers will not tend to generate a single price, but will generate a distribution of prices, if we accept that: (*a*) traders are heterogeneous—they have different time preferences, different abilities to process information, and different attitudes toward uncertainty; (*b*) price formation takes place over real time; and (*c*) the interactions of buyers and sellers create continuing changes in the range of bids and offers (Fusfeld 1988).

None of these neoclassical assumptions and their logical corollaries enable us to reach the real world. The perfect ordering of preferences and the perfect competition assumptions both imply that man is cognitively omniscient by origin and by result, while the homogeneity of goods assumption means that consumers, as cognizing agents, cannot see any subjective differences between different specimens of an allegedly homogeneous product for all occasions. All these assumptions contradict the fundamental cognitive properties that I have thus far posited for economic actors as real cognitive beings. Predictably, too, the assertion of these assumptions would mean that we have to deny not only the idea of price sensitivity (in the sense that I am developing here), but also the idea of consumer capital that I elaborated in chapter 6. Both of these concepts suggest a real world of much greater complexity than the world conceived by the perfect competition cum homogeneous product school. They are conceptually more powerful concepts that can help us to gain more insights into how consumers actually respond to the complexities they face.

The idea of consumer capital in the sense of the accumulation of knowledge and information about different consumption objects and consumption activities presupposes, even for a supposedly standard article, the possibility of the existence of heterogeneous perceptions of the subjective value of that article among different consumers or even to the same consumer at different moments. Consumer capital, in this view, is the relevant but well-ordered knowledge in the mind of the consumer that helps the consumer to sharpen his or her perceptions of value. Being relevant and well-ordered knowledge, it enables the consumer to form hypotheses about the level of utility that will be realized upon particular purchases and to screen competing offers. It provides controlling norms for appraising the results of consumption. Seen in this light, we might say that the better equipped a consumer is in respect to his or her consumer capital, the more sensitivity he or she should develop not only toward price differences and changes, but also over quality differences and changes. Differently put, the overall cognitive sensitivity of consumers should be enhanced as they build up their consumer capital.

As might be expected, suppliers under the regime of vigorous consumer capital formation have to compete on both price and quality terms, especially for products where it is difficult to project a supplier-specific image onto the mind of the consumer. The supplier who fails to compete effectively on price terms will naturally have to move toward the more specialized segments of the market where quality matters more significantly in the eyes of the consumer. Because the market acts to channel both price and quality information to consumers, a competitive market encapsulating more information is generally more favorable to the process of consumer capital formation. In turn, increased consumer capital will enhance the overall cognitive sensitivity of the consumer. Competition, in a nutshell, is a positive factor that sensitizes the consumer to value, although we need to add the qualification that competition in this sense is not equivalent to the sense of perfect competition implicit in neoclassical theory.

This thesis is, however, valid only partially, for consumers, no matter how experienced and well informed they are, grasp the subtle relationships between price and quality only within certain limits. Contrary to the neoclassical assumption, more information, even if it is provided free, is not always beneficial. As Simon contends (1976), increased information implies the increased need for screening.[8] As my previous analysis has shown, major conditions that prevail in the modern consumption economy (e.g., an increasingly sophisticated market with an expanding information base, rapid technological innovations and fast-changing products rendering previously built-up consumer capital obsolete, and an economy increasingly dominated by manipulative activities) can become negative conditions that discourage consumer capital formation. They are negative factors that numb rather than enhance the cognitive sensitivity of the consumer toward value.

In skill-intensive consumption, consumer capital, however, always has a positive role to play. I have said that consumers who are upgrading their skills tend to see more value in their consumption activities and tend to reap more satisfaction from their active participation in the consumption process. Commanding an expanding capital base and enjoying escalating satisfaction, consumers strongly expect more excitement ahead. As a result, their attention is increasingly directed toward the quality aspects of their consumption. Admittedly, consumers' sense of value will be sharpened by virtue of their heightened interests, but their expectation of greater future enjoyment means that they are generally more willing to share some of their "subjective surplus" with their suppliers by way of more readily accepting price increases, especially those increases that are accompanied by quality improvements such as additional novel features.

Indeed, the more positive the role played by consumer capital in con-

8. This was pointed out to me by an anonymous reader.

sumptions of this kind and the more wide-ranging that capital base is, the more important the subjective idiosyncracies of consumers become in their decision making. With more subjective components to dominate their decisions, consumers' cognitive asymmetries naturally tilt toward the quality end. The implications for suppliers' pricing are obvious. Suppliers have ample room to increase their product prices as long as they innovate by upgrading their products or improving their service. Naturally, they are motivated to do so, although the rate of price increases will be constrained by the forces of competition as well as by the consumers' heightened sense of value. Given the possibility of wide-ranging differences in subjective perceptions of quality among consumers, it is always easy for suppliers to skirt some of the competition they face by concentrating on particular segments of the market and by injecting (as much as possible) supplier-specific characteristics into their products.

Price Sensitivity and Manipulation

I have mentioned that, beyond a certain point, the development of the modern economy renders consumer capital formation (in the sense of accumulating substantive knowledge about consumption objects) less rewarding. To reiterate, the advent of the modern, affluent economy is partly responsible for the erosion of the price sensitivity of the consumer and for tilting his or her cognitive asymmetry toward nonprice aspects. The rapid launching of new products by suppliers quickly renders the existing stock of consumer capital easily obsolete and discourages vigorous investment in consumer capital formation. Experiences of rapid inflation imprint on the consumer that it may be wiser to spend when prices begin to rise but before the next round of price increases. Besides, the greater the proportion of disposable income of the average consumer that remains free or uncommitted, the less vigilant he or she is in spending such "aimless" money, because the return to vigilance becomes less rewarding.

This is to be expected. With more free money to spend, consumers can afford more errors in their consumption decisions because the marginal disutility of their errors decreases. As consumers move further toward socially guided consumption, they become more confused and vague with respect to what they truly want and with respect to how such vague wants can best be satisfied. Consumers still want to maximize utility, but the very quality of that utility becomes increasingly suspect. They may still be satisfied, but perhaps for a shorter time or with less intensity than expected. In particular, consumers are more prone to disappointment regarding those types of consumptions that derive their utilities largely from their exclusive values and are, therefore, of a "negative" nature. Indeed, the more consumption becomes dominated by social values, the more it will become erratic and unpredictable. Differently put, one might suspect that there is a chronic deterioration in the quality of the satisfaction consumers obtain as the level of their affluence rises. In such a state, one can expect consumers to spend even more freely, perhaps with the vain aim of recovering the kind of satisfaction and the quality of utility they once experienced. A consumer oriented in this direction is naturally more concerned about the quality or the exclusive value of the offers encountered than the prices attached to them.

These factors alone would have directed suppliers toward more nonprice competition. With the advent of extensive manipulation, the switch to this type of competition is overwhelmingly clear. With nonprice competition dominant, the attention of the consumer is increasingly being drawn to aspects of quality. As can be expected, the project of imprinting quality messages onto the consumer is very different from the more straightforward method implied in price competition. For effectiveness, it requires indirect hinting (soft selling) and repetition of the same message and, therefore, more organized marketing efforts. It works best by influencing the customer's sense of significance. In other words, the effectiveness of quality competition depends, coincidentally and in part, on the same skills and techniques of manipulation.

The effect of manipulation is that, through persuasion at the unconscious level, higher prices are accepted by the consumer as standing for higher values. This effect comes partly from the power of advertising, which is rooted in its ability to exploit the cognitive defects of the consumer. Formulated in the present context, advertising can be said to have the goal and effect of reducing the consumer's overall cognitive sensitivity, especially his or her resistance to upward adjustments of prices. It indoctrinates his or her prior decisions about what is valued before he or she encounters a choice situation. It persuades consumers to see more apparent value at the moment of decision by helping them to expand momentarily their imagination and powers of association. It diverts attention to nonprice factors in actual choice situations. In short, the consumer is to be disarmed, as far as possible, of his or her natural vigilance. The choice situations in which consumers make decisions are to be turned into occasions for consumers to rubber-stamp an offer rather than test the intrinsic value of the suppliers' offers.

Cost Insensitivity and Manipulative Pricing

The preceding analysis has important implications for pricing. In chapter 5, I explained why the modern, large, multiproduct firm has become more insensitive to its own cost structure with respect to its individual products and how prices are set by manipulative suppliers. To briefly reiterate, suppliers set prices in accordance with what they think consumers can be persuaded to accept with the aid of a manipulative budget. Prices that are set or targeted by a supplier can be seen to consist of the following components: (*a*) the basic cost of production plus an allocation of the firm's overhead; (*b*) the target profit margin; (*c*) a margin of error allowed for in the projection of the basic cost of production caused by the uncertainty of economic parameters that are involved in the production environment, particularly if prices are set far ahead of production or if long-range investments are planned with relatively meager current market data; (*d*) the projected manipulative cost; and (*e*) a margin of error allowed for the uncertain effects of manipulative actions. While components *a* and *b* are more straightforward and have more solid foundations, components *c, d,* and *e* involve highly subjective projections which are not so easy to define and which can differ substantially among various suppliers. As such, they may remain in flux throughout the life of a product. As a result, a clear-cut definition of the actual cost from moment to moment may turn out to be an impossible task. This, together with the difficulty of allocating overhead cost to a particular product, can account for the increased cost insensitivity of the modern, multiproduct firm with respect to its individual products at any particular moment. Expectedly, the less knowledgeable and less established suppliers are more uncertain of the margin of error for both their projected basic cost and manipulation cost. But even established suppliers whose experiences enable them to set lower safety margins for their projections cannot be very sure about the optimal level of manipulation and the margin of error to be allowed for, especially when they move into areas such as the protection of their market share or the retention of market leadership. With major components of their costs determined by highly subjective evaluations and given the potentially wide variations in these projections and evaluations, it is no wonder the modern consumer sector is characterized by greater degrees of price differentiation even for more or less standard consumer products, reflecting, as it were, cost insensitivities on the part of the suppliers. In its turn, cost insensitivities are the breeding ground for manipulation.

Under the regime of manipulation where consumers are persuaded that higher prices stand for higher value, price competition can be a self-defeating strategy. Under such a regime, price cutting beyond a certain point or even the very act of cutting prices might be interpreted by the consumer as an attempt to offer inferior quality. Instead of being suspected of offering inferior quality, suppliers who reduce their prices across the board might sometimes be seen as betraying a weak position, for example, being badly in need of cash. In the same vein, if a substantial innovation in a product offered by a supplier is not accompanied by a price increase, especially during a period of creeping inflation, the consumer might view it with the same skeptical eye and might question whether or not that improvement is only cosmetic.

Manipulation yielding increasing returns (Chamberlin 1966) favors larger scale firms. Since it is not easy to predict whether or not the consumer will respond in the same manner to the same set of manipulation techniques, the effects of manipulation can be erratic. There is, in other words, no clearly defined optimal proportion of manipulation cost in the overall cost. Naturally, larger scale firms are in a better position to absorb the margin of error and to continue to experiment with a new set of manipulative techniques. With larger firms dominating the market or different segments of a market, price competition will assume less importance. Pricing will be influenced more by administrative guidelines and by targeted levels of manipulation costs to be employed. Smaller suppliers, being price takers, are more prepared to compete by offering better quality or better service. These market conditions further suggest that price reductions become a dubious strategy, if not a counterproductive one, under the manipulative regime.

A Manipulation Theory of Consumer Price Determination

What, then, are the implications of widespread manipulation for price theory in the realm of consumer products? Under the regime of manipulation, there can be a range of possible costs for any given target price set by the supplier, depending on how different suppliers perceive the effectiveness of their manipulative actions and, thereby, how much they are going to spend on manipulative activities. Conversely, within a reasonable range, any price assigned to a particular product can be generally made acceptable to the consumer upon the application of a sufficiently sizeable manipulation budget, sometimes without even a repackaging of the product in question. With an important component of the cost of an item composed of a manipulation budget and as the effects of manipulation are uncertain, it is fallacious to talk, as classical economists do, of some invariable, constant factor over time that is commensurate with the value of a commodity.

On the other hand, since the consumer's subjective conception of value over less essential goods is a plastic one and is subject to different degrees of "engineering" by powerful, manipulative suppliers, it is equally fallacious to say that prices are determined only by the subjective valuations of individuals. Prices may still reflect subjective valuation or, to say the least, they have to be mediated via the subjective apparatus of consumers, but, over an ever wider range of goods, these valuations are subject to the persuasion of manipulative firms. This does not, of course, mean that consumers are reduced to passive agents incapable of independent judgments. But it is clear that the sovereignty of consumers, in the sense that they are indisputably masters of their own preferences, no longer holds. With the price sensitivity of the average consumer declining in a more affluent economy, we might posit a corresponding decline in consumer rationality, especially for goods embodying substantial conventional values.

With manipulative actions on the ascent, the price determination of consumer products in the modern economy becomes increasingly contingent on the management policies of large-scale, multiproduct firms. As more administrative considerations dominate the pricing process of these firms, prices of individual products tend to become more sticky. As prices no longer directly reflect basic costs, one can hardly tell the profit or loss position of an individual item in any precise manner at any particular moment. The decline of this cost sensitivity also means that the management becomes both less motivated and less well placed to alter existing prices. With the manipulative cost acting as a buffer, there is more room for other cost components to change without needing to raise prices each time the basic cost of production moves upward. Since manipulation takes time to have an effect, it is not advisable to change an existing price too often, for it will stir the suspicion of the consumer and undermine his or her confidence in the messages transmitted in the manipulation. In addition, there is the familiar argument that frequent alterations in prices raise administrative costs. All these considerations suggest, correctly or incorrectly, that prices once set are likely to remain stable, although one should not infer from the stickiness of individual prices that price levels will be stable for the consumption sector as a whole, as new products as well as repackaged and repriced products are continually pushed into the market.

To sum up, the role of prices undergoes important changes with the advent of vigorous manipulative activities in the consumption sector. Whereas prices can be interpreted to signal opportunities or to signal scarcities in a premanipulative state, prices no longer reliably serve these functions in an economy pervaded by manipulative activities. They are no longer as useful for inferring the basic cost of production or as indicators of genuine scarcities. Given that manipulative costs are rather arbitrary and not readily decidable, their presence distorts the function of prices as signals of opportunity. Given that manipulation is itself capable of generating scarcity through the subjective perception of the consumer, prices incorporating a significant manipulative cost are no longer reliably reflective of true scarcities.

With the manipulative factor playing a crucial role in dominating pricing decisions, the concept of equilibrium can be given a new interpretation. Whereas prices are still apparently subject to interactions between supply and demand, new equilibrating mechanisms engendered by more sophisticated supply-side factors related to the structure and objectives of large corporations give a new meaning to the concept of equilibrium. Clearing the market is achieved as much by price reductions as by the stepping up manipulation. Furthermore, with the advent of manipulation as one fundamental determinant of present-day consumption, price determination in a static economic system should no longer remain the central problem in the theory of value. The search for a system of prices that brings about equilibrium in an economy becomes a kind of misplaced ideal, as we learn that the importance of price as well as the mode of price formation is relative to the particular stage and organization of an economy, as well as to the particular mode of value formation prevailing in the economy in question.

Consumer Rationality in Crisis? Reflections on Some Fundamental Principles

With the proliferation of manipulative factors, the modern consumer can be characterized as being torn between two sets of opposing forces operating against each other. On the one hand, by virtue of their innate consumer interests and active capital formation, consumers are striving to maintain their rationality. In this regard, they are positively assisted by cooperative responses from rational suppliers as well as by the expanding market. On the other hand, consumers are goaded into less-than-rational states at the unconscious level by the manipulative environment that they have unwittingly helped to create and to which they are inescapably bound. Which direction consumer rationality will tend toward in the future is an interesting question that will have far-reaching consequences and should merit further research.

At the risk of oversimplification, we may say that manipulative factors have negative effects on the several strands of consumer rationality we have discussed. I said earlier that the idea of a weaker yet content-rich notion of consumer rationality can be defended on the grounds that consumers, while not mechanistically rational, are nonetheless pragmatically rational in that they do consider, as far as their cognitive resources permit and as far as such considerations do not go against the dictates of mental efficiency in their decision making, their broader interests when they face a choice situation. Such rationality could be seen to rest partly on some innate capacities that allow consumers to make the best out of a situation each time and partly upon their ability to efficiently and effortlessly retrieve concepts of value from the unconscious level, in spite of the fact that these values are not originally innate. Such an ability, however, turns out to be a two-edged sword, because it also permits the infiltration of values that are in conflict with his or her overall interests and permits these values to dominate.

With the advent of manipulation, it becomes more difficult for us to speak of situational rationality and of naturalized rationality. I have already dealt with these difficulties in depth and will not repeat them. It becomes, too, more difficult to speak of "correspondent rationality" in the sense of correspondence between ends and means. This is because the rise of affluence has dissipated the concept of ends in the minds of consumers. They surely know that they want to maximize utility, but what particular types of utility they really desire and how best they can achieve them is no longer something firmly in their grasp. This is particularly true as more of these ends are "imported," stealing into his or her mind; such imports may be only fleeting and of transient interest to and may be foreign to other parts of his or her value system. It is not surprising, therefore, that consumers might at times experience sharply diminishing marginal utility in some types of consumption, finding themselves disillusioned and at a loss about the real meaning of such consumption. Alternatively put, the advent of manipulation renders the idea of "reflective rationality" (e.g., Sen 1987) less easily attainable in the sense of a correspondence between our means and those aims that we are convinced of as worthy of our pursuit upon our reflection of them or our experience of them. This is because the project of manipulation is to set out to suppress, as far as possible, consumers' reflective faculties and to prevent them from reexamining their patterns of values.

But it would be prejudiced to conclude that it is no longer possible for us to speak of consumer rationality with the advent of manipulation. In some senses, consumer rationality is on the advance in the modern consumption economy. First, it is misleading to say that the manipulative firm is no longer interested in discovering what we really want as consumers. The continuing development of science and technology enables consumer rationality to be advanced in different ways. It renders possible the discovery of more knowledge about our real needs (e.g., certain types of medicine). It enables certain of our fantasies to come true (e.g., speed and ease of travel or ease of communication). In this connection, the advent of the large firm with a concentration of resources and with sophisticated rules of decision making is crucially important. Alternatively put, consumer rationality can be said to advance on the respective foundations of scientific rationality and procedural rationality. Of particular interest, too, is the fact that, given any known want that is expressed by the consumer, it is much easier for the present-day supplier to fill such wants than it was in the past. Clearly, this is one important aspect of consumer rationality that registers a significant advance in the present state of the modern economy.

I have discussed in depth how the modern consumer interacting with the supplier in a competitive market leads to the production of more consumer capital (and, of course, more producer capital as well). This aspect of consumer rationality will not repeated here. However, there is an important aspect of consumer rationality related to the learning factor implicit in the idea of consumer capital that should also be mentioned. In response to manipulation, more vigilant consumers will not fail to develop protective techniques. Such techniques could be taken as part of their consumer capital. They may choose to continue to deal with long-standing suppliers who insist on giving good value of money. Consumers may make efforts to suppress (as much as possible) impulse buying, or they may exploit special sales or avoid long-term commitments. With the loss of innocence, consumers should be able to dilute some of the manipulative influences that are imposed on them.

With consumer rationality torn between these opposing forces, what conclusion can be drawn out of my discussion? Or is seeking a conclusion a misplaced objective? Several points should become clearer from the preceding discussion. First, consumer rationality in particular and economic rationality in general, or broader still, human rationality in general are clearly in flux in the path of our evolution. We cannot sensibly speak of rationality as if there were some invariable standard to rely upon, while acknowledging that mankind as a whole is constantly evolving. Second, because we cannot speak of human rationality without bringing up the idea of human values and, given the peculiarities of human values such as plurality and conventionality, we probably cannot have a tenable monist account of rationality. Third, if rationality is inseparable from human values, it seems plausible to suggest that there must be both rationality-augmenting aspects and rationality-diluting aspects to any socioeconomic framework or institution that is rooted in certain human values that represent, in part, the convention of the time or of the place. The modern, large, manipulative firm is a case in point. It is capable, on the one hand, of imposing extensive manipulative power on consumers, but on the other hand, its resources and organization make the advance of knowledge and technology that would better the state of our consumption possible.

Given both the rationality-augmenting and rationality-diluting aspects of the modern, manipulative firm, can we come to any conclusion with respect to the overall level of consumer rationality in the present-day consumption economy? While accepting this as a question that cannot be satisfactorily answered without further research, the way we have formulated the issue seemingly biases us toward a more pessimistic answer, although that pessimism has to be heavily qualified. Because most of the pertinent points have been covered, I will not repeat them here. In short, the thrust of my argument is this. There is a basic unalterable asymmetry between the power of the consumer and that of the supplier. Whereas consumers cast the votes, they remain individuals in the realm of consumption. On the other hand, their counterparts, suppliers, are much better organized, increasingly so in the modern economy. While the final say of consumers and the existence of competition will limit the arbitrary manipulative power of suppliers, there are apparently no effective checks against the subversive power of manipulation, for the effective checks possessed naturally by consumers are gradually stripped away with the advance of affluence. Given increasing affluence and increasing domination by social convention, it is obvious that the marginal utility of consumption as a whole and, by corollary, the marginal disutility of errors made by consumers will be on the decline. With less consumer vigilance, we have no way but to accept, pending further research, a rather grim prognosis for consumer rationality.

Part 3
Toward a Cognitive Paradigm

CHAPTER 8

Cognition and the Place of Value Theory in Economics

The Centrality of Cognition

The preceding chapters show that by positing a more general theory of value, one that encompasses a theory of value formation (i.e., how utilities develop in the minds of consumers) and one that studies the relations between the architecture of human cognition and consumer behaviors, we can systematically explain features that are characteristic of the modern consumption economy without resorting to ad hoc hypotheses. For example, such a theory can be used to analyze the extensive use of advertising and marketing, the less-than-fully-rational behaviors of modern consumers, the orientation toward nonprice factors in competition among suppliers, the prevalence of the demonstration effect, the coevolution between the expectations of consumers and suppliers, the domination of the distribution function over the production function, and so on. Central to these explanations is the idea of cognition; namely, how the evolution and the structure of our minds affect the development of our value patterns, our judgments of utility, and, thereby, our decisions in consumption activities. All together, the host of explanations suggests that with a different theory of the mind, we seem to end up with a different theory of value and a different theory of price formation. And if a theory of value hinges on a particular theory of the mind, a promising research direction would be to examine alternative theories of the mind and to spell out the different theories of value they entail or embody. Cognition should, therefore, no longer be viewed as exogenous to economics. For more fruitful theorizing, it should be made part and parcel of the core knowledge in the study of economics. In order to further demonstrate the validity of this important assertion, I will review different schools of thought and show that their overall ineffectiveness in replacing neoclassical orthodoxy might be attributable to the fact that they do not involve the study of cognition or posit a tenable theory of the mind. I will also review the main patterns of contrast and complementarity between my theory and these different schools.

Evolutionary Economics

The heterodox school of economics that bears most ambivalent relations with neoclassical orthodoxy is evolutionary economics. One can find a number of diverse approaches under this label, especially from the standpoint of how they define their relations with neoclassical economics and the kind of evolutionary principles they employ or emphasize.[1] Common to these diverse approaches is, of course, their stance of positing a developmental perspective to economics as opposed to the "timeless" character of the neoclassical model, which is reminiscent of the mechanical model of Newtonian physics. Additionally, in spite of their differences, these diverse views often acknowledge their intellectual debt to Schumpeter. Nelson and Winter, for example, consider it appropriate to use the term *neo-Schumpeterian* to denote the kind of evolutionary approach they employ (1982). Generally speaking, the evolution metaphor is useful to economic theorizing in two ways. First, it provides a theory of natural selection, market competition being seen to be analogous to biological competition; only firms that are fittest will survive. Second, it supplies a theory of adaptation, namely firms adapt to the business environment and improve themselves in gradual steps to achieve better performance (see Nelson and Winter 1982).

Curiously, some evolutionary economists, while challenging the timeless character of the neoclassical framework and acknowledging the evolutionary approach as a more fruitful one in explicating economic phenomena, seek to fit mainstream economics into the evolutionary perspective. Kenneth Boulding, for example, contends that neoclassical price theory can be fitted into an evolutionary framework with great ease (1981, 87) on the grounds that implicit in the former is an ecological interaction of commodities that continually exercises a strong selective process. Boulding goes as far as showing that the mathematical and graphical apparatus of price theory can be derived from the ecological-evolutionary model (87–97), although he is fully aware of the fact that the theory of maximizing behavior and marginal analysis is essentially "Newtonian."

That neoclassical theory can easily be modified to fit the evolutionary perspective is also shown in the simple natural selection argument for profit maximizing firms being selected (see Friedman 1953). Considering the complexities involved in the process of evolution, the thesis is, however, too raw and simplistic to be capable of testing and falsification. A more refined approach is adopted by Nelson and Winter, who concentrate on the task of showing how orthodox theory, by virtue of its rigid assumption of rationality

1. See, e.g., Boulding 1981; Hicks 1969; Hirschleifer 1985; Mattews 1984; Nelson and Winter 1982.

and its simplistic assumption of maximization and equilibrium, obscures the essential features of economic change. In their view, the central concern of evolutionary economics should be to study the dynamic processes by which firm behavior patterns and market outcomes are jointly determined. Characteristic of such processes are search and selection, through the joint actions of which firms evolve over time with the condition of the industry in each period bearing the seeds of its conditions in the next period. As a result, economic change occurs through successful innovations adopted by the firm. Within an industry, individual firms are compelled to adopt new and more efficient techniques for fear that they might be displaced by firms that do.

Whereas Nelson and Winter confine themselves to the smaller task of producing a more realistic theory of economic change and growth, many other evolutionary economists are more anxious to see the entire neoclassical orthodoxy replaced by the evolutionary paradigm. This is particularly true of those economists who come under the label of "evolutionary political economy." These economists advocate an interdisciplinary, broad-based approach and a holistic framework as well as propose the study of social institutions other than markets, with the intent of eventually providing a realistic alternative to neoclassical economic theory.[2]

How effective is the challenge of evolutionary economics to the orthodox position? There is no clear-cut answer to this question. On the one hand, the fundamental insights of evolutionary economics are sound ones, for example, the notion of search, innovation, selection, and the long-term perspective it advocates are highly important. Hence, they contribute to our understanding of competition and technological development. On the other hand, apart from Nelson and Winter, who use an evolutionary theory to account for the phenomena of economic change, much of evolutionary economics is either a straightforward application of the Darwinian or neo-Darwinian metaphor to economic phenomena or a rhetorical gesture with insufficient conceptual or analytic rigor. For one thing, the idea of evolution is not always clearly explicated. Many applications of the idea are not even attempts to apply the principles involved in biological evolution. To many, the word *evolution* means little more than "development," "gradual change," or "process." Even a work as careful as Nelson and Winter's has not spelled out the evolutionary principles they pick, and it takes for granted that the principles they apply are accepted beyond doubt in the evolution literature. As a matter of fact, the idea of Schumpeterian innovation they advocate is, strictly speaking, not compatible with the Darwinian concept. In the latter view, organisms are molded by

2. As advocated, for example, in the tenets pronounced by the European Association for Evolutionary Political Economy. For details, see their official publication, *European Association for Evolutionary Political Economy Newsletter.*

their environment rather than actively searching for better conditions of life (see Wuketits 1990).

Another, more fundamental problem that besets evolutionary economics is that, within the realm of biology from which the idea of evolution springs, a number of controversies remain to be resolved. In spite of the numerous debates over and reformulations of the theory of evolution for more than a century, we have yet to come to an uncontroversial consensus. The recent decade, in fact, witnesses a new debate over different facets of the theory of evolution in biology, including fundamental questions about the mode, unit, and tempo of evolution. Controversies arose over the question of natural selection, namely, whether natural selection could plausibly be thought of as occurring at a number of different levels and on a number of different types of objects, from genes to demes to species, or should selection be restricted to the competition among individual organisms that is characteristic of Darwinian thinking (see Depew and Weber 1985). Important questions were also raised regarding the distinction between microevolution and macroevolution, especially over the possibilities of explaining the facts of macroevolution on the sole basis of our knowledge of the mechanisms involved in microevolution. Interestingly, it is also contended that a truly biological science will have to incorporate molecular biology, in particular findings in genetics. This means that new discoveries in evolution will be concerned not only with the demands of the environment on species, but also with the way the molecular structure of organisms functions to direct, cause, and carry out evolution (see Campbell 1985). In addition, it is also suspected that past theories of evolution are inadequate because they fail to take into account the self-organizing properties of complex systems, whose features are just beginning to be understood (Kauffman 1985). These controversies, among others, indicate that, even within the paradigm of biological evolution, there is a pressing need to clarify its fundamental concepts and instruments.

With these controversies far from being resolved, it is doubtful if evolutionary economists can come to terms among themselves about the precise meaning and use of the ideas involved in their evolution studies. This does not mean that the value of their work, such as that of Nelson and Winter, which is based on a concept of evolution different from that embodied in orthodox biology, should be belittled. But it seems obvious that until the very fundamental ideas of evolution are clear to both biologists and economists, any progress to be made in evolutionary economics will be seriously handicapped.

Another drawback of evolutionary economics is that while it can boast of its insights at a macrodynamic level, evolutionary economics is lacking a solid microfoundation. It is easy to extrapolate biological processes to economic activities, but the value of such exercises must be considered dubious until the fundamental controversies that plague the study of evolution are resolved. For example, since evolutionary economists do not have their own theory of value or price to offer, it is easy for neoclassical price theory to be made compatible with the evolutionary approach or to be given an evolutionary interpretation. It can readily be shown that the idea of equilibrium is, after all, not inconsistent with the dynamics of evolution and that the two ideas are, in fact or at times, complementary. Nor has evolutionary economics any theory of rationality to offer. But without its own theory of rationality, it is trapped in the paradox that if it takes without question the neoclassical model of rationality, it will have difficulty in explaining why some economic organizations that are as rational as others by definition are eliminated in the process of evolution. On the other hand, it would be strange to put those firms that are eliminated in the competition process on the same level of rationality as successful firms. Rationality and survival value, while seemingly compatible with each other, are not straightforwardly identical concepts.

One point to note is that, in terms of parsimony, neoclassical theory remains superior in comparison to the evolutionary economics we now have. As Nelson and Winter remind us, it is important to keep any evolutionary theory simple for maximal explanatory power. But evolution is clearly a highly complex process, and with more complexities being discovered in recent biological studies, it is doubtful that a unifying scheme will soon be forthcoming. But until we have a more unified evolutionary theory in general, there is little hope that evolutionary economics can compete with the formidable simplicity of the neoclassical framework.

Institutionalism

Closely affiliated with the evolutionary economists are the institutionalists and their descendants, the neoinstitutionalists. As a matter of fact, many economists who are called evolutionary economists are also called neoinstitutionalists. In chapter 6, I mentioned the work of Veblen. Without doubt, there is a close link between the theory espoused in this book and the basic tenets held by the institutionalists, in particular Veblen. I will return to such relations later in this chapter. In this section, I will first briefly examine the institutionalists' challenge to neoclassical economics and appraise the extent to which the challenge is a successful one.

While institutional economics is commonly and specifically used to denote the school of U.S. economic thought founded by Veblen, Commons, and Mitchell, it covers a wide spectrum of economists who hold that economic activities do not take place in a sociocultural vacuum and who hold the view that social institutions and values have profound impacts on the behaviors of individual economic actors. How social values are formed and how resource decisions are made by economic actors are thus key concerns that ultimately distinguish institutionalism from other schools of economic thought. Historically, the intellectual traditions that shape this mode of thinking include the critical attitude of the German historical economists and the U.S. philosophy of pragmatism as espoused by John Dewey, as well as Darwin's evolutionary thought. Together, these heritages foster in institutionalism a sharp and critical attitude toward conventional economics. Veblen, in particular, presents a devastating critique of neoclassical economics. In his view, neoclassical economics is preoccupied with static equilibrium, abstracted from sociocultural changes and their impacts on economic activities, and characterized by the adoption of a taxonomic approach. It woefully rests on the assumption of a hedonistic psychology of individuals, depicting them as passive, inert agents.

In opposition to the neoclassical position, Veblen and other institutionalists hold that the focus of economics must be on the analysis of the different processes by which modern societies develop their valuational systems and express emerging values in the formation of their resources decisions. Veblen, in fact, is particularly concerned with the modern business civilization that, in his opinion, signifies our frailty in the midst of institutions that are forced upon us but that no longer serve us well. To understand such impacts, economics must be studied in relation to how the entire institutional structure evolves over time. Such a route of inquiry has been continued by subsequent generations of institutionalists, including Adolf Berle, J. M. Clarke, Gardner Means, and Walton Hamilton and neoinstitutionalists such as J. K. Galbraith, Clarence Ayres, Gunnar Myrdal, and Gerhard Colm.

Similar to evolutionary economics, institutionalism upholds a macrodynamic and holistic perspective and, as such, is particularly attuned to the analysis of economic change. Institutionalism has many valuable insights to offer, but, unlike evolutionary economics, it does not have any foundational metaphor from which it can draw inspiration. In spite of this drawback, interest in institutionalism survives.[3] Indeed, questions about how institutional differences account for differences in economic performance in developing and socialist countries as well as about the multifarious relations between law and economics are now receiving increasing attention by serious economists.

The limitation of institutionalism and neoinstitutionalism, like evolutionary economics, lies in their lack of a strong foundation at the level of the individual actor's behavior. Notwithstanding Veblen's critique of the neoclassical's hedonistic conception of people and its utilitarian basis, his important insights (such as conspicuous consumption) could always, though not without arbitrariness, be accommodated within the neoclassical framework of

3. Paul Samuelson was of the opinion that institutionalism withered away some forty years ago.

utility optimization. Veblen's view that economic actors always succumb to social influences and values and hence act by imitation, while an important one, obscures the distinction between our rational and less-than-rational faculties. In other words, the institutionalists have to make up their mind about the limit of human rationality. They have to decide the extent to which they agree with the subjectivists and the neoclassical views in this regard. If they take an intermediate position, they have to answer the subjectivist's challenge that, in the ultimate analysis, what one chooses faithfully reflects what one truly values regardless of external influences. Without an explicit theory that posits under what conditions or by what mental apparatus economic actors resist or fall prey to social influences, the institutionalists are bound to end up with a lopsided view of the power of institutions and to exaggerate their influence. Without advances on this frontier, institutionalism will remain a fragmented conglomeration of important insights.

Post-Keynesian Economics

Convergent to both evolutionary economics and institutionalism is the post-Keynesian school. As can be expected, a number of economists can be labeled at once as institutionalists and post-Keynesians, depending on the kind of intellectual heritage they acknowledge. Depending also on how broadly the term is used, post-Keynesians can refer to economists ranging from students of Keynes to his sympathizers who agree broadly with a non-neoclassical reading of Keynes's doctrine. Needless to say, they all share the view that Keynes provides a revolutionary way of analyzing the real-world economy.

Although far from being a monolithic group, post-Keynesians are said to share certain fundamental tenets (see, e.g., Davidson 1981), in particular their opposition to the general equilibrium model of neoclassical theory. According to Davidson, the post-Keynesian school of thought may be summarized in three propositions (1981, 158–61): (*a*) the economy is a process in historical time; (*b*) in a world where uncertainty is unavoidable, expectations have an unavoidable and significant effect on economic outcomes; and (*c*) economic and political institutions play a significant role in shaping economic events.

In addition to these propositions, one might discern other common beliefs and concerns among the post-Keynesians. For example, post-Keynesians hold that, unlike risk, the uncertainty of the future cannot be adequately represented by probability statements. They are concerned about the distribution of income and power, particularly insofar as they are related to the problems of inflation. They give particular attention to the institution of money and its related institutions, for example, the banking system, time-oriented markets for goods and financial assets, money contracts for spot and forward transactions, and money-wage contracts. They hold that modern, money-based economies do not possess any automatic mechanisms whereby full employment of resources can be guaranteed. The existence of such an "underemployment equilibrium" is significantly attributable to the nature of the monetary institutions and also, in part, to how production is organized. In their view, unemployment is an inescapable characteristic of any money economy where liquidity considerations are involved.

All these are important insights, but, like evolutionary economics and institutionalism, post-Keynesian economics is more concerned with the macrofeatures of an economy than with the microaspects of individual behavior, except perhaps in the discussion of expectation formation and pricing. Indeed, the microeconomic foundations of post-Keynesian macroeconomic theories of growth and distribution have always puzzled critics who point out that, at best, post-Keynesian theory relies on a simple (and unexplained) mark-up pricing formula (see Kenyon 1979). This is, of course, an unfair allegation because one can say that while the post-Keynesians do not possess a general theory of price, they do have a specific approach to price determination, or, more specifically, a theory of the pricing behavior of firms. Post-Keynesians argue that the pricing behavior of oligopolistic firms in the manufacturing sector of modern economies can be explained by the demand of firms for funds from internal sources for purposes of investment expenditures. The firm is supposed to choose a mark-up that will yield a required level of retained profit that is capable of generating funds for investment plans, to be constrained by the condition that such a mark-up should not be out of line with the state of demand in a particular business climate. On this account, actual prices do not reflect current demand conditions. Instead, they reflect the funding requirements for the planned investment expenditure that the firm considers necessary for it to adjust its capacity sufficiently to meet anticipated future demand. In other words, the post-Keynesians hold a concept of price that is more in line with that of the classical political economists, in the sense that prices are basically production determined rather than demand determined (see Kenyon 1979, 40). This line of thought is very different from the one espoused in this book, which holds that prices, at least insofar as consumer goods are concerned, are neither production nor demand determined. Instead they are marketing determined, that is, prices are engineered by marketing organizations, especially those of a larger scale, that seek to manipulate the tastes and preferences of consumers.

How far have the post-Keynesians succeeded in dismantling or replacing neoclassical orthodoxy? Like the previously discussed doctrines, the insights of the post-Keynesians, while sound and useful, do not seem to have dealt a fatal blow to neoclassical economics. One important reason, again, is that the neoclassical model, holding an encompassing optimizing principle, can readily accommodate many challenges. For example, one can say that, after all, economic actors do not behave very much differently in states of certainty or uncertainty. They still rely very much on optimizing principles in handling their affairs. Their expectations about an uncertain future may be fuzzy, but, at any moment they are to make a decision about allocating resources, they will, wittingly or unwittingly, adopt the principle of equimarginality. If this is the case, post-Keynesian challenges could be treated as special cases that neoclassical orthodoxy has not yet handled, but is capable of handling with ease. For the main difference between conventional economics and post-Keynesian economics lies merely in their different assumptions about the characteristics of the economic environment instead of basic assumptions about human nature, although it seems implicit in post-Keynesian doctrine that economic actors are, in general, susceptible to the influences of social institutions. But how far such susceptibility goes is an unanswered question for the post-Keynesians.

Like other nonmainstream economics I have discussed, the post-Keynesian school accuses neoclassical orthodoxy of neglecting the profound importance of institutions. By itself, this is not a very effective accusation. For implicit in neoclassical doctrine is an ideal of the market institution, an institution that can be demonstrated in principle to result in the highest level of welfare for the economy as a whole. In its perfect state, the market is, therefore, what we should strive for and, conversely, any aberration is to be abhorred and corrected. In this view, the post-Keynesian account, like other heterodox accounts, can easily be interpreted as not inconsistent with the neoclassical position. It can be seen as supplying both the necessary and useful knowledge about the kinds of aberration that a market may face and that have to be corrected before it reaches its ideal state.

The Neo-Austrian School

The Austrians and their descendants, the neo-Austrians, claim that their perspective equips them with a more sensitive understanding of how the market economy works. This perspective can be said to consist in the following characteristics: (*a*) recognition of the importance and subjective character of knowledge, expectations, and learning in market processes; (*b*) recognition of the dynamic dimension and the discovery nature of competition as opposed to the model of perfect competition assumed by neoclassical theory; and (*c*) upholding the doctrine of methodological individualism and, thereby, the "meaningless" aggregation of economic categories.

Not all neo-Austrians, however, are in agreement with one another about the primacy of these tenets.[4] In general, most neo-Austrians would consider that what ultimately distinguishes them from other schools of thought, and in

4. Alexander Tabarrok recently argued that methodological individualism is more fundamental than subjectivism (1990).

particular from the neoclassical school, is their emphasis on the subjective approach to analyzing economic phenomena. This emphasis is concisely put by Lawrence White.

> The subjective approach to economic phenomena builds economic analysis upon the insight that every individual chooses and acts purposively, i.e., in pursuit of his purpose and in accordance with his perceptions of his options and for achieving them. This approach has been the hallmark of the Austrian school from its inception in the 1870s to the present day, though different members have defended their method in different ways. (1977, 4).

A major problem that haunts subjectivism and its core subjective theory of value, as I have pointed out, is that there is no way in which comparisons of utilities experienced by individuals can be objectively made. Neoclassical economists also uphold a subjective theory of value, but they claim to have circumvented the problem by using the conceptual cum technical device that actual prices realized in exchange can be taken as reliable if not infallible indications that the consumers' level of utilities derived from consuming the goods they receive and the level of utility of the money they have to part with are in a state of equilibrium. This device enables neoclassical theory to explain price formation and to derive the law of demand. Such a device is rejected by the Austrians, who consider it illegitimate to assert that, at the point of equilibrium, consumers will be prepared to make exchanges. In their view, only when consumers are persuaded that they will reap a surplus utility over and above the utility of money that is forgone, will they engage in exchanges. This is a valid argument in itself, but it lends little help to the Austrians who are anxious to develop a more sophisticated theory of price determination.

I have pointed out that the Austrians and the neo-Austrians do not possess a theory of value formation because, in emphasizing the thoroughly subjective character of human decisions, they unwittingly take on the position that human actors are fundamentally immune from external influences. For, the Austrians argue, there is no one agent who is in a better position to make a valuation about one's preferences. This view, leading to the proposition of consumer sovereignty, contributes, to no small extent, to the basic weakness of the Austrian school. It explains their reluctance to address how changes in institutions affect the value patterns of economic actors and how the latter's tastes change over time.

Not all modern Austrians, however, are happy with this position. A number of more liberal neo-Austrian scholars have been devoting considerable efforts to enhancing the explanatory power of the Austrian framework by positing more refined and realistic postulates about human behaviors that are compatible with the basic tenets of subjectivism or purposeful behavior, especially how people act under states of uncertainty or incomplete knowledge. In these endeavors, these scholars (e.g., Lachmann 1986) have not hesitated to incorporate sociological premises of different descriptions into their explanatory frameworks, especially those of Alfred Schutz, Max Weber, hermeneutics as well as the thoughts of scholars like Henri Bergson (see Moss 1987), which emphasize the interpretative nature of human action and human relations.

These are without doubt, commendable efforts, but they suffer from one basic difficulty. Since there is potentially a large set of plausible theories in sociology or psychology, one needs to ask by what criteria should these proposed theories be screened for use in economics. In other words, these scholars face the same "interface" problem between economics and psychology and are open to the same objections that their intellectual ancestors (e.g., Mises) raised about those who, in transplanting noneconomic premises into economics, unwittingly subject the autonomy of the latter to the former disciplines. In a sense, one can say that this is a paradox that plagues the Austrian position and inhibits its effort to expand its explanatory framework.

Modern Austrian scholars' search for a more realistic set of postulates about humanity arises, to no small extent, from their perception of one major weakness of the neoclassical school, namely the lack of realism in the latter's postulates. The insights these scholars offer are no doubt useful antidotes to the simplicity of the neoclassical framework. But the question remains of how far the Austrian school, in one version or another, is capable of providing an effective replacement for the neoclassical school? Alternatively put, can we legitimately say that there is a distinct Austrian paradigm? If such a paradigm is not forthcoming, could an expanded Austrian framework explain as much as neoclassical theory without tacitly using some neoclassical assumptions?

The answer is a controversial one. Kenneth Arrow, for example, is reported to say that, for the most part, the Austrians are merely stating in words what their neoclassical counterparts are saying in mathematics. That is, to the extent that Austrian economics is true, it is nothing new.[5] Arrow is, without much doubt, speaking from the side of the neoclassical camp. But there are others who are less partial. Laurence Moss, as I mentioned in chapter 3, for example, states that he does not believe that Austrian economics offers a separate and distinctive explanatory framework. Most of the main points of the modern Austrian critique, in his opinion, can be accommodated

5. See report entitled "Austrians and Stanford Economists," featured in "Dofflemeyer Lecture Series," in *Austrian Economics Newsletter* 12, no. 1 (1990):10–11, published by the Ludwig von Mises Institute, Auburn University.

by certain important modifications of the typical neoclassical explanatory framework. That is to say, there is no Austrian paradigm. True, neoclassical theory is inadequate for explaining institutional changes in society, such as the patterns of industrial organization or the processes of technological change. But the neoclassical model is highly useful, at least as a metaphorical device, for modeling certain types of rule-driven behavior. Its inadequacies can be made up for, in Moss's opinion, by the brilliant insights of the Austrians, in particular the notion of the creative entrepreneurial element in human action.

The view that the neoclassical and Austrian schools are highly complementary is not without an element of truth. The two schools hold a largely similar theory of rationality. From the Austrian perspective, economic actors are actors of purposeful behavior. On the essential nature of man, Mises says in his *Human Action* (1966):

> Human action is purposeful behavior. Or we may say, action is will put into operation and transformed into an agency, is aiming at ends and goals, is the ego's meaningful response to stimuli and to the conditions of environment, is a person's conscious adjustment to the state of the universe that determines his life. . . . Man is capable of subduing his emotions and impulses; he can rationalize his behavior. . . . He is not a puppet of his appetites. He arranges his wishes and desires into a scale, he chooses, in short, he acts (11–17). . . . Society is concerted action, cooperation. [It] is the outcome of conscious and purposeful behavior. (143)

To be rational in terms of acting purposefully, of making plans in accordance with one's perception of market opportunities and with one's available resources is, of course, not the same as being perfectly rational. But they are not inconsistent. Indeed, the difference seems to disappear once we take on a metaphorical, commonsense or instrumental interpretation of the neoclassical position. Besides, both schools are strongly rooted in the doctrine of methodological individualism, tacitly holding the belief that collective phenomena are the result of individual actions and not the other way round. These positions differ, to a significant extent, from the theory espoused in this book, which posits a theory of less-than-full rationality and a pattern of feedback causation between the individual and the collective.

While one cannot deny that many of the Austrian insights are based on theories about the human mind (Hayek himself explicates one in the Kantian tradition in his *Sensory Order* [1952]), it would be too far-fetched to say that their theorizing is based on a unified or commonly accepted theory of the mind. Their emphasis on subjectivity, on individual exploitation of opportunities, on creativity, and on entrepreneurship, while bearing some clear-cut images of people, do not allow them to speak of having a specific Austrian theory of the mind. Even if one insists that there is one, it is a theory that supports the idea that man is essentially a rational animal, an idea that does not challenge the neoclassical theory at its root in any serious way.

Behavioralism and Bounded Rationality

The neo-Austrians are not the only batch of economists concerned about finding a more realistic set of postulates to supplant the neoclassical set. I have mentioned the work of the "scientific" subjectivists who are intent on bringing into economics a set of more fruitful premises from realms such as psychology. As a matter of fact, a large number of neoclassical economists who are not entirely happy with the extreme neoclassical assumptions and who attempt to introduce piecemeal improvements within the bounds of the neoclassical framework (but using the same set of tools and techniques) could be broadly labeled as behavioralists.

This is particularly the case in the theory of the firm, where interesting progress has taken place. The advances are associated with improvements introduced to the objects of maximization. For example, Baumol proposes replacing profit with another simple objective, namely revenue (1959). Williamson proposes a more general model of managerial utility maximization, based on the notion that managers seek to maximize their own utility and the fact that separation of ownership from control gives rise to problems of controlling managers (1964). In more recent literature, this idea is incorporated in what is called principal-agent analysis.

At the risk of oversimplification, one could say that these "managerial" models, which typically assume that managers maximize a simple objective function subject to an arbitrarily given profit constraint, represent a subset of a broader behavioral approach that aims to introduce realism into the description of the actual decision-making processes of the firm. The thrust of the approach is to explain how firms, as complex entities, actually behave in the modern business environment. Cyert and March (1963), for example, contend that firms in general, and managers in particular, should not be regarded as a single cohesive group but, rather, as a coalition of individuals with conflicting interests. This mode of theorizing is, to no small extent, inspired by the work of Simon, who questioned whether the economist's notion of rationality is appropriate for the analysis of behavior in, say, situations of uncertainty. Simon contended that economic actors, by virtue of their limited cognitive abilities, can exercise only "bounded rationality" when making decisions in complex and uncertain situations. Rather than maximizing utility or profit, both individuals and groups are inclined to "satisfice," that is, attempt to meet certain attainable goals.

The behavioral approach, however, scores far greater success in offering alternative theories of the firm than in offering alternative theories of consumer behavior, in spite of the fact that there exists a vast literature on the empirical measurements of demand involving (at times) some behavioral assumptions. As a matter of fact, behavioral theories that are largely parasitic on the neoclassical framework (and thereby only able to improve marginally on the latter) fail to explain a wide array of consumer behaviors in general. The Lancaster theory that I mentioned in chapter 3 is a case in point. The reason for this asymmetry is that in the firm—a complex organization—individual participants can be generally depicted as rational, regardless of whether or not their "rational" acts are compatible with one another and whether, collectively, they will lead to an upgrading or lowering of the overall performance of the firm in question. This means that without compromising the basic tenets of neoclassical theory, it is possible to break a lot of new ground in studying a wide range of possible agency behaviors within the firm. This, however, is not the case as far as consumer behaviors are concerned, because within the highly restrictive regime of full rationality, the range of plausible theories about consumer behavior is clearly limited, as the consumer is essentially an individual making decisions for himself or herself.

Behavioralists who are intent on breaking new grounds in developing alternative theories of consumer behavior are, therefore, compelled to reject the neoclassical notion of rationality. As an alternative, they either embrace Simon's notion of bounded rationality or go beyond Simon's concept in positing, to different degrees, patterns of consumer irrationalities. In either case, they reject models that assume that the information-processing capabilities of economic actors are highly powerful, if not unlimited (e.g., compensatory models that assume that human brains function like multisensory pocket calculators; see Fishbein 1963; Rosenburg 1956). Indeed, one may say that the more the behavioralists' assumptions move away from the pole of perfect rationality, the better they are in a position to develop more realistic postulates about the behaviors of consumers, for example, about their resistance to change, about the strategies they employ in their acts of choice, and, equally important, about how their attitudes are shaped by their environments. In this regard, Earl's vivid portrait of the consumer is a most refreshing one.

> Being a consumer is not an easy role to play successfully, even in an affluent society. Consumers have to act in a complex, unsettled world where surprises are commonplace. . . . If opportunities are not to be thrown needlessly away, the consumer must be a skilled speculator and strategist. (1986, 1)

The kind of behavioral approach adopted by Earl, which he also calls a subjectivist approach, is novel and highly promising although not without difficulties. The main difficulties are the same as those faced by the neo-Austrians. They are, first, the choice of core assumptions within a supposedly huge range of possible alternatives, and, second, the delineation of the relations between these chosen assumptions (which are bound to involve theories of psychology or sociology) and other economic assumptions, in particular how changes in the former affect the autonomy of economics.

The behavioral or subjectivist approach of the more radical kind necessarily raises the question of how useful and relevant Simon's notion of bounded rationality is as a guiding concept. In recognizing the essential limitation of the information-processing capabilities of people, the notion of bounded rationality wisely advises against conventional economics for their unnecessary stance of making such tacit assumptions as perfect knowledge, perfect information, or perfect foresight. In proposing to concentrate economic discourse on a workable domain of rationality, for example, the domain of procedural rationality, it enables economists to make the most useful contributions out of the concept of rationality. Whereas we are obviously not perfectly rational, our rationality in handling a large part of our affairs is not to be doubted, especially those affairs that call for a careful or subtle calibration of utility and return. The crucial question, therefore, is whether the idea is of sufficient heuristic power to help economics develop a fully and truly behavioralist framework. In this regard, two related questions can be asked. First, how bounded is the rationality of the economic actor or, in our case, of the consumer. Second, how far does the irrational (or less-than-fully rational) side of man, which a theory of bounded rationality tacitly accepts, affect the rational side. The first question has not been directly answered by Simon, and the second question never seems to bother him. But answers to these two questions are obviously essential for an effective behavioral approach, and unless they are well considered and taken fully into account, any behavioral theory that purports to explain consumer behavior will easily be subject to the fashions of the day in other social science disciplines, in particular in psychology. Economics clearly needs its own theory of rationality, but one that is broad enough to encompass less-than-rational aspects. This, in turn, means that it needs a theory of the mind that can account for such characteristics.

The Resilience and Hidden Strength of Neoclassical Orthodoxy

The preceding survey is neither detailed nor exhaustive nor is it meant to be so. I have, for example, omitted the neo-Marxist approach, the hermeneutic approach (e.g., Lavoie 1989), the rhetoric approach (e.g., McCloskey 1985), or the humanistic approach (e.g., Lutz and Lux 1979). This is because the goal of the survey is to show, by way of example, the general thrust of criticisms made by the major heterodox schools and their overall directions in order to provide a broader context in which to place the theory espoused in this book. With this specific purpose in mind, this survey is conducted at a level that goes beyond the confines of value theory (in some cases, the heterodox schools do not have any explicit theory of value). Such generality is also needed in order to situate different theories and to define their interrelationships, within which context the importance or triviality of a value theory or the need for a more sophisticated one can stand out clearly.

On the whole, it is true to say (and the different schools have said it) that neoclassical economics suffers from two major flaws. Insofar as the cardinal characteristic of economic actors goes, neoclassical theory imputes to them far more rationality than they possess, to the extent of risking caricature, at times. The Austrians and neo-Austrians are quick to point this out and supply what, in their opinion, is a more true-to-life portrait of economic man, namely a purposeful, self-conscious, creative actor. To different extents, the behavioralists and the subjectivists also adhere to this view. As far as the economic environment is concerned, neoclassical theory is alleged to portray a timeless, unchanging environment, an assumption that omits not only historical factors, but also the influence of institutions on individual behavior. In addressing this flaw, evolutionary economists, post-Keynesians, and institutionalists propose postulates that reflect what they each perceive as the cardinal, defining feature of the economic environment—the forces of selection, the uncertainty of the economic environment, or the impact of institutions on economic decisions, respectively.

What these schools each supply are clearly important and sound insights and should be welcomed by neoclassical economics. One would, therefore, expect that with such forceful challenges, neoclassical orthodoxy would soon dissolve, to be replaced by a new, unifying theoretical framework or at least by a set of fragmented schools. Contrary to such an expectation, no dissolution of neoclassical orthodoxy is in sight. Sociologists of science, especially of the Kuhnian strand, have a lot to say about the resilience of neoclassical orthodoxy. For example, neoclassical economists are portrayed as too reluctant to give up their intellectual capital. As "normal science," neoclassical economics provides numerous puzzle-solving opportunities for its practitioners, to the extent that they become unwittingly trapped in a self-contained or self-propelling inertia, with few resources to look around for better ideas (see Eichner 1983).

These arguments are generally valid, but they are not devoid of bias. For it is just too easy to make a caricature of neoclassical economics on simplistic terms and to ignore its hidden strengths altogether. For a theory to reign over a discipline for such an extended period, there must be some deep, underlying reasons that support its dominating influence. On the other hand, it should be recognized that their brilliant insights notwithstanding, the different competing schools of thought also suffer from limitations of their own. We might, for example, note that the macrodynamic, real-time-based schools do not have, or have yet to evolve, a full-fledged theory of value and a supporting theory of rationality. This does not mean that they lack hypotheses about how individuals behave. But there is a clear asymmetry between the weight of the assertions they make at the macrolevel of economic change and those at the microlevel of individual behavior. The evolutionary economists, for example, have yet to reconcile the relationship between the idea of survival value and the notion of rationality or to show the limitations of survival value or natural selection. While firms do face the problem of survival, consumers are not under the same pressure. The institutionalists are correct in positing the impact of institutions on economic behaviors, but it is necessary for them to distinguish behaviors that are highly susceptible to institutional influences from those that are less so. Similarly, the post-Keynesians have yet to offer a theory of rationality in order to justify the difference in the way their economic actors behave in the face of uncertainty from their neoclassical counterparts. In contrast to these weaknesses, one may say that the neoclassical school is more robust. Before we further reexamine the strength of neoclassical orthodoxy, let us analyze again its weaknesses.

Neoclassical theory is regarded as embodying a theory of perfect rationality. Whereas this is often seen to be a negative feature (see chap. 4), it is possible to view the postulate in a positive light. First of all, the idea of perfect rationality can be interpreted metaphorically. In this interpretation, it is no longer necessary to take the economic actor to be a perfectly rational being in a literal sense. It merely suffices to say that he or she is always rational (e.g., Stigler 1981). The perfect rationality thesis is introduced because it is necessary to have this assumption to facilitate the building of formal models. Indeed, neoclassical economists can say that most criticisms of the notion of perfect rationality arise from their critics collapsing the instrumental value of the idea with its substantive conception.

Even if the idea of perfect rationality seems odd, it can still be justified on the ground that T. W. Hutchison proposes.

> The maximization-under-certainty postulate has proved, as a piece of simplicatory scaffolding, very difficult, or virtually impossible, to remove, while leaving standing any model or theory for which any significant degree of generality could be claimed. There is simply no general assumption to replace this oversimplified one. For there is, so to speak, only one set of correct expectations, or state of adequate knowledge, for each and every situation. But there is an endless variety of incorrect and inadequate ones, which are constantly changing and impossible to generalize about except in arbitrary terms. (1977, 80)

In other words, if we forgo perfect rationality, we are compelled to face the bigger difficulty that besets either the opposite pole of total ignorance or the intermediate areas of partial ignorance. Such a difficulty, as we have already observed, is well exemplified by the experiences of the radical subjectivists and the behavioralists in search of more realistic postulates that accept some states of partial ignorance.

In addition, the idea of substantive rationality can be further justified from the computational and optimizing theory of the mind that we can impute to the neoclassical model. Such an image of the mind has been the received doctrine in the realm of cognitive science until only recently. To anticipate my analysis a little, it may be said that seeing the mind as an optimizing apparatus justifies the perfect rationality principle that underlies much of neoclassical economics and, thereby, many of its formalisms. It also justifies the neoclassical theory of price determination, which can be interpreted as an instantiation of optimizing behavior in general.

I have said that the neoclassical approach has successfully dissolved the classical problem of value and has provided the most satisfactory solution to this problem thus far. It dissolves the classical problem of value because, in treating value as a subjective concept, the neoclassical approach clearly shows that it is futile to search after some absolute existence in the economic order outside the realm of the human mind. It provides the most satisfactory solution to the problem of value because it demonstrates that value is fully revealed in price in the state of market equilibrium and, therefore, can be taken to equate to market price in that state.

Although, as the Austrians have argued, it is of doubtful legitimacy to infer consumer equilibrium from exchange at known prices, the neoclassical solution is still highly attractive and not totally unreasonable, as long as we take the equation to be a kind of rule-of-thumb measure. Anyway, the epistemological price, if any, of this hypothesis is worth paying, for the benefits of the assertion are tremendous. First, the identity posited unifies the subjective preferences of individuals with the state of market prices in the real world. If subjectivity of preferences and choice is fully reflected and manifested in objective measures in the market, one could claim that the neoclassical theory of value has transcended its original status as a subjective theory. Having forged such a synthesis, neoclassical economists could easily explain why they no longer need to bother with the question of value in the literal sense.

Apart from transcending the subjective status of the theory of value, the unification has profound philosophical consequences. We can now view the equilibrium of prices in the market as tantamount to an equilibrium of subjective values in the minds of the market participants. Since exchanges consist in voluntary acts, an equilibrium of market prices and, by extension, an equilibrium of subjective values is an equilibrium brought about voluntarily by willing actors who seek to maximally realize their self-interests. Thus, market equilibrium implies the attainment of the state where individual participants' subjective values and their magnitudes have already been given maximal free interplay and the fullest possible expression, a state of affairs that can hardly be further improved upon from the vantage point of the collective whole. Although this is essentially a restatement of Pareto's thesis, this formulation commands an additional philosophical dimension not fully captured by Pareto.

Thus, from the utilitarian point of view, equilibrium in the market and, by extension, in the economy as a whole represents the state where maximal welfare for the collective is to be realized. This statement, of course, presupposes that the values held by the individuals are constrained by the material resources they are in command of and does not imply that a different distribution of resource endowment will yield the same pattern of values (see, e.g., Deaton and Muellbauer 1980; Sen 1982). But given any particular state of resource distribution among its economic actors, one could say not only that maximal welfare is realized by the economy in equilibrium but that the equilibrium itself should reflect the attainment of the most equitable state, in the sense that economic actors with given resources have been allowed the fullest possible opportunities to realize their preferred values, within the constraints of the opportunities, resources, and values of other actors. Thus, given any particular pattern of resource distribution, the market system in equilibrium is not only the most efficient system for the allocation of resources, but it is also the most equitable one and one that maximizes welfare for the system as a whole. Maximal efficiency, welfare, and equity are thus at once attained and unified under the neoclassical optimizing approach, which in turn can be seen to be supported by an instrumental theory of perfect rationality and a computational optimizing theory of the mind. No other competing school commands the same depth and breadth of unity and support.

From this vantage point, one could even defend the view that neoclassical theory does not necessarily require a macrodynamic, real-time dimension and that it does not find it necessary to bother about institutional changes. The neoclassical model, in effect, espouses a theory of market institutions. If equilibrium in the market or markets is capable of simultaneously attaining maximal efficiency, equity, and welfare, the market institution is the ideal institution that the real world should strive after. If there is any deviation in the real world from this ideal state, it is not the theory that is a problem. It is just that the real world is locked up in some disequilibrium state. There is surely a way to study these disequilibrium states and the neoclassical economists can say that they are actually moving in that direction, albeit a little belatedly. Whichever the case, theories of disequilibrium, whether static or dynamic ones, complement rather than replace the neoclassical framework, which alone sets the ideal and limiting standard.

On the same grounds, one could easily justify the view that neoclassical economists find it necessary to expend a colossal amount of energy and attention in theoretically proving the existence of equilibrium, as well as on the determination of equilibrium values in a perfectly competitive economy. The existence proof is important in that if we can unequivocally establish the proof, we can be assured, at least in principle, that the best possible state that we all yearn for, that is, one in which maximal efficiency, equity, and welfare can be simultaneously attained, does exist. It is just a matter of how this state can be identified and realized. Major intellectual investments expended on such proofs, therefore, can be justified on the grounds that they are the necessary first steps in building a truly solid base for economic theorizing. The rest will be smooth sailing once the foundation is established. Thus, the perfect rationality and perfect divisibility assumptions that neoclassical doctrine posits, but which render it so susceptible to challenge, can be further seen to be instrumentally essential to this important task and can be justified in this light.

In this interpretation, what appear to be the weaknesses of neoclassical orthodoxy, namely its unreality and its timelessness, are no longer weaknesses as such. They are necessary to supply the very theoretical foundation for economics without which any future empirical work would be piecemeal and lack a sense of direction. Thus, the challenges of the heterodox theories may be said to be misplaced, if not gross misunderstandings of the fundamental purpose of the neoclassical enterprise. Neoclassical economists need not disagree with these challenges, but it is not improper for them to insist that there is a more fundamental task at hand that needs to be dealt with if economic theory is to be placed on a firm foundation.

As I have previously shown, almost no heterodox theories quarrel with the neoclassical assumption of rationality in the relaxed version, namely, the economic actor is importantly rational rather than perfectly rational. This is an important agreement because this means that these heterodox theories are, at their roots, holding an image of people and the mind not radically different from that held by neoclassical doctrine. The only difference between them, therefore, are priorities and directions in their research programs: neoclassical economists seem more anxious to build a sound theoretical foundation by employing devices that are mistakenly seen as distortions of human nature. Although the heterodox theories seldom say it, they are actually espousing, to different degrees, the same principle of optimization that cuts across human behavior and the market order. This means that, even if neoclassical theory is to be overthrown, the basic foundation upon which neoclassical theory is built—namely, the assumption that the mind is an optimizing apparatus and economic behavior is optimizing behavior—is still alive.[6] Even if the hetero-

6. Curiously, but not altogether surprisingly, the optimization approach is also fully embraced by economists who are sympathetic to central planning (see, e.g., Kantorovich 1989).

dox theories should successfully replace neoclassical theory, the result will merely be a change in the direction and emphasis of research, for the basic components of the optimization paradigm, namely, rational man and his rational mind, remain unscathed. In other words, the perfectly rational man may be gone, but the optimizing approach—the foundational cornerstone of neoclassical orthodoxy—remains.

CHAPTER 9

The Mind as a Computational and Optimizing Apparatus

The optimization paradigm that runs through neoclassical doctrine is, of course, not new. Its major conceptual component, rationality, is seen to be the distinguishing essence of man by philosophers as early as Aristotle.[1] Indeed, the entire tradition of rationalism in Western philosophy could be said to be rooted in the recognition of this important fact. In this view, man and man alone can invoke a mode of thought that explicitly follows rules and arrives at conclusions that can be intersubjectively judged as either valid or invalid. Rationalism, proclaiming the cult of rational knowledge, values cognition whose paradigm is scientific cognition. In accepting cognition supported by reason alone, it rejects cognition based on revelation, divination, foreboding, prophecy, or crystal gazing. Though amply surrounded by evidence pointing to the irrationality of human beings in different realms, philosophers over a wide stretch of human thought have adhered to this notion that man is innately rational. In the least, they take it that human beings should strive for rationality and that they have the potential to do so. Such a preoccupation with the ideal of rationality had its greatest moment in the eighteenth century, when it was seen to be an essential feature of the ideology of the Enlightenment. In the twentieth century, the rationalist tradition finds new expressions in a few important developments, first, in the development of modern logic by Frege, Whitehead, and Russell, and, second, in the development of cognitive science. Indeed, the first generation of cognitive scientists, for example, Jerome Bruner, Herbert Simon, Allen Newell, and Jean Piaget, embraced an image of man that is decidedly rationalistic and elected to study issues that involve the abilities of human beings to reason validly.

Another major component of the optimization paradigm that also lends support to the idea of rationality is the idea of the computational mind, an idea that helped to give birth to present-day cognitive science.[2] The computational theory of the mind grows out of perceiving the brain as an information-processing apparatus, analogous to a computer. Briefly, the idea of computa-

1. This speculation was made by Bertrand Russell (quoted in Pylyshyn 1984, 257).

2. Other major motivations came from developments in contemporary logic, information theory, and cybernetics.

tion is that an elementary set of building blocks can be used to construct an unlimited variety of complex symbolic processes, and the vast diversity of mental symbols must be constructed out of finite means and rules (see, e.g., Johnson-Laird 1988). Two important theses supplement this theory. First, the mental representations posited by the theory, like the information contents of data and programs used in computer software, can be formulated independently of the physical instantiation of the brain's hardware, as is also the case of the computer. Second, our commonsense intuitions about the organization of problem solving, learning, and other cognitive tasks resonate with the way computer programs are organized, for example, in terms of goals and subgoals, self-monitoring, and self-modification (see Jackendoff 1987). In a nutshell, computational theory posits that, from the relatively simple cognitive functions (such as low-level vision or mental images) to the more complex modes of cognition (such as learning, memory, and thinking), our cognitive activities can be shown to be governed by principles that involve, in one way or another, rule-guided computations.

The idea of computation is not, however, uncontroversial, particularly if one considers the fact that cognitive science is still in its infancy compared with the other sciences. Whereas some theorists focus on symbol manipulation defined in terms of formal rules and take the general purpose digital computer as their inspiration, others emphasize parallel-processing computational networks whose behaviors are not defined by such formal rules. Similarly, whereas many computational theorists strongly believe that higher mental processes, for example, problem solving and memory are essentially computational phenomena, others are more cautious about such characterizations and the theoretical limits of computation. In the same vein, whereas most cognitive scientists are in favor of the position that computational questions are autonomous of physiology, there are those who champion the application of neurophysiological insights in formulating the basic outlines of their computer models (see Boden 1988).

In spite of these controversies, the fact that the mind is unconsciously and inherently computational in the broadest sense is not to be doubted. Indeed, the cardinal facts about the unconscious mind are that, in most situations, it is almost automatically and instantaneously capable of identifying and extracting crucial parameters from an environment, of subtly weighing the relative significance of these parameters, and of coming up with judgments that, on ex-post analysis, often turn out to conform to generally accepted standards of rationality. From these features, one could further infer that the mind is characteristically an optimizing apparatus, in the sense that it is capable of weighing, in any normal situation, the conflicting demands for efficiency, accuracy, and reasonableness of a judgment, and of supplying a set of specific criteria upon which the quality and scope of that judgment is circumscribed and by which that judgment is to be appraised. The need for the mind to develop the optimization approach, it may be further speculated, arises from the fact that the brain, being a finite-resource system and responding to survival pressures, has to structure itself in a way that it can allocate its limited energy in the most efficient manner.

Given that the mind can be characterized as an optimizing apparatus, the idea of calibrative or instrumental rationality as a guiding principle for the analysis of human behaviors, be they economic or noneconomic, is only natural. For if the mind is subtly capable of calibrating trade-off relations, the principle of equimarginality, upon which the rationality principle is generally based and fully embraced by conventional economics, can be said to rest on solid grounds of human cognition.

The Ratiomorphic, the Rational and the Logical Mind

Thus far, it seems that neoclassical theory can claim that, in embodying, albeit tacitly, the concept of an optimizing mind, it rests on completely solid ground. This claim, however, turns out to be a fragile one. This is because neoclassical theory, upon further scrutiny, actually embodies an extreme version of the optimizing mind in the sense that it is assumed to operate without any energy expenditure in the brain or, alternatively put, to be an infinite-resource system. This seems to be a harmless assumption and can be temporarily defended if we accept the instrumentalist point of view. But as I will show, there is a limit to how far we should invoke instrumentalism, for, unavoidably, any social science theory has to take a position about what it posits as the dominant features of the mind if it is to stand on solid theoretical grounds and sustain its claims. I have already shown the difficulties that beset this extreme view in chapter 4. To carry the critique further, I will make the following distinction between viewing the mind as a rational knowledge-processing system and viewing the mind as a "ratiomorphic" apparatus. In the former case, the mind is seen to be an inquiring system that seeks, selects, and processes data using the imaginative faculty of hypothesis formation, supported by the reasoning faculty that employs the laws of logic and formal rules of deduction and inference. In the latter case, the mind is seen as employing rules, whether they are strictly logical or not, that enhance man or, indeed, any biological organism's overall fitness for survival. More specifically, the term *ratiomorphic* can be used to apply to any animal's (or human's) activities that have a certain survival value but do not require consciousness, and the sum total of the logiclike or reasonlike mechanisms can be called the ratiomorphic apparatus (see Wuketits 1990). It comprises all organs involved in information gathering and information processing and it functions for the sake of survival through information processing and generally increases an organism's fitness. In this view, the architecture of the mind is the result of the long development of responses to evolutionary pressures. The innate mechanisms of calculating and experiencing the environment contained therein represent the outcome of evolution by natural selection.

This demarcation enables us to view the human mind as consisting of two distinct levels. At the ratiomorphic level, information is gained by a mechanism relating experiences to expectations as well as vice versa. This means that certain experiences are programmed, so to speak, by particular patterns of expectation. As a result, many of the decisions that trigger actions can be said to be programmed by expectations, to the extent that these decisions seem to be arrived at in a spontaneous and, therefore, seemingly effortless manner. This mode of operation is different from the level of the rational mind that consciously seeks rational knowledge. At this level, one may say that knowledge is gained through a conscious inquiry employing tools such as induction, hypothesis formation, deduction, and screening. Such a conscious process, which operates on the principle of trial and error, cannot be said to rest on any prefixed program (cf. Popper 1972).

As we can see immediately, the neoclassical mind does not model itself on either of the above. It is closer to the hypothetical model that logicians construct out of logical rules and principles. I have already analyzed this type of methodological error in my critique of ordinalism in chapter 2. These logical rules, as I will show shortly, are not the kind of rules that people employ in their ordinary reasoning and in their dealings with pragmatic affairs. As a matter of fact, the rules by which we handle our lives are largely ratiomorphic rules that are the outcome of our mind's natural response to the challenge of the environment. Hence, the mind that follows these rules is a far cry from the logical mind that we impute to the neoclassical position. On the other hand, the logical model that characterizes the neoclassical mind bears little affinity to the model of acquisition of rational knowledge, which operates largely on the rule of error elimination and which, for that matter, also is an effect of the evolutionary process, a feature that is not shared by the logical mind.

In defense, one might, however, contend that the neoclassical mind, in spite of its extreme assumptions, must somehow be related to these two models by virtue of the optimizing principle it embodies. For, after all, the ratiomorphic mind is operating on the principle of optimization and, hence, can be said to rest on the same principle that governs the neoclassical mind. This, however, is not the case, for the ratiomorphic mind is inclined toward different types of biases and "irrationalities" that are absent in the neoclassical model. On the other hand, one can hardly say that the rational mind that seeks rational knowledge closely follows the optimizing principle. True, the rational mind requires canons of logic to judge its products. But this is not the same as saying that it pursues the enterprise of inquiry on the principle of optimization. The neoclassical mind is, in contrast, merely a theoretical construct from our knowledge of formal logic and bears, therefore, little affinity to how our minds actually work at either level. Both the ratiomorphic and the rational mind amply apply the optimization principle, in particular the former, but one cannot make the claim that optimization is all there is to how the mind actually operates at these two levels without substantial qualification.

Biases in Human Reasoning

That the mind does not actually operate on the basis of the canons of logic only becomes apparent during the recent phase in the development of cognitive science. Empirical work on reasoning over the past thirty years has vigorously challenged the notion that human beings reason in a rational manner, let alone that they invoke some logical calculus in their reasoning process. Johnson-Laird and Wason, using some simple games (Johnson-Laird and Wason 1970 and Wason and Johnson-Laird 1972), show that the actual content of a problem, which should not make any difference for any syntactically governed apparatus, biases us even in apparently simple reasoning tasks. These findings challenge the idea that our minds are logical machines whose reasonings are independent of the specific information in a problem. This thesis is further supported by Johnson-Laird's analysis of the irrelevance of classical syllogisms to our ordinary thought processes. Syllogistic reasonings, he suggests, might work only if one were to have unlimited memory capacity and had mastered sophisticated mathematical notations (1983). In our day-to-day reasonings, we employ an array of techniques that avoid the explosion of combinatorial possibilities that plague conventional formal approaches to syllogistic reasoning. Instead, human beings employ what Johnson-Laird calls mental models in their reasoning processes (1983). These mental models consist of a variety of devices, techniques, or procedures that human beings separately or jointly use in arriving at their cognitive judgments but that may not be congruent to one another. On the whole, the more familiar the material and the richer the relevant schemata that are available, the more readily can one solve a problem.

Another challenge to the rationality of human reasoning is launched by Kahneman and Tversky, who demonstrate that there exist strong biases in the human cognitive system that should be taken into account in any theory of human reasoning. Instead of depending on logical rules, they show how heuristics and strategies guide the individual's reasoning in everyday life (Kahneman, Slovic, and Tversky 1982; Kahneman and Tversky 1984). People do not reach decisions in a way that is logically consistent or that obeys the laws of probability. People are not coherent in the way that it would be nice to believe they were. To support their thesis, Kahneman and Tversky develop a psychology of preferences that does not follow strictly from an economic calculation of gains and losses, but instead focuses on how individuals "frame" selections (1984). They also observe that the laws of probability are actually overwhelmed by the principle of representativeness. By way of example, they show that people are keenly attuned to the likelihood that someone with certain characteristics will also exhibit certain other characteristics, even though the added supporting details may render the resultant set of characteristics even less probable in absolute terms. In the same vein, Christopher Cherniak rejects the idea that any rational agent must employ a logic such as a complete, first-order deductive system (1984). To do so, one would have to marshal infinite resources. Instead, Cherniak argues for a standard of "minimal rationality," that is, one makes some but not necessarily all inferences that are appropriate and one even uses heuristics that are formally incorrect in order to arrive at a reasonable decision within a reasonable time.

These studies thus demonstrate persuasively, though not conclusively, the fallacy of taking the mind to be a logical machine, as is tacitly assumed by neoclassical orthodoxy. These studies do not deny that many of the strategies and heuristics that human beings employ are related to the optimization model, but, at the same time, they do not suggest that all modes of reasoning are of this type.

An Initial Paradigm of Mind and Value

A new paradigm of the mind in a full-fledged state, I must admit, is not yet at hand. Research in cognitive science is still too preoccupied with the computer analogy and too concerned with accumulating details at an empirical level to be ready for a grand conceptual synthesis. But the paradigm seems to be developing and the major elements of a forthcoming synthesis are already in place. A great intellectual flowering seems ready, awaiting the merger of evolutionary epistemology and cognitive science, the former to furnish a long-term perspective by which empirical findings in the latter could fall neatly into place. From the viewpoint of value theory elaborated in this book, it is clear that that such a potential synthesis, which my theory anticipates and draws some of its potential resources from, is of paramount importance. This is because any theory of value has to take a position, in one way or another, about what the most important features of the human mind are. A new theory of the mind, as I have shown, even in a crude sketch, will radically alter our formulation of value theory, in particular that aspect that is concerned with value formation.

The architecture of the mind that I posit differs radically from that of the neoclassical mind. Instead of being a perfect computational system and an optimizing apparatus, assuming an inexhaustible supply of mental energy and resources, our minds operate upon a multiplicity of principles and with only limited resources. Our minds no doubt command colossal information-processing power, but they are also characterized by a number of limitations. For example, our search system may be highly efficient, but there is no guarantee that we can recover any one particular memory. The orientation toward speedy access to and retrieval of data in the memory, made possible by and probably also contributing to the distributive organization of the brain, means that the same system cannot simultaneously have the most effective screening mechanism to check the quality or desirability of its retrieved output. Considerations of energy expenditure also compel any retrieval of data from our memory to be of a limited range, because it seems that the mind has increasing difficulty holding added units of data for conscious comparison and appraisal. The capacity for learning that is characteristic of the human mind means that the ratiomorphic mind of man faces, of necessity, the trade-off between its opening up and becoming sensitive to a wide array of data input and its keeping the processing of such inputs at a low level of energy expenditure. In other words, while the architecture of the mind is rendered suitable for learning in the course of evolution, it is also rendered susceptible to penetration by different kinds of inputs.

Such an architecture of the mind, permitting the infiltration of inputs and values into the largely unguarded, unconscious stratum, means that our mental maps are characteristically fragmentary. On the positive side, such an architecture facilities the transmission of information and the process of socialization, leading to the creation of a diversity of cultural conventions in the human species. However, it is the same architecture that permits the existence of a compartmentalized value system and the easy domination of our behavior by certain types of conventions. This distinctive malleability of man, attributable to the distributive, open-ended structure of the brain can, in turn, be seen as the cause or the outcome (or probably both) of our cultural evolution (cf. Popper and Eccles 1977). While we are not yet able to ascertain conclusively the direction of this causal relationship, we can safely say that the human brain, which is a product of biological evolution, has further developed in ways that render it amenable to the process of cultural evolution. It is clear that in this very process a number of trade-offs in its structure appear, reflecting the different demands of the respective modes of evolution upon it.

If the mind is molded by the evolutionary process so that it becomes highly sensitive to and dominated by social values and conventions, then it is obvious that developments in the structure of human values, which tend toward multiplicity and diversity, affect in no small way how our minds work in the human environment and, thereby, how we behave. The institutionalists and post-Keynesians are entirely correct in their assertions that social institutions are important determinants of economic behavior, although they do not begin their analyses from a theory of the mind.

A fragmentary state in the ratiomorphic mind is clearly not the end-state. Our biological urge for attaining the highest level of fitness naturally drives our minds toward striving for some kind of unity in the different compartments of our mental maps, regardless of whether or not such unity exits. In a sense, we may say that man's succumbing to some overarching belief systems or ideologies, independent of how reality actually is, stems from the dominant urge of the ratiomorphic mind to reconcile conflicting values in spite of the fact that, in so doing, its rational counterpart must be suppressed. Much of our irrationality, including how we adopt certain kinds of worldviews or how we succumb to the bombardment of certain marketing messages, can be said to grow out of these deep-rooted biological and cultural conflicts in the different compartments of our minds.

That consumer rationality is susceptible to being weakened by the socialization process has profound consequences on the evolution of the modern consumption society. It explains the proliferation and effectiveness of marketing and advertising in modern business, the subversion of the sovereignty of the consumer, the creation of "apparent" values, the emphasis on nonprice competition, the rise of the "manipulative firm," the domination of the production function by the distribution function, and the power of the distributor-producer in the present-day consumption economy. I have already elaborated these points in chapter 6 and will not repeat them here.

The Intellectual Lineage of the Present Theory

This book has shown that a theory of value cannot be separated from a theory of the mind. It shows that the neoclassical theory of the mind, which supports its elaborate logical edifice, is significantly flawed. In contrast, my value theory is grounded on a radically different conception of the mind. Although this new conception is still in its initial stage, the basic ingredients have already emerged in the current phase of cognitive science as well as in evolutionary epistemology, a discipline that is defined as "an epistemology taking cognizance of and compatible with man's status as a product of biological and social evolution" (Campbell 1974, 413).

Rooted in the fact that the mind is a result of biological evolution and that it anticipates and responds to cultural evolution, a value theory built on these facts inevitably adopts the properties of the "evolutionary" mind, with its natural strengths and limitations. If the mind is an evolutionary artifact, it is only obvious that a value theory that is grounded in this concept takes on an evolutionary character. In this connection, the perspective of my value theory is congenial to that of present-day evolutionary economics. Notwithstanding this affinity, there are, however, important differences between them, in particular in the way they draw on knowledge of evolution. Evolutionary economics, on the whole, adopts an extrapolative strategy, building an economics by mapping evolutionary principles in the biological domain onto the economic domain. While this strategy can easily yield a number of insights, not all of them are relevant and some criteria need to be set up to screen out irrelevant mappings. In general, evolutionary economists are eager to adopt the most obvious biological principles, and they tend to ignore the multi-dimensional complexities involved in cultural evolution, particularly those facets that operate under principles that are distinct from those that govern biological evolution. In contrast, my evolutionary approach, beginning with the studies of the evolution of the mind and a view to studying the formation of value, takes evolutionary knowledge not as exogenous principles to draw inspiration from, but as an inherent part of the fundamental knowledge of economics. As a result, it should avoid the previously mentioned pitfalls that beset evolutionary economics.

Apart from drawing intellectual resources from evolutionary epistemology and cognitive science, the value theory espoused in this book draws, to different extents, inspiration from different schools of economics. From neoclassical orthodoxy, it accepts the importance of the optimization principle and the optimizing mind that puts this principle to work. Thus, I do not repudiate the idea of optimization or ignore the source of the strength of neoclassical economics. Instead, my theory benefits from understanding the limitations of building an economics based solely on this principle. By seeing the mind from a long-term, evolutionary perspective, my theory enables us to appreciate that both the ratiomorphic mind and the rational mind employ principles that go beyond the straightforward notion of optimization. Of particular importance, my theory helps to distinguish conditions under which the optimization principle is effectively and abundantly employed (e.g., under well-structured situations) from conditions under which the principle is of little relevance (e.g., in the processes of value formation).

The long-term perspective and the idea of the susceptibility of man to social influences that my theory espouses mean that it is very much in accord with the post-Keynesian tradition and also that of the institutionalists. My theory, however, is able to add insights in two important respects. First, it is capable of explaining, from the level of the mind, how such susceptibility arises. Second, it is also able to analyze the limits of such susceptibility (e.g., the human mind is still a powerful optimizing apparatus in most well-structured situations). As a result, my theory is able to avoid the pitfall of espousing an extreme position, as is the case of some institutionalist versions.

In broad outline, my theory is also compatible with the most important insight of the behavioralists, namely, the idea of bounded rationality. The theory, however, goes beyond the behavioralist position in two ways. First, it is more specific about the extent of bounded human rationality, especially its ability to offer hypotheses that may explain how such bounds arise from the architecture of the mind. Second, it ventures beyond the bounds of rationality and looks more systematically at the irrationalities therein. Thus, my theory is distinct from the work of Hebert Simon, who also advocates the concept of bounded rationality. Simon is one of the founding fathers of cognitive science, which, in its first phase, was characterized by a logical and computational bent. Although Simon late modified his position (e.g., in his formulation of neoclassical theory as holding a concept of substantive rationality) and espoused a more tenable concept of procedural rationality, his concept of the mind is still basically a computational one. Hence, his conception of bounded rationality is distinctly different from my conception, which is based on a dynamic, evolutionary mind that allows the generation and proliferation of irrationalities.

While my value theory accepts ideas from and is generally sympathetic toward the Austrian and neo-Austrian position, it differs from their position in many important respects. Many of these differences have been analyzed and will not be repeated. It is sufficient to say that the my theory, while acknowledging the importance of subjectivity, does not stop at emphasizing the importance of this characteristic. In attempting to link a theory of value to a theory of the mind, I want to elucidate those mechanisms and features in the mind that significantly and objectively affect the formation of values. Ignoring this link, the Austrian scholars are not inclined toward developing a theory of value formation, and, as a result, they do not produce a theory of value and a theory of rationality that either differs very much from or can effectively challenge the neoclassical position. Without a theory of value formation, the Austrians tend to view value as a purely endogenous matter in the mind. They are thus compelled to ignore the systematic social factors or developments that goad human behaviors, especially at a less-than-fully conscious level. These drawbacks can be further attributed to the fact that the Austrians do not themselves develop a theory of the mind or that they hold one that is not sophisticated enough to enable them to see order out of what they may perceive as intractable subjectivity.

From this brief survey, we can say that the present theory, in many respects, is able to make up for the deficiencies of both the orthodox as well as the different schools of heterodox thoughts. It does this both at the methodological and the substantive levels. At the methodological level, it shows that important economic theories, both macro and micro, must be related to theories of rationality, which, in turn, must be related to theories of value in the broad sense, namely, how values arise in the first instance in the human mind. In turn, theories of value must be related to the foundational stratum of the theory of the mind. Alternatively put, any economic theory, if it is to be based on a sound foundation, must take a position with respect to how the mind functions or how it is constituted, at least insofar as economic actions are caused or directed. At the substantive level, my theory proposes an evolutionary and realist theory of the mind that fills much of the gap left by other theories, especially in the explanation of the formation of value and the limits of human rationality, upon which new theories of price behaviors and consumer behaviors can be readily developed. These theories, as I have shown, command much more systematic explanatory power than their earlier counterparts. In this regard, what I have offered is nothing more than a first and crude sketch of a rich repertoire of potential theories that have yet to be developed.

Some Philosophical Ramifications

The new theory proposed in this book points to the development of a new paradigm in economics, one that we can call the "cognitive paradigm." It shows how explicitly contrasting different theories of the mind will lead to different theories of value, rationality, and price. One may perhaps say that what ultimately divides major schools of economic thought from one another is not their superficial features, but what theories of the mind they explicitly or implicitly espouse. The analysis in this book should have demonstrated this point amply.

It seems clear, but nonetheless should be made more explicit, that any theory of rationality by which economic actions are to be judged critically depends on a theory of value in the broad sense. In discourses about the animal world or about human behaviors during the subsistence phase of man, there is no need to make the distinction between rationality and value, for what value one can discern is confined to survival and any behavior, innate or learned, that is oriented to enhancing fitness for survival must be deemed rational, although it is questionable whether it makes any sense to label such behavior rational. In the modern world where values proliferate and where values held among individuals are in conflict with one another or in conflict with collectively held values, the question of rationality becomes a real and important one. A value theory, therefore, is important not only in that it provides the basis for the formulation of the notion of rationality, but also in that the study of the very nature of values that prevail in an individual or in society enables us to determine or hypothesize the extent to which irrationalities rule in that individual or society.

If the discourse of value should precede the discourse of rationality or if the discourse of value should dictate the formulation of the notion of rationality, we have an additional case against the primacy of the notion of optimization. This lends support to the idea of instrumental rationality that is embodied by neoclassical economics. For optimization, in the final analysis, is nothing but an operative principle and presupposes a well-defined value system or a set of clear-cut ends for its effective application. If it should happen that (and it does seem quite obvious) the values and ends in question are fuzzy in themselves or in their relationships, or if such values and ends are to be called into question by their holders from time to time, or if such values are of such an insidious nature that their formations are not at all conscious to their holders, then it seems only logical that we should first study their character and their formation. We should not assume that such a problem has already been solved and that we are left merely with the problem of selecting and refining the tools to be used in attaining such known ends. The foundational question of values and their associated problems should obviously come before the solutions to be sought and what tools we should use to seek such solutions.

We have seen that the modern consumption economy is laden with conventional values fostered by suppliers. The conventional character of these values means that the notion of equilibrium is no longer a fruitful concept, and may be an unreliable one, in describing the state of an economy. If values are largely conventional by nature, a market equilibrium attained under such values is likely to be a contingent phenomenon. There is no guarantee that the equilibrium attained is a unique or a natural one; there is no assurance of recurrence or permanence of this state. If this is the case, it serves little purpose to focus on the question of whether or not an equilibrium exists or what equilibrium prices are. This again confirms my thesis that the study of the nature of value should come before the tools we use in theorizing about or describing the economy. It also clearly shows that, if we are serious about building an economics that can reflect the complexity of the modern economy, there is no way to escape confronting the problem of value in the broad sense. It thus seems that value theory, rather than price theory, remains the first and foremost problem in economics.

Bibliography

Addleson, M. 1986. "Radical Subjectivism and the Language of Austrian Economics." In *Subjectivism, Intelligibility, and Economic Understanding,* ed. I. Kirzner. New York: New York University Press.

Amihud, Y., and B. Lev. 1981. "Risk Reduction as a Managerial Motive for Conglomerate Mergers." *Bell Journal of Economics* 12:605–17.

Arrow, K. J. 1963. *Social Choice and Individual Values.* 2d ed. New York: Wiley.

Arrow, K. J. 1979. "Values and Collective Decision Making" In *Philosophy and Economic Theory,* ed. F. Hahn and M. Hollis. Oxford: Oxford University Press.

Arrow, K. J., and F. H. Hahn. 1971. *General Competitive Analysis.* San Francisco: Holden-Day.

Bailey, S. 1825. *A Critical Dissertation on the Nature, Measures, and Causes of Value.* London.

Baran, P. A. 1957. *The Political Economy of Growth.* London: Penguin Books.

Baren, P. A., and P. M. Sweezy. 1966. *Monopoly Capital.* London: Penguin Books.

Baranzini, M., and R. Scazzieri, eds. 1986. *Foundations of Economics: Structures of Enquiry and Economic Theory.* Oxford: Basil Blackwell.

Baumol, W. J. 1959. *Business Behavior, Value, and Growth.* New York: Macmillan.

Becker, G. S. 1976. *The Economic Approach to Human Behavior.* Chicago: University of Chicago Press.

Becker, G. S. and K. M. Murphy. 1986. "A Theory of Rational Addiction." Working paper no. 41, Center for the Study of the Economy and the State, University of Chicago. Photocopy.

Blau, P. 1977. "A Macrosociological Theory of Social Structure." *American Sociological Review* 83:26–54.

Blaug, M. 1973. *Ricardian Economics: A Historical Study.* Westport, Conn.: Greenwood Press.

Boden, M. A. 1988. *Computer Models of Mind.* Cambridge: Cambridge University Press.

Boulding, K. E. 1981. *Evolutionary Economics.* Beverly Hill: Sage Publications.

Buchanan, J. M., R. Tollison, and G. Tullock, eds. 1980. *Toward a Theory of the Rent-Seeking Society.* College Station: Texas A&M University Press.

Campbell, D. T. 1974. "Evolutionary Epistemology." In *The Philosophy of Karl Popper,* ed. P. A. Schilpp. LaSalle, Ill.: Open Court.

Campbell, J. H. 1985. "An Organizational Interpretation of Evolution." In *Evolution at a Crossroads,* ed. D. J. Depew and B. H. Weber. Cambridge, Mass.: MIT Press.

Chamberlin, E. H. 1966. *The Theory of Monopolistic Competition.* 8th ed. Cambridge, Mass.: Harvard University Press.

Cherniak, C. 1984. "Computational Complexity and the Universal Acceptance of Logic." *The Journal of Philosophy.* 81:739–58.

Coats, A. W. 1976. "Economics and Psychology: The Death and Resurrection of a Research Program." In *Method and Appraisal in Economics,* ed. S. J. Latsis. Cambridge: Cambridge University Press.

Coats, A. W. 1983. "The Revival of Subjectivism in Economics." In *Beyond Positive Economics,* ed. J. Wiseman. London: Macmillan.

Coats, A. W. 1987. "Economics and Psychology: A Resurrection Story." in *Psychological Economics,* ed. P. Earl. Boston: Klumer.

Colander, D. C., ed. 1984. *Neoclassical Political Economy: The Analysis of Rent-Seeking and DUP Activities.* Cambridge, Mass.: Ballinger.

Cyert, R., and J. G. March. 1963. *A Behavioral Theory of the Firm.* Englewood Cliffs, N.J.: Prentice-Hall.

Davidson, P. 1981. "Post-Keynesian Economics." In *The Crisis in Economic Theory,* ed. D. Bell and I. Kristol. New York: Basic Books.

Dawkins, R. 1988. *The Blind Watchmaker.* London: Penguin Books.

Deane, P. 1978. *The Evolution of Economic Ideas.* Cambridge: Cambridge University Press.

Deaton, A., and J. Muellbauer. 1980. *Economics and Consumer Behavior.* Cambridge: Cambridge University Press.

Debreu, G. 1959. *The Theory of Value: An Axiomatic Analysis of Economic Equilibrium.* New York: Wiley.

Depew, D. J., and B. H. Weber, eds. 1985. *Evolution at a Crossroads: The New Biology and the New Philosophy of Science.* Cambridge, Mass.: MIT Press.

Dobb, M. 1973. *Theories of Value and Distribution since Adam Smith—Ideology and Economic Theory.* Cambridge: Cambridge University Press.

Durkheim, E. 1938. *The Rules of Sociological Method.* Trans. S. A. Solovoy and H. J. Mueller. Chicago: University of Chicago Press.

Earl, P. E. 1983. *The Economic Imagination: Toward a Behavioral Analysis of Choice.* Brighton: Wheatsheaf Books.

Earl, P. E. 1986. *Life-style Economics: Consumer Behavior in a Turbulent World.* Brighton: Wheatsheaf Books.

Earl, P. E. 1987. *Psychological Economics: Development, Tensions, Prospects.* Boston: Klumer.

Edgeworth, F. Y. 1881. *Mathematical Psychics: An Essay on the Application of Mathematics to the Moral Sciences.* London: Kegan Paul.

Eichner A. 1983. *Why Economics is Not Yet a Science.* London: Macmillan.

Elster, J. 1983. *Sour Grapes: Studies in the Subversion of Rationality.* Cambridge: Cambridge University Press.

Elster, J. 1986. *An Introduction to Karl Marx.* Cambridge: Cambridge University Press.

Elvee, R. Q., ed. 1982. *Mind in Nature.* New York: Harper and Row.

Etzioni, A. 1986. "The Case for a Multiple-utility Conception." *Economics and Philosophy* 2:159–83.

Feyerabend, P. K. 1975. *Against Method: Outline of an Anarchistic Theory of Knowledge*. London: New Left Books.

Fishbein, M. A. 1963. "An Investigation of the Relationships between Beliefs about an Object and the Attitude toward that Object." *Human Relations* 16 (August): 233–39.

Fishburn, P. S. 1974. "Lexicographic Orders, Utilities, and Decision Rules: A Survey." *Management Science* 20:1442–71.

Fisher, I. [1892] 1965. *Mathematical Investigations in the Theory of Value and Price*. New Haven: Yale University Press.

Friedman, M. 1953. *Essays in Positive Economics*. Chicago: University of Chicago Press.

Fusfeld, D. 1990. "The Single Price Theorem." In *Research in the History of Economic Thought and Methodology*. Vol. 7, ed. W. Samuel. Greenwich, Conn.: JAI Press.

Gabor, A., and C. W. J. Granger. 1966. "Price as an Indicator of Quality: Report on an Inquiry." *Economica* 33 (129): 43–70.

Galbraith, J. K. 1967. *The New Industrial State*. Boston: Houghton Mifflin.

Gardner, H. 1985. *The Mind's New Science: A History of the Cognitive Revolution*. New York: Basic Books.

Georgescu-Roegen, N. 1954. "Choice, Expectations, and Measurability." *Quarterly Journal of Economics* 68:503–34.

Georgescu-Roegen, N. 1982. "Utility." In *Encyclopedia of Economics*, ed. D. Greenwald. New York: McGraw-Hill.

Goode, W. J. 1978. *The Celebration of Heroes: Prestige as a Social Control System*. Berkeley: University of California Press.

Gossen, H. H. 1854. *Entwicklung der Gesetze des Menschlichen Verkehrs und des daraus fliessenden Regeln fur merschliches Handeln*.

Granit, R. 1982. "Reflection on the Evolution of the Mind and its Environment." In *Mind in Nature*, ed. R. Q. Elvee. New York: Harper and Row.

Hahn, F. H. 1973. *On the Notion of Equilibrium in Economics*. Cambridge: Cambridge University Press.

Hahn, F. H. 1980. "General Equilibrium Theory." *Public Interest*, Special Issue, 123–38.

Hansson, B. 1968. "Choice Structures and Preference Relations." *Synthese* 18:443–58.

Hausman, D. M. 1981. "Are General Equilibrium Theories Explanatory?" In *Philosophy in Economics*, ed. J. Pitt. Dordrecht: Reidel.

Hayek, F. A. 1952. *The Sensory Order: An Inquiry into the Foundations of Theoretical Psychology*. London: Routledge and Kegan Paul.

Hayek, F. A. 1983. *Knowledge, Evolution, and Society*. London: ASI Research Ltd.

Heiner, R. A. 1986. "The Economics of Information when Decisions Are Imperfect." In *Economic Psychology*, ed. A. MacFadyen and H. MacFadyen. Amsterdam: Elsevier Science Publishers.

Hennings, K. H. 1986. "The Exchange Paradigm and the Theory of Production and Distribution." In *Foundation of Economics*, ed. M. Baranzini and R. Scazzieri. Oxford: Basil Blackwell.

Hicks, J. R. 1939. *Value and Capital.* Oxford: Oxford University Press.

Hicks, J. R. 1969. *A Theory of Economic History.* Oxford: Clarendon Press.

Hirschleifer, J. 1985. "The Expanding Domain of Economics." *American Economic Review* 75:53–68.

Hollander, S. 1987. *Classical Economics.* Oxford: Basil Blackwell.

Hutchison, T. W. 1977. *Knowledge and Ignorance in Economics.* Oxford: Basil Blackwell.

Jackendoff, R. 1987. *Consciousness and the Computational Mind.* Cambridge, Mass.: MIT Press.

Jaynes, J. 1976. *The Origin of Consciousness in the Breakdown of the Bicameral Mind.* London: Allen Lane.

Jevons, W. S. [1871] 1970. *The Theory of Political Economy.* Ed. R. D. Black. New York: Penguin Books.

Johnson-Laird, P. N. 1983. *Mental Models: Toward a Cognitive Science of Language, Inference, and Consciousness.* Cambridge, Mass.: Harvard University Press.

Johnson-Laird, P. N. 1988. *The Computer and the Mind.* London: Fontana.

Johnson-Laird, P. N., and P. C. Wason. 1970. "A Theoretical Analysis of Insight into a Reasoning Task." *Cognitive Psychology* 1:134–48.

Kahneman, D., P. Slovic, and A. Tversky, eds. 1982. *Judgment under Uncertainty: Heuristics and Biases.* Cambridge: Cambridge University Press.

Kahneman D., and A. Tversky. 1982. "The Psychology of Preferences." *Scientific American* 246:160–74.

Kahneman, D., and Tversky, A. 1984 "Choices, Values, and Frames." *American Psychologist* 39:341–50.

Kaldor, N. 1972. "The Irrelevance of Equilibrium Economics." *Economic Journal* 82:1237–55.

Kantorovich, L. V. 1989. "Mathematics in Economics: Achievements, Difficulties, Perspectives." *American Economic Review* 79, no. 6: 18–22.

Katouzian, H. 1980. *Ideology and Method in Economics.* New York: New York University Press.

Kauffman S. A. 1985. "Self-Organization, Selective Adaptation and its Limits." In *Evolution at a Crossroads,* D. J. Depew and B. H. Weber. Cambridge, Mass.: MIT Press.

Kenyon, P. 1979. "Pricing." In *A Guide to Post-Keynesian Economics,* ed. A. S. Eichner. New York: M. E. Sharpe.

Kirzner, I. M. 1986. *Subjectivism, Intelligibility, and Economic Understanding.* New York: New York University Press.

Kosslyn, S. K. 1980. *Image and Mind.* Cambridge, Mass.: Harvard University Press.

Kuhn, T. S. 1970. *The Structure of Scientific Revolutions.* Chicago: University of Chicago Press.

Lancaster, K. J. 1966. "A New Approach to Consumer Theory." *Journal of Political Economy* 74:132–57.

Latsis, S. J., ed. 1976. *Method and Appraisal in Economics.* Cambridge: Cambridge University Press.

Lavoie, D. 1989. "Understanding Differently: Hermeneutics and the Spontaneous Order of Communicative Processes." Paper presented at the conference, "Carl Menger and his Legacy," Duke University.

Lachmann, L. M. 1986. "Economics as a Hermeneutical Discipline." Paper presented at the conference, "Interpretation, Human Agency, and Economics," George Mason University, Fairfax, Virginia.

Leibenstein, H. 1950. "Bandwagon, Snob, and Veblen Effects in the Theory of Consumer's Demand." *Quarterly Journal of Economics,* May, 183–207.

Loasby, B. J. 1976. *Choice, Complexity, and Ignorance.* Cambridge: Cambridge University Press.

Lutz, M. A., and R. Lux. 1979. *The Challenge of Humanistic Economics.* Menlo Park, Calif.: Benjamin/Cummings Publishing.

Marcus, A. J. 1982. "Risk Sharing and the Theory of the Firm." *Bell Journal of Economics* 13:369–78.

Marshall, A. 1923. *Principles of Economics.* 8th ed. London: Macmillan.

Mattews, R. C. O. 1984. "Darwinism and Economic Change." *Oxford Economic Papers* 36:91–117.

McClosky, D. N. 1985. *The Rhetoric of Economics.* Madison: University of Wisconsin Press.

Menger, C. [1871] 1981. *Principles of Economics.* Ed. J. Dingwalland and trans. B. F. Hoselitz. New York: New York University Press.

Menger, C. 1934. *Collected Works.* Vol. 1, *Grundsätze der Volkswirtschaftslehre.* Reprint. London: London School of Economics.

Merton, R. K. 1957. *Social Theory and Social Structure.* New York: Free Press.

Mill, J. S. [1848] 1967. *Collected Works.* Ed. J. M. Robson. Toronto: University of Toronto Press.

Miller, G. A. 1956. "The Magical Number Seven, Plus or Minus Two: Some Limits on our Capacity for Processing Information." *Psychological Review* 63:81–97.

Mises, L. v. 1966. *Human Action: A Treatise on Economics.* 3d ed. New York: Henry Regnery.

Mishan, E. J. 1961. "Theories of Consumer Behavior: A Cynical View." *Economica,* n.s. 28:1–11.

Moss, L. S. 1987. "The Modern Austrian Critique of Neoclassical Economics." Paper presented at Waseda University, Tokyo.

Nelson R., and S. Winter. 1982. *An Evolutionary Theory of Economic Change.* Cambridge, Mass.: Harvard University Press.

O'Brien, D. P. 1975. *The Classical Economists.* Oxford: Clarendon Press.

Pareto, V. 1906. *Manuale di economia politica, con una introduzione alla scienza sociale.* Milan: Società Editrice Libraria.

Pasinetti, L. K. 1981. *Structural Change and Economic Growth: A Theoretical Essay on the Dynamics of the Wealth of Nations.* Cambridge: Cambridge University Press.

Pasinetti, L. K. 1986. "Theory of Value: A Source of Alternative Paradigms in Economics Analysis." In *Foundations of Economics,* ed. M. Barangini and R. Scazzieri. Oxford: Basil Blackwell.

Popper, K. R. 1960. *The Poverty of Historicism.* 2d ed. London: Routledge and Kegan Paul.

Popper, K. R. 1963. *Conjectures and Refutations: The Growth of Scientific Knowledge.* London: Routledge and Kegan Paul.

Popper, K. R. 1972, *Objective Knowledge.* Oxford: Clarendon Press.

Popper, K. R., and J. C. Eccles. 1977. *The Self and its Brain.* Berlin: Springer International.

Pylyshyn, Z. W. 1984. *Computation and Cognition: Toward a Foundation of Cognitive Science.* Cambridge, Mass.: MIT Press.

Ramsay, F. P. 1931. *Foundations of Mathematics and Other Logical Essays.* London: Kegan Paul.

Ricardo, D. 1951. *Works and Correspondence.* 11 vols. Ed. P. Sraffa. Cambridge: Cambridge University Press.

Richter, M. K. 1971. "Rational Choice." In *Preference, Utility, and Demand,* ed. J. S. Chipman, L. Hurwicz, M. K. Richter and H. F. Sonnenschein. New York: Harcourt.

Ricoeur, P. 1978. *The Rule of Metaphor.* London: Routledge and Kegan Paul.

Robbins, L. 1935. *An Essay on the Nature and Significance of Economic Science.* 2d ed. London: Macmillan.

Robinson, J. 1978. *Contributions to Modern Economics.* Oxford: Basil Blackwell.

Roll, E. 1974. *A History of Economic Thought.* 4th ed. Homewood, Ill.: Irwin.

Rosenberg, M. J. 1956. "Cognitive Structure and Attitudinal Effect." *Journal of Abnormal and Social Psychology* 53:367–72.

Rorty, R. 1979. *Philosophy and the Mirror of Nature.* Princeton: Princeton University Press.

Rumelhart, D. E., and J. L. McClelland, eds. 1986. *Parallel Distributed Processing: Explorations in the Microstructure of Cognition.* 2 vols. Cambridge, Mass.: MIT Press.

Samuelson, P. A. 1948. *Foundations of Economic Analysis.* Cambridge, Mass.: Harvard University Press.

Schelling, T. C. 1960. *The Strategy of Conflict.* Cambridge, Mass.: Harvard University Press.

Sen, A. K. 1971. "Choice Functions and Revealed Preference." *Review of Economic Studies* 38:307–17.

Sen, A. K. 1976. "Rational Fools: A Critique of the Behavioral Foundations of Economic Theory." In *Philosophy and Economic Theory,* ed. F. Hahn and M. Hollis. Oxford: Oxford University Press.

Sen, A. K. 1982. *Choice, Welfare, and Measurement.* Oxford: Basil Blackwell.

Sen, A. K. 1987. *On Ethics and Economics.* Oxford: Basil Blackwell.

Senior, N. [1836] 1938. *An Outline of the Science of Political Economy.* London: George Allen and Unwin.

Shand, A. H. 1980. *Subjectivist Economics: The New Austrian School.* Exeter, Devon: Pica Press.

Shearmur, J. 1983. "Subjectivism, Falsification, and Positive Economics." In *Beyond Positive Economics?* ed. J. Wiseman. London: Macmillan.

Shepard, R. N., and J. Metzler. 1971. "Mental Rotation of Three-Dimensional Objects." *Science* 171:701–3.

Sherer, F. M. 1980. *Industrial Market Structure and Economic Performance.* 2d ed. Chicago: Rand McNally.

Simon, H. A. 1976. "From Substantive to Procedural Rationality." In *Method and Appraisal in Economics,* ed. S. Latsis. Cambridge: Cambridge University Press.

Smith, A. [1776] 1976. *An Inquiry into the Nature and Causes of the Wealth of Nations*. Ed. R. H. Campbell, A. S. Skinner and W. B. Todd. Oxford: Clarendon Press.

Sowell, T. 1974. *Classical Economics Reconsidered.* Princeton: Princeton University Press.

Sperry, R. 1983. *Science and Moral Priority.* Oxford: Basil Blackwell.

Spiegel, H. W. 1983. *The Growth of Economic Thought.* Englewood Cliffs, N.J.: Prentice-Hall.

Sraffa, P. 1960. *Production of Commodities by Means of Commodities—Prelude to a Critique of Economic Theory.* Cambridge: Cambridge University Press.

Stigler, G. J. 1961. "The Economics of Information." *Journal of Political Economy* 69:213–25.

Stigler, G. J. 1981. "Economics or Ethics?" In *Tanner Lectures on Human Values.* Vol. 2, ed. S. McMurrin. Cambridge: Cambridge University Press.

Stigler, G. J., and G. S. Becker. 1977. "De Gustibus Non Est Disputandum." *American Economic Review* March:76–90.

Strong, N., and M. Waterson. 1987. "Principals, Agents, and Information." In *The Economics of the Firm,* ed. R. Clarke and T. McGuinness. Oxford: Basil Blackwell.

Tabarrok, A. 1990. "Subjective Value Theory: A Reformulation." *Austrian Economics Newsletter* 12:5–9.

Taylor, D. A. 1983. *Mind.* London: Century Publishing.

Thaler, R. M. 1980. "Toward a Positive Theory of Consumer Choice." *Journal of Economic Behavior and Organization* 1:36–60.

Townshend, H. 1937. "Liquidity Premium and the Theory of Value." *Economic Journal* 47:157–69.

Tversky, A. 1969. "Intransitivity of Preferences." *Psychological Review* 76:31–48.

Utton, M. A. 1979. *Diversification and Competition.* Cambridge: Cambridge University Press.

Veblen, T. 1898. "Why is Economics Not an Evolutionary Science?" *Quarterly Journal of Economics* 12:373–426.

Veblen, T. [1899] 1953. *The Theory of the Leisure Class: An Economic Study of Institutions.* Rev. ed. New York: Viking Press.

Vollmer, G. 1984. "Mesocosm and Objective Knowledge: On Problems Solved by Evolutionary Epistemology." In *Concepts and Approaches in Evolutionary Epistemology,* ed. I. M. Wuketilits. Dordrecht: Reidel.

von Neumann, J., and O. Morgenstern. 1944. *The Theory of Games and Economic Behavior.* Princeton: Princeton University Press.

Walras, L. 1874. *Elements of Pure Economics.* Translated by W. Jaffe, 1954. London: George Allen and Unwin.

Wason, P. C., and P. N. Johnson-Laird. 1972. *The Psychology of Reasoning: Structure in Content.* Cambridge, Mass.: Harvard University Press.

Weintraub, E. R. 1985. *General Equilibrium Analysis: Studies in Appraisal.* Cambridge: Cambridge University Press.

Williamson, O. E. 1964. *The Economics of Discretionary Behavior: Managerial Objectives in a Theory of the Firm.* Englewood Cliffs, N.J.: Prentice-Hall.

Wiseman, J., ed. 1983. *Beyond Positive Economics?* London: Macmillan.

White, L. H. 1977. *The Methodology of the Austrian School of Economics.* Auburn, Ala.: Ludwig von Mises Institute of Auburn University.

Woo, H. K. H. 1986. *What's Wrong with Formalization in Economics? An Epistemological Critique.* Fremont, Calif.: Victoria Press.

Woo, H. K. H. 1990. "On the Notion of Epistemic Opportunity Lost." *Methodus* 2, no. 1 (June): 33–37.

Woo, H. K. H. N.d. *The Place of Metaphysics in Philosophy.* Manuscript.

Wuketits, F. M. 1990. *Evolutionary Epistemology and its Implications for Humankind.* Albany: State University of New York Press.

Author Index

Subject Index